Sundial of the Seasons

BOOKS BY HAL BORLAND

The Outdoors

An American Year
This Hill, This Valley
The Enduring Pattern
Beyond Your Doorstep

People and Places

High, Wide and Lonesome
The Dog Who Came to Stay

Fiction

The Amulet
The Seventh Winter
When the Legends Die

Folklore

Rocky Mountain Tipi Tales
The Youngest Shepherd

Poetry

America Is Americans

SUNDIAL OE

J. B. Lippincott Company

THE SEASONS

A Selection of Outdoor Editorials

from The New York Times

 by Hal Borland

Philadelphia & New York

For Barbara, especially in Autumn

I gave you emeralds in May and amethysts in June;
July I gave you turquoise skies and silver stars and moon.
December will bring Diamonds, but before the frosty cold
I give you coal-hot rubies and October's molten gold.

Foreword

I doubt that anyone thought, back in the Fall of 1941 when I wrote an editorial about oak trees, that *The New York Times* and I were planting an acorn from which would grow a forest. I certainly didn't. But from that first outdoor editorial have grown more than a third of a million words about wind and weather, time and the seasons, man and his natural environment. In this volume I have chosen 365 out of a total of close to 1,200 of those pieces to assemble into a kind of almanac of the outdoor year—any outdoor year—as seen through one countryman's eyes and mind.

Since I have arranged the entries to this book's purpose, they do not follow the sequence of their original publication in the *Times*. And although the book covers a typical year day by day, it does not begin with January 1. To me, the calendar we use to satisfy the keepers of vital statistics is an arbitrary reckoning that ignores the seasons. I live with the natural year, and since this book is a consequence of that life it begins with the vernal equinox, in March. It begins with Spring.

As for the individual entries, I think of them as reports by an observer with an interpretative turn of mind who happens to be following the oldest continuing story known to man, the story of man and his natural surroundings. No matter how insistently we herd ourselves away from the land, many of us have a deep, innate need to know that the land is still there and that the seasons still keep to their eternal sequence. Cities crumble, machines rust away, governments rise and fall, but mountains still stand, rivers flow to the sea, grass clothes the hills, trees become woodlands, the sun rises and sets and the moon persists in its phases. It is about such matters that these pieces were written.

I am sure that as editorials they have solved no political crises, swayed no elections, had no noticeable effect on the tax rate, and never averted or even eased international tensions. That, to be sure, has not been their purpose. If pressed for a profound reason, I should say that they were written to suggest a somewhat longer sense of time and a different perspective than are prompted by the daily headlines. If man and his knotty human problems seem somewhat minimized in them, that is because they reflect the view of the world from where I stand.

My vantage point is a rural countryside in the lower Berkshires, specifically the hill-and-valley farm where I have lived and worked for a good many years. A considerable part of the world is visible, both literally and figuratively, from my own hilltop. I may not be able to see the towers of New York or London or Moscow, but instant communication and the daily mails keep me in constant touch with them. I do live far enough from the crowds, however, to somewhat mute the daily sounds of mass emotions and ease the infective tensions of nervous trauma. It is possible here to see that birds and trees and insects still outnumber people, despite exploding human populations. And I am constantly reminded of forces beyond the eager hand of man: Seasons and weather, sunlight and darkness, the urgency of growth, the fertility of the seed and the egg, the inevitability of time and change. It is obvious, day by day and hour by hour, that man and all his works, both those magnificent and those frightful beyond comprehension, still do not constitute the whole of life or the greater part of activity upon this earth. These observations and beliefs are fundamental to the viewpoint that must permeate this book, since the book is inevitably a part of me.

A number of the outdoor editorials have been reprinted in anthologies and textbooks and I have adapted material from them for use in two of my own books; but this is the first time a volume of them has been assembled in their original form. Despite the temptation to revise, I have let them stand almost exactly as they originally appeared. I have moved a comma here and there and I have muted the few topical references, but otherwise they are unchanged. I have, however, indulged in occasional footnotes, some to clarify a point, some to admit error and make amendment, some for my own amusement. And I have noted the few occasions when a piece was written elsewhere than here at home. Also, for the readers interested in such detail, I have assembled a special index at the back of the book listing each piece and the date of its original publication in the *Times*.

I wish to thank two editors, Charles Merz and his successor, John B. Oakes, for unqualified freedom to write what I chose and as I wished. And I thank *The New York Times* for permission to use this selection of my outdoor editorials in this form.

H. B.

Salisbury, Conn.
1964

Contents

SPRING

 MARCH

A Seed and an Equinox
March 22

No one will deny the wonders and magnificence of astronomy, one of the great sciences which endure as a monument to man's powers of reason and observation. But the annual recurrence of the vernal equinox makes one aware of hidden forces so accurate and so sensitive that the observer can scarcely escape a feeling of awe and wonder. All around one are the evidences of sensitivity to time and the stars that make any human science pale a little by contrast.

Man has known for a long time the fixed sequence of star and planet, sun, moon and tides. But how can a seed "know" when to begin to sprout? How can sap at the roots of a tree "know" when comes the proper time to start that mysterious movement upward toward twig and waiting leaf bud? What moves a bulb to muster forces and send up shoots to catch the sunlight and begin to manufacture food for the plant? What mysterious force prompts one seed to wait in its sprouting till all danger of frost is past, while another sprouts at that precise moment when its stem and leaf can survive 10 degrees of frost but not 12 or 15?

We have answers, of a sort, in terms of warmth and length of daylight; but those are, in final examination, observations of response, not of ultimate cause. We have elaborate apparatus to measure sun's warmth and soil's moisture and even sap pressure. But how does a grass seed measure such critical conditions? Somehow they are measured by all living things which spread leaves and manufacture chlorophyll. They "know" when the equinox comes, when Spring arrives, when they should respond. Man studies a clock and a star to learn such basic simplicities.

A New Year   *March 23*

Now it can be told even in Gath, published in the streets of Askelon. Spring is here, by the calendar at least. It arrived well before yesterday's dawn, when few of us were up to see the planets wheel into line or hear the muted creak of the trunnions as the old earth swung slowly over to face the sun. The change came in the dark of early morning, and the day didn't look much different from the day before. But it brought the vernal equinox, and now it's Spring. In the records, at least.

There was a time when this was the occasion of a new year as well as an equinox and a new season. To those close to the land and the weather, such a system of accounting would still make more sense than having New Year's Day in January. What is there to look forward to in January but snow and cold? If the calendar makers had wanted their year to start with a blizzard, they should have chosen the Winter solstice, which often brings a storm but which does see the daylight begin to lengthen. But the choice missed solstice as well as equinox, so we have nothing to celebrate now but Spring.

However, it is a new year down where it really matters. The roots know it, and the bulbs and the seeds. The time is at hand when the green and growing world makes its own calendar. This is a new year, the newest season of the year, any year and all years. What is newer than a young new leaf? Or a pussy willow? Of course this is the time of the new year that matters! Everything alive knows it and begins to respond. Spring, which is the year just opening its eyes and lifting green fingers to the sun, was born yesterday. Happy New Year!

The Vital Willows   *March 24*

Weeping willows are great amber fountains beside the ponds, and along the watercourses at least a dozen varieties of lesser willows glow red and russet as though some secret incandescent fluid coursed their stems. Willows respond to the season in a wondrous way for all to see. The sap rises and the twigs almost pulsate with their translucent color. The amber of the weeping willow is a live, warm color that steadily verges toward green as the leaf buds begin to open. The red that suffuses the stems of the brookside shrub called hoary willow is as ruddy as the blossom, soon to come, of a swamp maple. And other willows, tree and bush, show most of the colors between that greening amber and the full-bodied red. And those colors will continue on the willow stems until the leaves are there—not on the stems, really, but in them, suffusing them.

This color, this particular look of vitality, is not deceiving. The willows may lack the staying power of the oaks, but they outnumber and outgrow the oaks ten to one. Given half a chance, they will bind almost any stream bank, protect it from flood and erosion. Given a sand bar for footing, the willows will convert it into an island complete with fertile soil. The almost microscopic seed of the willow is wind-borne and its vitality lasts only a day; but a willow branch will take root in any moist soil, and a willow fence post becomes a brand new tree in a season or two.

The warm, translucent color in the willow stems beside the pond and in all the valleys is one of the most vital of all Spring colors. It is the essence of leaf and shade, stem and growth, root and bough, pulsing there before your eyes.

The Song of the Brook *March 25*

By the end of March the brooks are speaking a new language, chattering of change and singing quiet songs of the season. There is every reason that they should, for of all the waters of the earth, the water of the brooks is most alive, most quickly responsive to the shift of the sun and the urgencies of the earth. Life may have first appeared in the warm seas of the ancient past, and the boglands of today are reminders of such beginnings. But it is the live waters of the brook that talk of eternal Springtime.

The boglands are the quiet nurseries, at least until the redwings and the peepers begin to shout. What happens in the bogs has an air of mystery, of fundamental matters proceeding in elemental silence. The brooks are eloquent of that stage when life acquired a voice and the earth began to throb with achievement and jubilation. If the voice of the brook was not the first song of celebration, it must have been at least an obbligato for that event.

True, the voice of the brook is no more than the sound of water flowing downhill. But an oriole's song is only the throb of an avian throat, for that matter. Reduce it to an explanation and the song remains, whether it is the song of a bird or a brook or the wind. No song can be explained out of existence, any more than grass can be explained away by talk about green chlorophyll or a catkin disposed of by calling it an inflorescence. The song of the brook remains, a voice of change, a psalm of the surgent season.

The Daylight Stretch *March 26*

Now that the days begin to stretch, both morning and evening, the land and sky seem to stretch, too, and so do those who live close to the land. The countryman, whose eye has been on the end of Winter, now can look all the way to next Fall. When he goes out to the barn to do the morning chores, he can look across his fields and see corn planted and sprouting, pastures green, hayfields lush. He glances at his machinery shed and hears the mower clattering, the baler chomping, sees the corn picker going down the October rows and delivering a stream of yellow ears into the trailer wagon. He looks up at his silos and smells that fermenting smell of new ensilage. All this the last week in March.

There's day-to-daying, but there's also season-to-seasoning, and you sense it strongest when you have the earth underfoot. There's still snow back in the hills, and there's melt and mud to come before there will be mellow soil and the whole demanding urgency of growth. But the signs are here, right now, without a new leaf in sight and without one oriole greeting sunrise. The substance of change is there in the earlier dawn, the later sunset, and a man doesn't need an almanac to tell him.

One of these evenings the peepers will be out and yelping. And one of these days that crimson glow will appear in the lowlands where the swamp maples grow. Then the green will start. A man can't see it yet with his eyes, but it's as clear as that early sunrise to his understanding. He can see beyond tomorrow now, and beyond next week. He begins to stretch with the daylight.

The Interim   *March 27*

The yearning for mild days and the look and feel of Spring is as natural to man as March begins to merge with April as is the urge of a migrating bird to fly north. That is why we watch hopefully for the big signs and make so much of the little ones. We see a crocus clump in full bloom at last and exclaim over it as though it were a whole garden of flowers. We see half a dozen early bees gathering pollen in the purple chalices and want the honey smell of clover blossoms to be here tomorrow.

Celandine, a roadside weed, begins to show green leaves, and it is a hopeful miracle. Chickweed shows green at the edge of the garden, and instead of pulling it, as we will persistently in another month, we almost welcome it. Daffodil tips show cautious inches, and we peer for buds. We watch the iris swords beginning growth and wonder why the peonies aren't yet showing that stout crimson hope of furled shoots. We see the fat buds of the lilac and know, but can't quite believe, that they won't be opening into leaf and blossom for several weeks, at least.

We are Winter-weary, and the lengthened daylight is only a taunt, not yet the reality of Spring. This is what used to be sulphur-and-molasses time and now is capsulated-vitamin time. This is the interim, the painful pause between the seasons, no longer Winter, we hope, and not yet really Spring. Give us a few 60-degree days in a row and we will practically burst into either leaf or song. We have had enough of that white stuff. Now we want that green stuff, that chlorophyll. That is the basic reason we welcome April so eagerly. April has a green sound to it.

Succession   *March 28*

There is a succession in the days, now, that quickens the human heart. Whether they are gusty days or days of calm, chill days or days of deepening warmth, they have the air of change. No two days are alike. Sometimes it seems as though the season were trying a variety of moods, play acting in a dozen different parts, eager to be Spring and reluctant to be no longer Winter. But the very indecision is itself the mark of change.

The hardy plants of Spring reflect the trend. Daffodils are well up and hyacinths have broken ground. Crocuses have spread their color to the temperamental winds. Beneath their mulch, the peonies are showing pips of crimson. Flower buds are so fat on the forsythia that when a shoot is brought indoors its golden bells open almost overnight. And mountain pink is full of fat buds awaiting only a few successive days of April sun. There is the amber glow, luminous and almost translucent, in the willow withes.

You walk through the garden, still largely bare and waiting, and you see these things. And you look down a long hillside and you feel them, feel the pressure of succession, the slow but certain urge of change. Growth is there in the earth, at the grass roots, at the twig ends. The green world is waiting, already in the making where the mysterious chemistry of sap and chlorophyll has its origins. And the heart responds, already sensing the seedling, the new shoot, the Summer's dappled shade. April whispers from the hilltop, even as March goes whistling down the valley.

The Voices   *March 29*

The silence is ended. It was the silence which began with the last scratchy note of the last katydid, progressed with the brittle-dry scuffle of leaves in the roadway, deepened with the echo of owl hoot and fox bark. At its greatest depth it was a silence in which one could hear the whisper of snowflakes falling. Now it ends in the song of flowing water and the almost tentative voice of the pond frogs.

Those, of course, are the obvious voices. So, too, are most of the bird songs which now precede the great chorus. The early robins sing at dawn, even though their song seems to lack the smoothness it will have in May; and the crows jeer, as though at the robins; and the jays scream at the crows. Sparrows which have sung little through the cold months seem to have found their old songs again, or at least a few of them. And from the reeds down by the pond comes the half-harsh, half-liquid *ka-chee* of blackbirds newly arrived from the Southern marshlands.

The subtler voices call for listening, however. They only now begin to manifest themselves, but it is they that will make the very air vibrant in the months ahead. Find an orchard or a meadow and sit down and listen—still more important, feel with all your senses; and you will be aware of them. They are the outriders of the great insect horde—the ants, the first hungry bees, the earliest beetles and the minute flies which tap the opening buds for sustaining sap. They barely hum, now; but back of them is the whole season's insect life and loudness, waiting only a proper warmth to hatch and begin to hum or shrill. The silence is ended and will not return until the frost bites deep in another Autumn.

❧ The reference is to the red-winged blackbird, *Agelaius phoeniceus,* of course, and this version of the call is arbitrary, as are all phonetic versions of bird song. Some hear it as *o-ka-lee,* or *kon-ka-ree.* Aretas Saunders, in his *A Guide to Bird Songs,* says this song consists of "one to four gurgly, liquid, musical notes followed by a trill, or more rarely a series of rapid notes connected by liquid consonants." In a later entry in this book there is a discussion of bird songs and human attempts to put them into words.

The Spring Furrow   *March 30*

Some years the Spring plowing doesn't get under way until late April, or even May; but this year has been different. The robins came north several weeks ago—those that hadn't spent the Winter here—in great flocks. They salute the sunrise, they scatter over the pasture lands, and they follow the chuffing tractors and the plows, certain that Spring plowing is done specially for them. Go out into the open country and you can see the black furrows open to the sky. You can also smell the fragrance of fresh-turned loam, which is like no other smell in the world—earthy, rooty, elemental. It is the smell of Spring, of growth. Few farmers will admit it openly, but one reason for Spring plowing is to open up the fields and free that fragrance. It is better than any storebought tonic for a man who lives with the land.

Plowing is hard work, but not nearly as hard with modern machinery as it was with a team of horses and a walking plow. But even in the old days there was a sense of accomplishment in following the furrow, in seeing the smooth turn of fresh soil from the polished moldboard. The ability to turn a smooth, straight furrow was, and still is, a gauge of the farmer's skill. The expression "He plows a straight furrow" was long in the language and is still heard occasionally. But only farmers and gardeners know the vernal smell of a fresh furrow. It does something to them.

Anyway, April is not quite here and the plows are busy on many a hillside and many a flat forty. That doesn't mean there won't be frost, hard frost, still to come. It does mean that deep frost is out of the ground and that the smell of Spring is there waiting, the smell of the Spring furrow newly turned.

Dawn   *March 31*

Dawn comes early, almost an hour earlier than it did when March began. It is a crisp dawn, icy around the edges, and every roadside pool of yesterday's melt is filmed with a brittle, glassy pane. The pasture brook that chattered all afternoon and into the frosty evening is reduced to a whisper, the flow from the hillside's persistent drifts awaiting another midday's warmth. Turf that was soggy underfoot yesterday now is crusty to the tread. Dawn and dusk, day and night, abide by the season's deliberate rhythm of change.

A robin scolds in the young daylight, then sings a tentative song. Another robin answers. A blue jay flies to a leafless maple, gray against the sky, and twitters a Springsong that hasn't one jeering note. Two redwing blackbirds, fluffed fat against the chill, talk hoarsely to each other in a willow whose cautious catkins are still half sheathed. A cardinal whistles, waits, then whistles imperiously as though summoning the sun. Winter's silence has ended, but Spring's jubilation is still to come.

It is five-thirty. The sun rises just a trace north of east, ten days past the equinox. A man's breath twinkles, a faint cloud in the frosty air, and a trail of thin mist rises along the whispering brook. Four black ducks skim the naked treetops, wings swiftly beating, necks outstretched, silent as shadows. A man faces the sun, feels its glow, and knows that March, like the snow on the wooded hillside, is fraying away, flowing down the brooks, making way for April.

 APRIL

The Beginnings *April 1*

Peepers in the moist lowland shrill of April. In the warmth at the foot of the stone wall the earliest daffodils are ready to open, and a few red maples have already burst bud. Things are happening, the vernal change. Color will soon return, the bright pennants of Spring, the blossoms of a fresh and burgeoning world.

But the great change comes before the time of full flowering. The deep wonder lies in the beginnings. The bud itself is the major miracle. To watch the upthrust of a daffodil shoot, to see it take form as a sheathed blossom-to-be, to see that bud grow and take on the warmth of color—there is the synthesis of Spring. Once open, it is a flower, color to delight the eye, perfected beauty. But also, once open, it begins to fade, imperceptibly for a few days but slowly fading nevertheless.

Thus it is with a bud, whether it be of an eager maple blossom, a violet, a tulip, or the delicate anemone of the woodlands. Spring is there within it, and such perfection as shapes the leaf and the flower. But it is the process of Spring that constitutes the miracle, the way a pin oak tree stands on a hillside, fattening buds along its twigs and branches, and comes with slow deliberation to that time when all the little leaf points appear from the bud scales, and there stands a tree fringed out, no longer in bud and not yet in leaf. Or the way a beech unfurls its lance-point buds, or the way a shagbark hickory unclasps its amazing capsules. Or the way bloodroot comes to flower, and Dutchman's-breeches.

There is April, in the swelling bud. There is Spring. There are the deep wonders of this season, not in the flower but in the flower's beginnings.

April and Robins   *April 2*

People who can't tell a bald eagle from a vulture know what a robin looks like, and they know that when robins strut the lawn April must be here. April just isn't April, in this part of the world, without robins. Spring couldn't come without them.

The robin long ago became a kind of national bird without a shred of legal backing. It didn't need legal proclamations, for the robin is one of the best known and widely distributed birds in all these United States. Perhaps most important of all, it is a cosmopolitan bird, equally at home in a city park, on a suburban lawn and in the open country. Unlike most other thrushes, it prefers to nest near a house. Being a comparatively large bird, big as a blue jay, and a conspicuous bird with its black head and cinnamon-red breast, the robin simply can't be overlooked. Besides, robins love to strut. And to sing, preferably from a street-side tree.

The robin's song is often underrated, probably because the robin is so common and so vocal. But the robin, after all, is a thrush, and the thrushes are accomplished songsters. The robin sings long, loudly and rather deliberately. Its notes are clear and rich in tone. And no two robins sing exactly the same way; they vary their songs, put the phrases together differently. An individual robin may sing as many as ten different songs, varying with the time of day.

Robins are already singing in many places. Their chorus will increase day by day. After all, it is April, even to a robin.

❧ Robins again. There are a good many robins in this book, just as there are a good many robins in the United States except where DDT has decimated them. The American robin, *Turdus migratorius,* is a thrush and a wholly different bird from the European robin, *Erithacus rubecola,* which is about the size of our larger warblers. Both have red breasts, which apparently is one reason the early colonists here, remembering the robin redbreast at home, called the American thrush by the same name.

The Songless Songster   *April 3*

Even people who like all kinds of birds seem to merely tolerate grackles after they have seen the first dozen or so in early Spring. Just looking at a grackle, this seems rather strange, for a grackle is a large, graceful black bird with a beautiful iridescent sheen on its feathers. It has a graceful tail, it is well proportioned, it flies well. It struts when it walks, and it walks instead of hopping, as a robin does. It comes north early in the Spring.

Having said that, you have about exhausted all possibility of praise for a grackle. And just about then the grackle, which is technically classified as a songbird, opens its mouth and makes a noise. As an individual bird, a grackle can croak, squawk, make clattery noises, but it can't sing a note. A flock of grackles is an offense to the ear. Some have likened their noise to that of a fleet of squeaky wheelbarrows. Others think of rusty gate hinges, thousands of rusty gate hinges.

Give the grackle credit, though. He doesn't sail under false colors. The very name "grackle" goes back in origin to European words meaning "croak" and "garrulous." He has been grackling a long time, and everybody has known about it. Even his Latin name has a kind of grackle sound: *Quiscalus quiscula quiscula,* harsh and repetitious. He undoubtedly got his common name from the farmers who knew him best, who watched him in the Springtime, when insects were plentiful and grain was scarce, and in Summer, when grain was plentiful and insects had no lure.

Anyway, the grackles are here, clattering away. And pretty soon there will be some songbirds that can really sing.

The Legendary Peeper

The scientific name of *Hyla crucifer,* the tiny tree toad with the shrill, bell-toned April voice, reaches back into Greek legend. Hercules, says the legend, was fond of a boy named Hylas. While they were adventuring with the Argonauts, Hercules sent the boy to bring water from a spring; but the water nymphs captured Hylas and thereafter he lived in the water, calling for Hercules in his sweet young treble voice. Ever since, that voice has been heard in swamp and bogland in the Spring of the year.

There is really nothing very strange about the hyla we know except that it is a very small frog with a very large voice. It lives and grows much as any other frog, from egg to tadpole to adult frog. It hibernates, and it emerges in the burgeoning Spring hungry for food and a mate. It belongs to a family very old upon this earth, and in a sense it represents the very Springtime of life.

We usually call this small tree frog the Spring peeper, but there are other common names. On Martha's Vineyard it is the pinkle-tink, and on Cape Cod it is the pinkwink. Both names are, to a degree, imitative of the hyla's call. But no name can more than hint at the sound, which is at once clamorous and exultant and strangely musical and yet quite unmelodic. A chorus of Spring peepers close at hand can be a din of disorganized sound; yet from a little distance this same chorus can be pulse-lifting and rich with the warmth of Spring itself. There's nothing else quite like it. That is why we listen for it year after year, personify it into legend, cherish it as the very voice of another Spring.

The Certainty

There is a certainty about beginnings that is inescapable. We see them around us now, as always when Spring creeps across the land, beginnings and continuances that build the substance of faith and belief. Who can long have doubts when he stands beside a greening meadow, or walks through a woodland stirring with the slow vigor of Spring, or even when he sees the complex beginnings of a daffodil thrusting up from a hidden bulb?

There is not only certainty but purpose in these matters. The maple never puts forth oak leaves, nor does the bulb which last year bore a daffodil ever send up an iris bud. We know these things as certainly as we know that rain falls and brooks flow downhill.

Man is wise and constantly in quest of more wisdom; but the ultimate wisdom, which deals with beginnings, remains locked in a seed. There it lies, the simplest fact of the universe and at the same time the one which calls forth faith rather than reason. Plant a seed and it grows and puts forth blossom and fruit and comes in time to seed again. Thus the cycle is completed, seed to seed, fact to fact, with growth and beauty between. Probe into the seed, however, and you come to the germ. Probe into the germ and you come to the point where you must say, "This is the source. Growth begins here." But beyond that source lies faith, the ultimate beginning.

There are countless ways of phrasing it, in the language of the preacher, the philosopher, the scientist. But whoever speaks, he must come at last to the point where the one certainty is the beginning, and beyond that he must call on the understanding that is faith itself.

Beyond   *April 6*

Ever since the first Spring that ever was, man has stood at this season with awe in his eyes and wonder in his heart, seeing the magnificence of life returning and life renewed. And something deep within him has responded, whatever his religion or spiritual belief. It is as inevitable as sunrise that man should see the substance of faith and hope in the tangible world so obviously responding to forces beyond himself or his accumulated knowledge.

For all his learning and sophistication, man still instinctively reaches toward that force beyond, and thus approaches humility. Only arrogance can deny its existence, and the denial falters in the face of evidence on every hand. In every tuft of grass, in every bird, in every opening bud, there it is. We can reach so far with our explanations, and there still remains a force beyond, which touches not only the leaf, the seed, the opening petal, but man himself.

Spring is a result, not a cause. The cause lies beyond, still beyond, and it is the instinctive knowledge of this which inspires our festivals of faith and life and belief renewed. Resurrection is there for us to witness and participate in; but the resurrection around us still remains the symbol, not the ultimate truth; and men of goodwill instinctively reach for truth. Beyond the substance of Spring, of a greening and revivifying earth, of nesting and mating and birth, of life renewed. Thus we come to Easter and all the other festivals of faith, celebrating life and hope and the ultimate substance of belief, reaching like the leaf itself for something beyond, ever beyond.

Two by Two   *April 7*

Regardless of the weather, you can begin to count on the season when the birds pair off and start looking for nesting sites. Man puts it in his own terms when he speaks of "a young man's fancy," but the vernal urge is universal, not merely man's possession.

The robins begin to strut the lawn and pastures in pairs and the flocks will soon break up. You seldom see a bluebird without seeing another close by. Bluebirds, of course, are notable as family birds and are often spoken of as exemplars of domestic happiness and devotion. The house wrens have begun to court with song and flutter, and even the chickadees are taking to the woods again, two by two. In some places the flickers are pairing off and inspecting all the hollow trees in the area with the critical eye of apartment hunters. And the downy woodpeckers who still come to the suet boxes for a handout now come in pairs and seldom are long apart.

As they went into the Ark of Noah, two by two, so they return now and prepare for the time of nesting and brooding and raising the families. And the morning songs are mostly mating songs, for that is their urge and purpose. That song will rise to a chorus with the growing season, bird song and bee hum and Spring flowers opening. It's all a kind of celebration of life itself and life's own Springtime, with a background of peepers chiming in with their own two-by-two chorus. For even the frogs know that Spring is essentially a matter of one and one, endlessly repeated.

Wild Goose   *April 8*

The geese are on the wing, moving north with April. You hear them in the night, like small dogs yelping in the far distance. You see them in midmorning, a penciled *V* against the sky, high overhead and pointing northward. You pass a country pond and see them in late afternoon, resting and feeding, gray bodies and long black necks with white chin straps sharply outlined against the luminous water. You hear them gabbling in the dusk.

Robins return and sing paeans to domesticity. Peepers emerge from muddy hibernation and shrill the boglands with celebration of life's resurgence. But the wild goose comes north with the voice of freedom and adventure. He is more than a big, far-ranging bird; he is the epitome of wanderlust, limitless horizons and distant travel. He is the yearning and the dream, the search and the wonder, the unfettered foot and the wind's-will wing.

True, the goose is no songster, by any stretch of the imagination. He is neither brilliant in color nor really spectacular in flight. He is neither romantic thief nor colorful villain, neither wastrel nor philanderer. We call a fruitless errand a wild-goose chase and we use his name as a synonym for stupidity. Yet the cry of the wild goose and the sight of a migrant flock can send our hearts and imaginations winging. It may have been by chance that the goose feathered the winging arrow and quilled the poet's soaring pen; but we doubt it every Spring when the wild geese come gabbling north again.

The Dawn Chorus   *April 9*

Enough of the migrant birds are back again to make quite a chorus at dawn. Hardy week-enders who are already going to the country may think such birds begin to sing soon after midnight, but the countryman, whose day starts early, knows this is something of an exaggeration. The robins, for instance, do get up before the sun, and the sun now rises soon after five o'clock; but 5 A.M. isn't exactly midnight. Not in the country, at least.

For anyone who really appreciates bird songs, this dawn chorus is the top concert of the day. From now until mid-June the birds will be singing most of the morning, and some of them will be celebrating sunset and dusk as well, but their best performance comes early in the day. It starts with the first thin light of day, when a few birds awaken and begin to call. As they get answers they seem to feel encouraged. Calls become tentative songs. The light strengthens and so do the songs. The birds open up their repertoires.

As sunrise approaches the chorus becomes enthusiastic. Then there is a pause, as though all the birds were awaiting some great event. Suddenly the sun is there on the horizon and the wait is over. Every bird in every tree begins to sing. The earlier chorus was only a preliminary. This is the main event. The birds sing as though it were the first dawn that ever was and they must celebrate.

For about an hour the chorus is magnificent. Unless one wants to sleep, of course. But who wants to sleep in the midst of such celebration? A new day has begun, and everyone should celebrate. In the country, at least.

First Bloom   *April 10*

The rains of April have a different feel from the rains of March. They are not warm rains, really, but they are no longer the icy rains that threaten momentarily to turn into snow or sleet. The rains of April soak the hillsides and swell the streams, but most of all they strengthen the root and encourage the bud. The high-hung bud in particular.

The old saying credits April's showers with bringing the flowers of May, and that is true enough. But before the violets come, and the Dutchman's-breeches, there is a great host of other flowers. They are not the kind that send us hurrying to the fields to pluck and admire; but the early bees know them for what they are.

Look down along the brook, now that the April rains have come, and you will see that the impatient willows are dangling fat catkins, the gray tassels of Spring. Turn to the damp lowlands where the swamp maples have stood in Winter nakedness for so long, and you can see the haze of red from their opening buds. And where the spicebush grows in a tangle of undergrowth there is a greenish-yellow mist of small bloom along the branches.

These are the flowers of April, the blossoms that come before the leaves. They reach for the early sunlight, and it is the mild rain of April that gives them encouragement. Other flowers, the groundlings, will be along in time to make late April and early May a colorful delight. Anemones will be dangling delicate white petals in the wind almost any day now, and dogtooth violets will spatter the bogs with flecks of gold. But it is the high-hung flowers, the bloom on the bough, that April showers first encourage.

The Beginning   *April 11*

It's a long story and away back, but the man—or woman—who domesticated the first peas undoubtedly did it to have something to plant before it's really time to plant a garden. Peas are a perfect excuse to go poking in the ground before the frost is really out or the melt fully absorbed. Peas are very satisfying to the person who must feel Spring come as well as see it and hear it, feel it in the soil.

Many gardeners and most farmers are that way about Spring and the soil. The farmer gets out and plows just as soon as the soil will turn from the moldboard. He has to feel the soil too. It's his world. He is rooted in it as surely as his corn and oats, and he can walk across a field and know the degree of Spring right down to the day and hour. So he plows, and he watches the crows and the robins and listens to the song sparrow and the phoebe, and knows the seasons are turning as properly as the soil there at his plowshare.

Maybe it's because Spring really comes from inside. Inside the earth as well as inside the man. The sun prompts it, but if there wasn't anything inside to be prompted, there wouldn't be any Spring. But there's the seed, there's the bulb, there's the bud, and there's the hope and confidence in the human heart. There's the whole essence of belief, the whole surge of life and growth, which answer the summons. State it any way you will, and pick your own cause and effect; but there's where you come out, year after year. A gardener plants peas and a farmer plows a field for corn because they know it's time to do those things. Because something in them responds to sun and rain and the whole summary of Spring's beginning.

The Empty Boast   *April 12*

One of the emptiest of man's boasts is that he has mastered his environment, this earth on which he lives. Spring after Spring he sees the floods come, sometimes minor, sometimes major and disastrous, but always water overflowing and invading land that man doesn't want flooded. And despite dams, dikes, diversion channels and all manner of controls, the streams from brook to river still have their way, and about all that man can do when the floods come is issue warnings and help people get out of the way of the water. Not even an orbiting weather satellite can divert the inundation.

Actually, man's own works have created more floods than they have controlled, despite all the hopeful planning. Every time a woodland is stripped, runoff is increased and streams are further swollen. Every time a bogland is drained, another reservoir for excess water is destroyed. Every time a valley is "reclaimed," an old flood plain is taken away from a river and that river's capacity is lessened. And every yard of new pavement covers a yard of soil that would absorb its share of potential flood water.

Flood control is a compromise, always, an attempt to restore old balances. Weather can upset all the balances. An extra foot of snow or an extra inch of rain can bring devastation to a whole river valley. It sometimes seems that nature is determined to show man who is in control. Nature has no such purpose, of course, but man might well temper his boasts from time to time. Especially when the floods come.

Spring Is for Laughter   *April 13*

It won't be long now, it can't be long, before Spring shows its full face and keeps it in sight. And of all the Spring tonics ever brewed, the sight of Spring itself is the most effective. Spring is bright and new and shiny, anything is possible, and you can laugh. You don't even have to take the weather seriously after the middle of April; you know it will even out pretty well.

So before long we can open the windows wide and let Spring in, and we can go out to the park or sit on a hillside and let Spring into us. And high time. It's time we looked beyond the human perimeter. You can't be suspicious of a tree, or accuse a bird or a squirrel of subversion or challenge the ideology of a violet. And once you find that out, you can begin to laugh again, both the laughter of sheer delight and the laughter of amusement at absurdity. We haven't had much laughter of that kind in quite a while.

We've had a long Winter, and not only in terms of weather. Humankind has achieved a kind of mass cabin fever. Life has been a serious matter, so serious that we got to forgetting that man can make a very funny fool of himself being serious. And taking other foolish men seriously. It has become a political crime, somehow, to laugh at some of the performers. Maybe we can now get outdoors and begin to smile and chuckle and laugh discreetly. At the animals first, and the birds, but eventually at men. And eventually we may recover our perspective, if enough of us begin to laugh at those who have so long insisted on being taken seriously with their absurd performances. It's time we opened a lot of windows. It's time we laughed again, in delight as well as relief. It's time to be rid of a few inhibitions and a lot of suspicions. It's time for Spring.

🌿 Winter's rigors and March mud often make early Spring a time of human cantankerousness and absurdity. Usually we can laugh off such antics, but the performance of the United States Senate's Subcommittee on Internal Security in the Spring of 1954, when this entry was written, made laughter unfashionable if not actually criminal. This editorial provoked several letters suggesting that the author was unpatriotic, perhaps even subversive.

April as It Is   *April 14*

Taken on its own terms, April is a welcome period of transition from March to May, a time of hope and promise. But, despite a persistent myth, April is seldom sweet and gentle, devoted to bee and blossom, especially here in the Northeast. How that myth began is anybody's guess, but its origins probably lie in England. Chaucer spoke of "April with his showers sweet," Stevenson wrote of "April come to bloom," and Browning yearned, "Oh to be in England, now that April's there."

The fact is that our April is not England's April, never was and probably never will be. Of our own poets, Robert Frost came closest to the truth when he said that April could be "one month on in the middle of May" or "two months back in the middle of March." Frost knew many Aprils and had few delusions about the seasons. Even Stephen Vincent Benét, speaking in urban terms, called it "grimy April."

True enough, April can be lovely, spangled with bloom and the newest of young leaves. It can be, and usually is, melodied with the voice of song sparrow and robin, redwing and oriole. And the call of the Spring peeper is the very voice of April. But April can also be cold rain, raw wind and, on occasion, snow. The cruelest aspect of April's tantrums, however, lies in the way they sometimes frost our hopes and expectations. We want to believe in that myth of gentle April. We want May in April. We are tired of Winter's cold leftovers. Given a taste of Spring in April, we want a full meal of it. And that's the gist of this whole matter of April.

The Fires of Spring   *April 15*

The fires of Spring are aglow in the swamps and along the damp valleys where the red maples root in the deep silt washed down from the hillsides. Maple buds have opened, and the warm crimson outlines every twig, a deep blush of color at a distance, a mass of ruddy florets when seen close by.

Look down any hillside now and you see them. The trees stand silvery gray against the massed brown of oak and ash, but their outlines are clear as the swift strokes of a pastel crayon. They flame with the deep red of an October apple. It is like a haze among the branches, almost an aura, and it seems an even deeper shade when seen against the blue of a clear April sky.

Red maples are insistent trees, insistent in their bold color. Last Fall they flared like candle flames, lighting the valleys with every shade of red. When a gusty wind swept through their branches, it swept their leaves away like a stream of embers whipped out of an open fire. Other maples might achieve a touch of scarlet, but here was the splash of red and scarlet and crimson and ruby and garnet, almost gaudy in its generosity.

Now comes the color again, the Spring color that precedes the lushness of the leaves. It will linger, and a warm amber will soften it as the florets mature; and the ground beneath the trees will turn crimson as the florets fall. Then the leaves will come, and the winged fruits, red as the blossom, will come swirling down on amber vanes. And the twigs themselves will show crimson, the same deep, insistent red, as the leaves unfold. For here is sunrise and sunset, here is the flame of the ruddy ember, on the branch.

Birch Haze   *April 16*

The gray birches are now preparing the green haze that will soon spread over the old hillsides, the first gauzy garments of Spring in the treetops. Before the birch haze appears, of course, the swamp maples are in bloom, crimson and all shades of red and orange; but that is blossom, not leaf. And the swamp maples are lowlanders, while the birches sweep up the slope where the mower has skimped his work, any slope where there is a rootbed.

The gray birches are the rabble of the birch family, with neither the dignity nor the endurance of the big white birches. They move in on wasteland and hillside pastures, strike root in a season and grow like weeds. Their purpose seems to be to clothe the land, create leaf mold in unlikely places. After them come the oaks, the maples and the white pines, but first come the birches. Their shallow roots loosen the soil, their leaves shade and enrich it. When they lose it to the tougher trees, they move on.

Gray birches grow tall and slim. They shed a constant freight of twigs. When the winds come and the heavy snows, they bow and tangle and they fall and rot; but their roots send up new shoots. They do not give up easily. Loggers pass them by except for spool wood or pulp or for kindling fuel. Farmers are forever warring with them in their pastures. Small boys swing on them. Woodpeckers mine them for food. They are of slight importance in man's economy, but nature's economy needs them.

And in Spring they are beautiful. The haze of young birch leaves is the very color of Spring. It is in the making now.

The Flicker   *April 17*

If the common names given to a bird indicate anything about its standing in public affection, the flicker stands high on the list. He is known as the yellow-shafted woodpecker, the golden-winged woodpecker, the pigeon woodpecker, Old Clape, the high-holer, Old Yellow-hammer, the wood-pigeon, Heigh-ho, Wick-up, Walk-up, the yawker bird, the hairy wicket, and probably several other names, most of them accompanied by affectionate adjectives.

Flicker, the most common name of them all, comes from its wavy flight. It flickers along. And it is unmistakable, big as a big, chunky robin, conspicuously barred in black and white above and speckled below. It has a scarlet patch on the crown and a black crescent on the lower chest. When it flies, the undersides of the wings have a golden touch from the bright yellow shafts of the wing feathers.

The flicker is known practically all over the United States, though it migrates from the cold northern country in Winter, even from the Adirondacks and the Berkshires. One reason for its wide range is its adaptability. It can forage on lawn and pasture with the robins, it can work the trees in true woodpecker fashion, or it can steal a little grain or fruit. And it will nest in a box or even on the ground if it can't find a suitable hole in a tree.

It's a friendly bird, though it can't sing worth a nickel. Even the other birds seem to recognize its friendship, for it will flock on occasion with robins or bluebirds or even with swallows and sparrows. It isn't generally known as a Spring bird, but back in the hills it isn't really Spring until the flickers return, yarruping and flickering and hammering and being generally companionable.

Marsh Marigold April 18

You have to get your feet wet to find the biggest and earliest marsh marigolds. They grow in the swamps and boglands, by preference, though they are occasionally found in stream margins. But they are worth a little wetting, for they are the purest gold that early Spring provides, breath-taking golden yellow.

The first of them are beginning to open bud now, with flowers like giant buttercups. The resemblance is no accident, for the swamp marigold belongs to the same family as the buttercup of the meadow. The Latin name, *Caltha palustris,* means "marsh cup." However, there is little resemblance between the foliage of the two plants. The marsh marigold leaves are shaped like big violet leaves.

Some call them cowslips, for no understandable reason. The true cowslip belongs to the primrose family and has no resemblance whatever to the marsh marigold. And, of all the flowers of Spring, only the buttercup itself can rival the marsh marigold in color. Its big, waxy petallike sepals are almost as big as a twenty-five-cent piece, however, and make the buttercup look like a dwarf in comparison.

The place to find them is where the giant marsh violets grow, preferably where running water warms their roots. The swamp with a slow flow is an ideal place, for the water flows without much current. There the marsh marigolds will grow in great clumps, on the oozy margins and even in the shallow water itself. There they bloom with a splash of color that can make late April a heart's delight even in a chilly season. And before they are gone, the big violets will begin to carpet the bogland with purple.

Blossom on the Bough April 19

If they never bore a bushel of fruit, the peach trees and the plum trees of this land would be well worth cherishing simply for the beauty of their blossoms. They are among the earliest of all our fruit trees to bloom, often putting forth flowers while the leaves are still shrugging their way out of bud. Indeed, in a good year the trees become pink or white before they are really green.

The peach blossom is a rare shade of pink which could, with one more blush, become crimson. At the base of the petals, in fact, it does verge into crimson. It is like a wild rose and it has a fragrance as dainty as its color. It is often as large as the little field roses that spread red-veined petals in the meadow in June. Its petals are softer than silk, this peach flower, and its multitude of stamens might be spun of some rare plastic which reflects the pink of the petals.

For individual show, the plum blossom can't compare with that of the peach. It isn't half the size, to begin with, and it has no color. The plum blossom is simply a little white five-petaled flower with a tuft of long-stemmed stamens. But it comes in groups; the whole tree is clustered with bloom. And its fragrance can sweeten a whole hillside, of an evening, a spicy fragrance sweet and tanged and reminding you of honey oozing from the comb. The reminder is no accident; when the plum tree is in full bloom it has more bees than blossoms.

Plums are beginning to bloom now, and so are peaches, to the glory of the countryside. Happy the man who owns such a tree, or even lives where he can see one and walk out and lets its fragrance sweeten his soul.

Dutchman's-breeks *April 20*

Dutchman's-breeches are in bloom on stony hillsides where the sun has begun to warm the soil beneath the leafless trees. The little white breeks tipped with gold sway on their slender stems, and the gray-green foliage feathers out around them as graceful as fresh fern fronds.

There is a dainty grace about Dutchman's-breeches, both in flower and leaf, that is matched among the early Spring flowers only by the rue anemones. And the anemones seem fragile; they lack the jaunty air of the breeks, which, although they quickly wither when plucked, give the air of being firmly rooted in April and able to stand up to anything that April brings.

Botanists call them *Dicentra cuculearia,* from the Greek which means "double-spurred." The reference is to the flower's shape. Actually, it has four petals. Two of them are joined to make the somewhat heart-shaped sack, which is technically double-spurred. The other two petals are inside the sack, very small and designed to protect the stamens.

The flower's shape makes it a natural host to the early bees, particularly the early bumblebees, which are its chief agents of cross-fertilization. Honeybees visit the breeks, but they can't quite reach the nectar, while the bumblebees can. Early butterflies also find a welcome there.

In another month the squirrel corn, *Dicentra canadensis,* which is a cousin of Dutchman's-breeches, will be in bloom on the same banks. But just now it's the season of the breeks themselves, jaunty as any Dutch boy in fresh-laundered pantaloons.

Grass   *April 21*

Of all the everyday plants of this earth, grass is the least pretentious and the most important to mankind. It clothes the earth in an unmistakable way. Directly or indirectly it provides the bulk of man's food, his meat, his bread, every scrap of his cereal diet. Without grass we should all starve, we and all our animals. And what a dismal place this world would be!

Grass is simplicity itself. Not the simplicity of the uncomplicated unicellular life of stagnant water, but specialized simplicity unmatched in the fields. All the grasses, even the corn and wheat and barley and oats, have achieved a kind of perfection by eliminating nonessentials. Their stems are seldom branched. Their leaves need no stem of their own, and they are long, tapering, economical expanses of chlorophyll. Their flowers have dispensed with petals, scent and honey, since they need neither bee nor butterfly to pollinate them. The wind does that job. Even their ovules are very simple, and their carefully rationed pistils. The flower's purpose is to make seed, not show, and it does it most efficiently. Even the roots of grass are uncomplicated.

So there it is, the simple grass, perfect for its purpose and found almost everywhere that plants can grow. It may vary into a hundred species, but never does it complicate itself too much. It grows tall, as bamboo. It grows generous, as corn. It grows lush and cool, as bluegrass. It is a weed sometimes, but it is a lawn, a pasture, a hayfield, a thousand-acre ocean of wheat. And now it greens the earth again, Spring in the lifting blade, everywhere.

Why? *April 22*

Before we are caught up in daylight saving again, these Spring-dusky evenings are a good time to ponder vernal questions. Before long many of us will be busy with lawn mowing and gardening, which leave little time for deliberate answers.

Why do crows get up so early in the morning? And why are they so energetic about it, and so vocal? Are they trying to get their pieces spoken before the real songsters get settled and tuned up? After a long and presumably hungry Winter, why aren't fish more eager for the kind of food fishermen offer them in April? Why does a thunderstorm in April seem so loud? Because we haven't heard one in so long? Or is it because there are few leaves on the trees to break the echoes? Why doesn't chickweed winterkill?

Why are woodchucks so glad to find any kind of pasture greens and early weeds in April and so insistent on eating only garden stuff in May? And June. And July. And August. Why, for that matter, are woodchucks? Couldn't foxes and other predators find some other dietary item if woodchucks were omitted from the menu? Do blue jays really lose some of their color in Spring, or do they merely look drab when compared to a bluebird? Why don't the warblers migrate just a little earlier, to brighten things up?

Why did anybody ever introduce the starling, which is not an American native, to this country? The red-winged blackbird can't sing a real song, but is there a cheerier sound in the April marshes than its rasping call? Why does celandine bloom so early? What makes dandelions so hardy? Why don't more birds eat more wasps? What wakes up the ants, and the moles, and the no-see-'em gnats? Why can April be so changeable? Why?

🐦 For several years I wrote a "Why?" every few months, and I have included a number of them in this volume. Their questions were not intended to be taken too seriously, and the answers often were obvious. I wrote them in part for my own amusement, in part because they voiced questions often asked. *The New Yorker,* in its issue of Nov. 26, 1955, printed an amusing piece about one of the "Why?" essays, answering the questions in accurate scientific detail. It was a splendid bit of dead-pan satire.

April Evening   *April 23*

The daylight is longer, much longer, now, and the dusk itself has a persistence that it lacked two months ago. Then the sun hovered for a brief moment on the western horizon, plunged out of sight and left the world to darkness. Now it seems to hover there several moments, and it vanishes in a glow that lingers, a soft twilight that fades slowly into darkness.

And the stars come slowly into sight instead of bursting into full glow. The Dipper rides high, almost directly above the pole-star, and Cassiopeia and Cephus are down near the horizon. In the south Leo stands high and Scorpius and Libra are low. But all of them are patient about their coming. They can wait for the frog trill to reach its evening peak.

The evenings are full of sound now, too; not only the frogs but a few of the birds can be heard after sunset. It is yet too early for the insect chorus, but life is up and stirring. You can sense sounds that you cannot yet hear, and you know that dusk does not clamp down with the deep silence.

Perhaps the most noticeable change of all is in the evening silhouettes. The trees begin to have substance now instead of mere skeletal shadows. Maple leaves are spreading. Even in the deep dusk you can see less starlight through the apple trees. The shape of shade to come is almost evident. And with this substance comes a new voice in the wind. The dry rustle and rasp of branch on branch gives way to the whisper of little leaves, each grasping at and fluttering in the downhill breeze. It is a live sound, for the evening itself has come to life.

The Moment   *April 24*

This is the moment, that moment which may last for a day or a week, depending on the wind and weather. It is the time when tree green trembles between wary bud and opening leaf, when a few hours of concentrated sunlight could almost change the face of the land. The canopy that will be Summer shade and next Autumn's vivid color is there on twig and branch, ready to unfurl. And even that statement is so local, so circumscribed by geography and weather, that it was out of date yesterday a hundred miles from here and probably will be out of date this morning somewhere within reach of a stoutly flung stone.

And that in itself is a measure of the delicate poise of the moment. A chilly wind can prolong it a little longer in one valley; across the hill in the next valley an afternoon of sunlight can mist a whole woodland with such green as we have not seen in a twelvemonth. The tracery of maple blossoms opening has been like the brushing stroke of a pastel crayon across the treetops in the lowlands, and the tiny bloom of spicebush has twinkled, stardust in the lower woodland. The osiers and the willows have been amber and ruby and then have ventured into first leaves, among the most eager of all the trees and bushes, along the watercourses.

And now the others are waiting, the birch, the beech, the ash and elm, and the maples especially. The oaks are later, cautious ever to fringe themselves with delicate pink and fugitive orange and then with green. But this is the moment when it is beginning to happen, one place and another; that breathless moment when new green leaves first open toward the sun.

Mr. Towhee   *April 25*

Some call Mr. Towhee the chewink and some call him the ground robin. Both *towhee* and *chewink* are supposed to represent the first two notes of the bird's characteristic call; and, as further proof of the fallibility of words in transcribing bird calls, Thoreau set down the same notes as *hip-you* and Seton heard them as *chuck-burr*. Few other bird calls have been so variously interpreted.

But nobody is confused for long about the bird himself. Richly marked with glistening black head and neck, clean white breast and belly, and rich chestnut-red sides, Mr. Towhee is a jaunty fellow almost as long as but slimmer than a robin. His mate is almost as vividly marked, with warm brown where the male is black. They make a striking pair in any field or back yard. But it is their vigor that most often makes them noticed. A towhee in a patch of dead leaves can make as much fuss as a bantam rooster. Only a fox sparrow can equal him for such activity, and the towhee is the more efficient of the two. He scratches the ground with alternate feet; the fox sparrow scratches with both feet at once.

For all his nervous activity, the towhee is easily imposed upon, especially by cowbirds. Some say that more cowbirds are hatched by towhees than by any other species. And still the towhee is a happy companion to have around. He comes north in April, almost as sure a sign of Spring in these parts as the bluebird. He doesn't sing like an oriole, quite, but he makes the world a brighter place. Who cares what words he sings, as long as he struts and flirts his eloquent tail?

The Digger

Some people are like ants. Give them a warm day and a piece of ground and they start digging. There the similarity ends. Ants keep on digging. Most people don't. They establish contact with the soil, absorb so much vernal vigor that they can't stay in one place, and desert the fork or spade to see how the rhubarb is coming and whether the asparagus is yet in sight.

Anyone knows that you can't just go out and work in a garden at this time of year the way a farmer does in his field. You have to woo a garden, from the very first day, testing its moods and giving your own moods a chance. There's no hurrying the relationship. When you've planted your first peas, you've done enough to start. After that you have to deliberate on where to put the next peas, and the spinach, and the lettuce. You need a warm afternoon for deliberating. And on cold days it's too cold to dig.

Rome wasn't built in a day, nor was Agricola's garden, or whoever it was that Horace wrote about. If you dig a garden all at once, you have no energy left to plant it. Do it bit by bit and you will have strength to pull the weeds later on.

There's no denying these truths once you stand with your feet on the soil and the spade in your hands. Such philosophy springs directly from the earth. The time will come when there's no other way out—you either dig and rake and plant or you give up. But on a warm afternoon in late April, well, let the ants do the hurrying. They don't know any better. Besides, they don't know rhubarb from pokeweed. A man does, if he's a gardener. And it's his duty to keep tabs on the rhubarb. The spade will be right where he left it when he gets back—if he ever does.

Lilacs

The lilac is not an American native, but few flowering shrubs are more typical of the American dooryard. And few are more pervasive with their fragrance or more generous with their blossom. May and lilacs are almost synonymous, and lilacs and apple blossoms are an inevitable pairing. Late April and the green of lilacs is one of the warmest greens on the landscape.

The lilac is native to Persia, but it has been known in Europe since the sixteenth century and it came to this country with the early colonists. It has been cherished by every generation of American householders. It stands today beside countless cellar holes, particularly in New England, testimony to some vanished housewife's hunger for blossoming sweetness. The houses are gone, the families scattered, but the lilacs persist, blooming May after May, for the hardihood of those old bushes is amazing.

The way of a lilac's leafing is one of Spring's miracles, particularly the opening of the terminal buds. They always come in pairs, and often through February, always through March, they seem on the verge of opening. They poise there, swelling with each day that is not down to zero. Then come the first warm days and they begin to open. Inside is a whole complex of miracles, not only tiny leaves but whole heads of blossoms, pin-point small at first but so full of color that they seem to stain the new leaves purple. The bud opens, the leaves unfold, and out of those terminal buds come stem and leaves and blossoms by the individual hundred, each full of sweetness and color. For that is the generous way of the lilac, queen of the American dooryard.

The Contact   April 28

A garden has two purposes. One is to grow vegetables which feed the gardener's body and flowers which warm his heart. The other is to satisfy his need for intimate contact with the earth and growing things. Which of these purposes is more important can be disputed endlessly, but eventually the answer lies in the gardener. Perhaps, if one ever arrives at the truth of the matter, they are of approximately equal importance; as has been said many times, man does not live by bread alone, nor by lettuce and carrots and beets and potatoes and broccoli. Man happens to be a sentient person as well as a hungry animal.

By the end of April the real gardener must get his hands in the soil. Planting seeds is a good and profitable exercise, but what he needs, down in his very marrow, is contact with the earth and communion with the rootbed of life. Atoms and molecules are all very well in their place, but soil, humus, compost, earth teeming with the sources of growth, are vital beyond measure. You don't have to know the chemistry of soil or the physics of molecular structure to feel the surge of life beneath your fingertips. You dig, you rake, you plant and you are participating in the ultimate, mysterious miracle.

Such participation is at once humbling and exhilarating. You become a partner of sun and wind and rain. You acknowledge the great forces, the primal urge. You become somewhat master of a plot of earth, encourage it to do your bidding, and eventually you reap, if you are fortunate. But at planting time you chiefly commune with the earth and cooperate with the elements and take part in Spring itself. You make contact with life.

A Promise   *April 29*

By April's end there is no doubt of the season. Early or late, it is definitely Spring, and no matter how dogged have been the frosts back in the hills, no matter how deliberate have been the early flowers, May is at hand and the grass is green and the buds are opening, leaf and petal. Robins sing, daylight lingers, and the world gets on with its vernal business.

A late Spring means a busy May. Nature always catches up with herself, somehow, before June arrives; and if there is much to be done, it is done in a hurry, once a start is made. Late April is, at best, only a beginning, a bursting of bud and a preparation for major matters. Before we are quite aware of it, the trees will be in full leaf, the earliest blossoms will be past, and June will be hurrying across the hayfields.

It is perhaps significant that April, back at the root of the word, meant "the open air," the air out-of-doors. So it is only reasonable that we should expect much of April after Winter and March, when the open air was somewhat less than hospitable. April is an opening up, not only of the bud but of the heart, for of all the seasons this is the one in which we have the most urgent need to participate. We must have a part in the new awareness, the partnership with time and sunshine. Man is more than a shrub or a vegetable, but he, too, needs Spring.

So we come to the end of April, even a chilly April, with bird-song around us and some of Spring's color; and we feel the strengthening sun, we sense the opening buds, we know again that no Winter lasts forever, no Spring skips its turn. April is a promise that May is bound to keep, and we know it.

End of April   *April 30*

By the end of April the commitment is complete. Late Spring or early, we are on our way into the fullness of mid-May, and June will come billowing across the meadows before we know it. Meanwhile there are a lot of things to be done. All the buds have to open, all the acres of chlorophyll have to be spread in the sunlight, all the early blossoms have to unfurl. The earth has to get on with its vernal business.

One thing about it, though, is that man hasn't much to do with what happens. The farmer, who lives closer to the land and the seasons than anyone else, knows this down deep in his bones. He knows that the seasons make their own calendar, and he knows that all he can do with Spring, really, is recognize it when it comes and cooperate with it. He can't leaf out a tree or liven a root or sprout a seed. But if he does his part he can be sure that nature will do its part—most of the time. So he plows, in season, and he plants and cultivates, and usually he gathers a harvest.

That's why the countryman is out in his fields right now. The season says it's time for him to be there. He has a partnership with time and the weather, but they are the ones who give the orders. We all have such a partnership, though the farther we get from the land the more difficult it is to admit it. Humility doesn't come easy. But where is the man who can say he had any hand in late April or early May? All man has really done is give the months their names and call this season Spring.

 **MAY**

May Baskets   *May 1*

Do youngsters anywhere still hang May baskets, or has May Day become wholly a date of social significance?

There was a time when May Day meant sentiment. It was preceded by a busy week when young fingers were weaving baskets and small cornucopias out of colored paper. Between spells of basketmaking, scouting expeditions were made to the woods and fields, to see how the season went with wild flowers. And at least one trip was made to the candy store.

On April's last day, as late as possible, the scouting expeditions were followed up. Purple violets, preferably those big, dark, long-stemmed ones which grow at the edge of the swamp, were picked. Dogtooth violets were gathered. And windflowers, if any were to be found. Spring beauties were sought, and Dutchman's-breeches. And the most delicate of young fern fronds were gathered for garnish. All were carried home in the dusk and stowed carefully in cups and glasses of water.

May Day morning called for early rising. In the bottom of the basket or cornucopia were put a few jelly beans left over from Easter, a few gumdrops, and at least one heart-shaped wafer candy printed with coy words of affection. Then the flowers were added till the basket brimmed with beauty. And at last, before breakfast if possible, the trip was made to Her house, where the basket was hung on the doorknob. The bell was rung and the basketeer ran like mad, to hide around the corner until She came and found the tribute.

That was May Day, in the morning, when there was sentiment in the date. The candy might be cheap, the flowers somewhat wilted; but the sentiment was real. What ever happened to it, anyway?

Violets for May Day   *May 2*

The violet isn't the first Spring flower—hepatica, bloodroot and anemone, to name but three, come earlier; but when the first violets bloom we can count on Spring. After the violets comes the whole flood of flowery May. The earth celebrates the season.

Violets have been known and cherished since antiquity. The Persians loved them. The violet was the flower of Athens, and Ionia was named for it. The Romans used violets in medicines and love philters. In ancient England the violet was a symbol of modesty and constancy, and American Indians knew it as a symbol of love and courage. The first colonists felt somewhat at home when they found violets among the wild strawberries in the fields, for they had picked violets in English meadows as children.

America's violets range in color from deep purple through the shades of lavender and include both yellow and white ones; but the deep purple ones with heart-shaped leaves grow almost everywhere. In a moist meadow they make their way among the grasses and clovers. In a bogland they grow rank, with stems sometimes a foot long. They creep into suburban gardens as though borne on the wind. They flourish at the country roadside, particularly in May.

Bees collect violet nectar. Early butterflies patronize their lunch counters. Youngsters used to gather them by the handful for May baskets. The rest of us just appreciate them and their warm generosity of bloom. Particularly when late April stands undecided between the seasons. Then we pick a few violets and know what time it really is.

A Boy and a Brook   *May 3*

Travel the country roads on a weekend, when school is not in session, particularly the hill roads beside the brooks, and you will see him. The boy beside the brook, the boy with a bait rod or a fly rod and a special light in his eye. Note that it isn't a willow pole he has, nor a twine string with a bent pin. Chances are you can look all season and never see that fictional young fisherman. If he ever did exist, which is doubtful, he is gone now. This boy beside the brook isn't being picturesque; he's fishing. He probably has a nylon line, and he knows his leaders, his wet flies and dry ones, and the way to use a worm. He also knows the water, the coves, the eddies, the ripples, and he knows fish.

Country boys have been fishing for a long, long time. It's a part of their growing up. Listen to a middle-aged man in waders and within five minutes he will say, "When I was a boy," or, "Thirty years ago," and tell you the exciting things that happened right over at that bend or at the mouth of that brook. He has special memories, and now and then he will even share them. Not only of fish and fishing, but of sunlight on water, and shadblow in bloom, and misty dawns, and days that were full of April, or May, or June.

If you ever wondered why fishing is probably the most popular sport in this country, watch that boy beside the brook and you will learn. If you are really perceptive you will. For he already knows that fishing is only one part fish. Unless you too were a fisherman when you were young, you may never know the other components, but you can sense them a little, just watching. That boy probably won't tell you. He's a little bashful about such things. But he will remember, all his years. And so will you, just seeing him, seeing that look in his eyes.

The Miracle of the Bud *May 4*

The earth teems now with the unseen miracle of new roots grop-
ing downward and young shoots reaching for the light and sun;
but all around us, in plain sight, is the equal miracle of the buds.
Out of the buds, so countless and so commonplace, come this
world's green leaves, its wealth of bloom, its surging growth of
twig and branch and stem. The miraculous surrounds us now.

Who would think, seeing the brown twig-tip buds of the lilac
in December, that in those Winter-dormant buds was packed such
a freight of leaf and stem and blossom as now reveals itself? Man's
most astonishing machine could not pack so much into so small
a space, let alone free it at a proper time and in a precise order.
Who, glancing at the nobby twigs of a pear tree in March, would
believe that silvery leaf and milk-white blossom were stowed there
for May? Who, passing a brook lined with swamp maples in ice-
locked January, would believe that the minute buds on those
branches would turn a valley crimson with blossom and then
green with shade?

Look at the dogwood, which defied the Winter with twig-end
buds like praying mantis heads and now is full of white-butter-
fly bloom and green squirrel-ear leaves. See how the willows,
which rattled cold twigs, seemingly bare as bones, in the February
wind, come to kitten-soft catkin and then to a whispery mist of
slender leaf. Watch the beech tree feather out in green gauze.
See how the birches achieve catkin and shimmery green of heart-
leaf. See the astonishing way a hickory unpacks its pink-sheathed
buds, putting the magician to shame for his parsimony. Look, and
know the miracle of the bud, the wonder packet of green life.

The Profundity of May *May 5*

Apple blossoms are pink and white in the orchards, and the bees
are working overtime. Violets bloom in the lowlands. Dogwood

whitens in the woodland, and along the gray stone walls the windflowers blow, the bloodroot still blooms and jack-in-the-pulpit and trillium open big, new leaves and prepare exotic blossoms. The brook runs bankfull; the pond laps at its high-water mark. April's rains are past and May is, initially at least, full of growth and sunshine.

And there is the profundity of May. There is a notion that anything with a depth of meaning must be hard to understand, must be written in an obscure language and reserved for the few. Yet here is May, a time of tremendous fundamentals and miraculous matters, all of them spread before us, flagrantly demanding attention. Its language is as simple as a new leaf or a buttercup flower.

Here is the fundamental of life, the whole process of germination and growth. Here is flowering and fertility and life preparing its own renewal. Here are sunlight and water being turned into food, photosynthesis, an even more profound process than atomic fission; and it goes on in every blade of grass, every tree leaf, every weed in the gutter, no more secret than sunlight. Here is abundance, and growth and beneficence, so much of it that the world seems hard put to contain it all. It constantly spills over, outreaching itself in abundance.

And there is another of the simple profundities of May. One of the fundamental laws of the world itself is plenty, not scarcity; production, not destruction; growth, not stagnation.

❧ My own apple trees are particularly responsive to the weather and may come to bloom any time from the last week in March to the third week in May. That is why apple blossoms are mentioned several times in this chapter. They usually open the same week as the lilacs, however. And when apples bloom I go out to look for, and always find, the first blossoms on the showy orchis, *Orchis spectabilis*, one of the most beautiful of all our small orchids.

Bluets *May 6*

Bluets are in blossom on upland pastures, and along back-country roadsides are patches of them that look like frost in the fresh green grass of early morning. They look frosty despite their name, for bluets are not blue at all; they are white with a faint tinge of lilac at the edge of the petals, and their centers are golden yellow. They are tiny, four-petaled flowers, seldom more than half an inch across, and they grow on stems about six inches long. In some places they are known as Quaker-ladies; elsewhere they are often called innocence. They grow from Maine to Georgia and west as far as Michigan.

Botanically, bluets are called *Houstonia caerulea*, and they belong to a strangely varied family, the madders. That family includes the coffee tree, the cinchona, from which we obtain quinine, the madder itself, from which a red dye is extracted, and the partridgeberry, that modest creeper of our Eastern woods. The family also includes those sprawling, prickly, inconspicuous-flowered weeds called bedstraw and goose grass.

Bluets are the smallest of the madders. One bluet in bloom is of no consequence at all. But bluets grow in patches, huge patches, and in the mass they are unmistakable and demand the eye. Violets, the low, short-stemmed meadow violets, often grow in the same meadow with them, but the violets have to be searched out in the grass, while the bluets make a display. They are helped, of course, by the smaller butterflies which cross-fertilize them, and on a clear, calm, sunny day the grass will be white with bluets and the air will be gay with fritillaries, clouded sulphurs and painted ladies—May at its best.

The Rush of Bloom *May 7*

It always comes with a rush, and always it surprises us with the extent of its generosity. It is as though we forget, from year to

year, how many blossoms there are, how pink an apple tree is in full bloom, how white is dogwood and how purple are lilacs. Then the warm days come, the buds open, the little leaves appear; and almost before the world has turned green it is covered with flowers on bough and branch.

This is one of those particularly spectacular dogwood years, and the weather has been right. The woodlands gleam with the creamy white leaf petals, so clearly visible while maple leaves are still miniatures, ash leaves are still opening, and hickory leaves are yet half encased in their silken sheaths. Dogwood is like a vast swarm of white butterflies in the Spring woods.

And lilacs, in the dooryard or at the roadside, seem to have outdone themselves. Perhaps there are no more blooms than usual, but it seems so. And their color seems deeper. The great purple flower heads nod with the night's dew and bow low after a rain and lift themselves regally in the sunshine; and at evening they flavor every breeze with the too-sweet wine of Spring.

The apple trees are past their prime, but they still stand like giant bouquets across the valley. And now they begin to strew their beauty on the wind, the petals streaming with every gust and whitening the new grass beneath the trees. Theirs is the sweet confetti of Spring's festival.

The rush is upon us, swifter even than the tide of green. And every year it goes too swiftly. Perhaps that is why we forget. Or it may be that we forget simply that we may be awed and delighted afresh each year.

The Wonder   *May 8*

Now comes a time of particular satisfaction with the green and fertile world. The brown hills are green again. Shade thickens in the valleys. Apple orchards are full of fragrant bloom and pear trees stand clothed like brides. Lilacs perfume the evening air, and peonies bud and shoot up like fabulous beanstalks. In the deep woods the trillium nods with crimson flowers and jack stands in his green pulpit and lady's slipper opens its moccasin flower. Violets attempt to purple the earth, and anemones persist in clouds of white for days after their early season should have ended. Elms are full of little leaves. Dogwood gleams, creamy white. Maples, which seemed to dally so long with blossom, now are clothed in green.

And the soil, the garden soil that lay wet and chill so long, begins to warm up. The gardener can make obeisance to it and feel response. There is life in that soil, now, the strength of Summer and the growing season. You feel it with your fingers, somehow, a vitality waiting to be tapped. The forces of growth are there, waiting for tillage and seed and understanding.

It is this sense of natural forces that is so satisfying. The tree bursting bud for a million leaves, the bursting into bloom, the grass covering a whole hillside. Migrating birds come in swarms, guided by some instinctive force, back to the homeland, the nesting grounds. The air fairly pulses with growth and life.

Later we will be so shaded, so overgrown, that the senses will become a little numbed. It is now that we are most aware of these things, now when brown memories are so clear and the bright change is so new. It is now, when leaves are still new and flowers still full of Spring, that the satisfaction and the wonder have their glow.

A Time to Look and Listen   *May 9*

This is the time of year when anyone who will look and listen can't avoid the suspicion that something beyond man's restless activity is at the heart of things. The countryman plowing a field or planting corn knows that he is working with forces greater than the horsepower of his chuffing tractor, and the city person, if he looks at the grass and trees in the nearest park, knows that his meat and vegetables didn't grow there in the corner market. There's the matter of soil and sun, of the earth and the sky. There are seeds and buds and there is germination and growth. There are urgencies and processes far older than the plow or the reaper, and they are at the root of all life as we know it. Man would perish without them.

Spring isn't really an object lesson. Nature is not in the teaching business. Nature is change and growth and all kinds of life, proceeding in its own way. But if man can't see that he is not indispensable, especially in the Springtime, he is blind indeed. Grass grows, trees flourish, birds nest and animals give birth without the need of one furrow turned or one pen built. Every meadow and woodland proves it, and every treetop and riverbank.

Man gets so busy with his own affairs that he forgets. The noise he makes with his own machines tends to drown out the quiet, fundamental voices. But if all the machines rusted away, the green and quietly busy world would still be here, going about its own business. Maybe Spring is a time for man to listen, a few minutes, and look, and even ponder a few questions about his own omnipotence.

Dandelions *May 10*

See the pretty dandelions, blooming everywhere. Is there a finer yellow to be seen anywhere around? The answer, though not exactly responsive, is that the dandelion is a pest, a nuisance, an interloper and several other things, all preceded by adjectives. Especially if the answerer is a man with a cherished lawn. People who like their lawns don't like dandelions, though the fact remains that the dandelion flower, viewed dispassionately, is as pretty as, say, a calendula or an aster. Furthermore, the dandelion is good to eat, if you like cooked greens. Not as tasty as some things not half as good for you, perhaps, but good Spring fare, fully as tasty as rhubarb or a lot of other beneficial Spring herbs.

The thing about the dandelion is that it has so many offspring. How can so flimsy a little puff of down and so minute a seed possess such vitality? Let one beautiful dandelion go to seed at the far corner of your lawn today, and tomorrow you have dandelions all over the place. The chicory you grow in the garden for a salad green isn't that proliferating, and chicory is a cousin of the dandelion. Several other salad greens are of the same family, and they don't take over the place even if you let them go to seed. You have to plant them and cultivate them and coddle them.

But not the dandelion. It will grow in a crack in a cement sidewalk. It will grow on an ash heap. Neither flood nor drouth seems to discourage it. The lawnmower merely provokes it to greater effort. You fight dandelions all week end, and late Monday afternoon there they are, pert as all get out, in full and gorgeous bloom, pretty as can be, thriving as only dandelions can in the face of adversity.

The Rose Kin Come to Bloom   *May 11*

First came the shadbush, its bloom like a shimmering white mist in the woodland, breath-taking in its beauty. Then early pears came to blossom, virginal as white chiffon in moonlight, each tuft of bloom set in a richness of silver-green leaf. Next the apple trees unfolded their pink-tinged buds to glorify the hillsides and the pristine valleys, pink and white and dawn-sweet against the chorus of greens that means mid-May. Soon the chokecherries will hang out their fat fluffs of frothy blossom. And then the pink pasture roses will glorify the fence row and meadow margin, sweet as June and lovely as a smile; wild roses, the only ones that still carry the family name.

For all of them are roses, of one kind and another. All came, the paleobotanists tell us, from a common plant back in the misted past when the blossom was a new adventure in plant evolution. Those five petals and that wealth of stamens are a family characteristic, and so is the fruit, whether it be an apple or a rose hip, a pear or a Juneberry. Adam knew the apple, in some form.

But now, in May, the fruit is a minor matter for tomorrow, next month, some future time of harvest. Now the rose kin all around us are sheer beauty, and we ask no more of them. Orchards are massed bouquets. Woodlands are adorned with the rose cousins in full glory. The petals shimmer. The pollen lures the bees. The May sun dances and the May air sings in celebration.

Adam may not have eaten the apple, but in May we can be sure that Eve wore apple blossoms in her hair.

Getting Down to Roots   *May 12*

The anemones are blooming in the woods, late this year with a late, cool Spring. Those who shy at botanical names may insist on calling them windflowers, which is a good enough name. But if you trace the botanical name back to its origins you come out at the same destination. The botanical name of the windflower is *Anemone trifolia. Anemone* comes from the Greek word that gives us *anemometer,* an instrument for measuring the wind. Even in Greek, the name is windflower, and the *trifolia* part simply means "three leafed," for this particular anemone's leaves are usually three-parted leaves.

Not all botanical names are so obvious; but the lady's slipper, which we commonly call the moccasin flower, also has its parallels. Botanically the lady's slipper is Cypripedium. Trace the word back to its Greek origins and you find the Greek words for "Venus" and "buskin." A buskin was a moccasinlike slipper. So there it is, Venus' buskin, lady's slipper, moccasin flower, the same thing fundamentally no matter what the language.

Or take bloodroot, which still blooms along some roadsides. The botanical name is Sanguinaria, straight from the Latin. In Latin, *sanguineus* is the word for "blood." Sanguinaria was an herb which stanched bleeding. The root of the bloodroot happens to be blood red, but it exudes a stringent, orange juice once used to check bleeding. Or examine crane's-bill, the wild geranium. Botanically it's a geranium. Trace down the word "geranium," and you go back again to the Greek, to the word for "crane," a bird with a long, slender beak, the same shape as the wild geranium's seed pod. Crane's-bill or geranium, it's all a matter of language.

The Thrasher   *May 13*

He has many common names, thrasher, brown thrush, fox thrush, mavis, sandy mocker, song thrush, ground thrush, red mavis, French mockingbird. But most of us know him simply as the brown thrasher, big cousin of the catbird, northern cousin of the true mocker. We even forgive him for starting to sing well before dawn, unless he perches just beside the open bedroom window, which he seldom does.

He is longer than a robin, and slimmer. His crown and back are rich cinnamon-brown, his throat and belly pale buff streaked with the same brown of his back. His beak is long, his eye is bright. But it is his voice that distinguishes him. He is a true thrush.

It is not right to speak of the thrasher's song, for he has many phrases which he puts together a hundred ways. And he knows he can sing. He enjoys his own voice, puts his whole self into it, twitching, jerking, almost leaping from the highest branch as he sings. Ecstasy almost overwhelms him. And his trademark is the repeated phrase. Give him five minutes and he will give you five complete songs, each long and intricate, each with almost every phrase repeated as he goes along. His voice has the tones of flute, piccolo, violin, sometimes even of clarinet. And it lacks the raucous jeer of the catbird.

True, he likes fruit. He also likes insects, beetles and such. And he seldom frequents the garden. He prefers the edge of the woods, the highest tree and the top twig. There he sings morning and evening, for hours at a time. He rests at midday and for a time during the dark of night. But his mission is song. He glories in song. He lives for it. And most of us find May a better month for his return.

The Green Land *May 14*

We think of this as the time of Spring flowers, fruit blossoms, lilacs. Actually, it is the time of leaves, the time of the countless greens which have not yet settled and matured into the standard green of Summer. This is the time when there is a whole spectrum of green across the land, when the whole world is dappled and misted as with a gently drifting haze whose color ranges from greenish yellow to greenish blue.

See the hills. On the ridges stand the pines and hemlocks and spruces, the dark masses of shadowy needles that not long ago, against the gray sky and the white snow, looked almost black. Now they are a deep, vivid green, warming with the lighter green of new needle tufts fresh from the bud scales. Just below them stand the birches, feathery with new leaves still so small you can see the white boles through their haze of lemony green. Then the poplars, a faint shade darker and twinkling in the breeze, already showing the silvery undersides of their young leaves. And the elms, darkest of all, and the maples, a fresher green than the elms.

See the valleys, with their emerald of urgent grasses, their pink and white of apple blossoms, white of wild plum, vivid yellow-green of willow. And the deep green of violet leaves, the light green of day lilies, the insubstantial-looking mist of varied greens on the osier bushes, the viburnums, the briars of all kinds. Even the river is green, reflecting its own green banks.

Green, the color of growth, of surgent life, enwraps the land. New green, still as individual as the plants themselves. Cool green, which will merge as the weeks pass, the Summer comes, into a canopy of shade of busy chlorophyll.

Laughter on Wings *May 15*

For sheer poetry of flight the barn swallows unquestionably deserve the laurel. Their mastery of the air is absolute, and there isn't one motion of their wings and long, forked tail that lacks perfection. Theirs is a kind of lyric flight that makes one understand the meaning of exquisite grace. They give ultimate meaning to the feathered wing.

But for laughter in the air, for lilting song of motion that makes the heart rejoice, watch the swallows' cousins, the chimney swifts. The swifts are neither as beautiful nor as graceful as the swallows. Some have described them as "cigars on wings," and they are a kind of sooty-olive color, looking almost brown in the air. Their tails are short and rounded, their wings long and slim. But they fairly twinkle in flight, swooping, dodging, racing. And they often chitter as they fly, almost as though laughing at their astonishing performance.

A flight of chimney swifts is like a crowd of children, gay with freedom and dancing in delight. They make flight seem like a fresh discovery, a talent never before known. You can predict the patterns of the swallows, like a perfect ballet; but the swifts improvise from moment to moment as though too exuberant to be confined by patterns. They make up their flight songs as they go along, exultant, practically jubilant at being alive and a-wing. They celebrate the miracle of flight.

Mister Mimic   *May 16*

Other migrants come and go, but the catbird comes with the violets and stays for the late asters, and virtually all the time he is here he contributes to the gaiety of his neighbors. He is here now, and he is in fine form, celebrating the sunshine, jeering at the rain, demanding attention and deserving it.

He is our northern "mocker," cousin of the brash mockingbird of the more southerly regions, and he has almost all the real mockingbird's talents. He seldom uses them all, however, particularly the talent for sustained song. For he is a clown, an unregenerate mimic with what might be called a keen sense of the ridiculous. A phrase or two of sweet song and he must pause, as though to say, "Pretty, huh? But now listen!" And he will make a complete travesty of what he has just sung, finally jeering at it. He has an operatic voice, but he uses it for scat singing.

And he likes an audience. He picks a nesting site near a house, by preference, and he will offer all kinds of vocal inducements to get human attention. Once he has it, he opens his bag of tricks. A show-off, no less; an adolescent with no self-consciousness whatever; a bird who seems to have the character of a party cutup. He is as capricious as the weather, and that may be why we like him.

The robin is sedate, the oriole is a serious fellow, the blue jay is a blustering egocentric. But the catbird is a quick-witted entertainer who seems to find life a vastly amusing enterprise. Nothing completely dampens his spirit, and his world never seems to be going to pot. The only time we resent him is when we can't rise to match his mood, and that, after all, is our fault, not his.

The Sequence   *May 17*

The bees are out and humming, and at evening the whippoorwills are calling; the orioles are loud and happy, there's shade in the woodland, lilacs are fading and peonies are in bud. It's mid-May, and only yesterday it was March.

But mid-May is, within a day or two, always this way, year after year. The variations are almost too minor to show up on a chart. This is the way it happens. And we know it's going to happen, just as sure as moonrise. Cause and effect and the age-old sequence, the first peepers, the last frost, the first violets, the chorus of robin song, daffodils, tulips and azaleas, and after that the whole flood of bloom.

We see it, and we forget; and next year we wonder when are the dates. We have early Springs and late Springs, and we fear for plants and flowers and debate the time to put seed into the ground. But somehow the plants know, and the buds, and they don't forget—because it isn't memory with them, not the kind of memory we know. It's fundamental, a response to the rhythms of time and the life of green and growing things. It's a part of the order that keeps the days and nights, the seasons and the years, in their immutable sequence.

We speak with a degree of awe of the fixity and order of the stars. But nobody ever stood off even one light-year and charted the seasonal sequence of a violet plant or a bumblebee. Maybe we are too close to such things to feel a proper awe. But there they are, and there they have been for a long, long time, marking off the seasons, needing neither clock nor calendar for guide.

Five Crimson Doves   *May 18*

Wild columbines are in bloom, enriching the shade-dappled ledges with gold and scarlet and spangling the air with the early butterflies they attract. Unseasonable heat has hurried them past their prime in many places, but where the shade lies deep in the hilly woodlands they will be glorifying the rest of May and even early June.

The columbine belongs to a big and widely varied family, the crowfoots, and is kin to buttercup, marsh marigold, anemone and larkspur. Its strange blossom, with its five spurs, those deep, red nectar pouches, has long appealed to the imagination. Botanists call it Aquilegia, seeing a resemblance to the eagle's beak in those spurs. The common name comes from the Latin name for "dove," *columba,* and reminds us that country folk long ago thought that those spurs looked like five tiny red doves perched in a huddle of golden sepals. Whatever the name, the flower is unique. And it seems almost to float in the air on its thin stem above the dainty blue-green foliage.

The columbine is not a picking flower. It is a wildling and it belongs in the leaf mold on the rocky ledges, along with hepatica and the anemones. It's a flower to admire where it grows, as much a part of the hillside woodland as the wood thrush and the drumming partridge. Here and there it creeps down to the quiet back roads, and often it grows beside the busy brooks that only fishermen know. But mostly it keeps to the rocky hillsides, companion of the birches and the bloodroot and wild ginger. And always it glorifies May, a gold-and-crimson bangle for a fine May day.

Salamander Weather   *May 19*

Go into the woods on a rainy May day, when the air is warm and the rain is a comfortable rain and a leisurely one, and if you watch your path you will probably find a salamander or two exploring the complex world of grass-stem forests. Small creatures they are, not much longer than a man's finger, and a beautiful orange-red in color. Rain-washed, they have a bright, flowerlike hue, almost translucent. And they are leisurely in their movements.

Biologically speaking, they are of the ancients, related to the amphibians, great and small, that crept from the waters of long ago and found the lands of this earth good. Around their cousins in Europe grew persistent legends. They were so cold-blooded, said casual observers a few centuries ago, that if they were tossed into a fire they could quench that fire at will, and they could emerge unharmed. And it was said also that they lived on air, and for that reason must have magical powers of health. Thus they came to have a place in the darker arts of healing and incantation.

Actually, they are neither mysterious nor fireproof. They are cold-blooded, true enough; but that is their quasi-reptilian nature. They live on the small insect life of their humble world and they hibernate through the cold season. They are harmless to human-kind, as harmless as the little sand lizards that skitter at the road-side in the desert country of the American West. And as those small lizards are varicolored gems of animal life in the desert, so are the orange salamanders in the damp woodlands when violets bloom and warm May rains send rills down the hillsides.

❧ These colorful little salamanders are technically known as newts or efts, and the Latin name is *Diemictylus viridescens*. They are hatched in the sluggish water of a pond or swamp, spend two or three years on land, usually in damp woods, then return to the water and become permanently aquatic. On land they are orange-red, but when they become aquatic their color changes to yellowish-green with red spots.

Chokecherries   *May 20*

Chokecherries come to blossom and back-country roadsides and thin woodlands are warm and pungent with their odor and bright with their white cylinders of bloom that hang like puffy pendants from the twigs. It's a poor woodland that lacks them, almost anywhere in America, for the chokecherries adapt themselves to almost any soil and make small choice among the hills and valleys to an altitude of 4,000 feet or more. Our Northeast is full of them.

Only by liberal stretch of the imagination can the chokecherry be called a fruit tree. It bears cherries which ripen in September, and there are those who make chokecherry jelly. There are even small boys who eat chokecherries, though the cherries are so astringent that they pucker the mouth and shrink the tongue. And their juice is, in effect, a dye on clothing and fingers, almost as firm a dye as the juice of black walnut hulls. Nobody eats chokecherries as a dessert.

And the trees, usually small and twisted, are of no commercial value except as firewood. Possibly some early furniture makers used chokecherry boards now and then, but the bigger cherry trees were more favored and provided bigger and better lumber. The tree never amounts to much and often is host to tent caterpillars and other unwelcome pests. It gets scant welcome in well-kept woods.

Yet it persists, thanks to the birds who eat the cherries and plant the seeds along fences and in the woods. It thrives where more valuable and less showy trees give up. It is a weed tree, if one must be completely truthful. But in May, when it is in bloom, it has beauty and pungent fragrance. Perhaps that is its excuse for being.

The Green Canopy *May 21*

Of all of May's swift changes, perhaps the most miraculous is the way the great green canopy is spread along every tree-lined street and in all the woodlands. Buds burst, inconspicuous blossoms hasten through their brief cycle, and the leaves appear. At first mere flecks of green—every shade of green there is—the tiny leaves droop on soft stems, still too young to hold up their heads. The stems strengthen, the leaves expand, and before we know it the trees are rustling in the breeze, dancing in the sunlight, pattering in the rain. The trees are in leaf again.

To us who live beneath them, leaves mean shade, ease to tired eyes, the pleasure of soft contours where a few weeks ago there were only stark skeletons of branches. But to the trees the leaves mean life and sustenance. Each leaf is a spread of chlorophyll, that green magic which traps sunlight, air and moisture and converts them into starches and sugars. Every tree is a complex factory, yet the leafy process is completed with so little fuss that we are unaware of it. We pay the leaf less heed than an unfurling flower, yet it is the leaf that creates the basic food for everything alive.

There they stand, the miraculous trees, shimmering now in new leaf, already busier than man's huffing, puffing factories. We pay them passing tribute for their cool shade and green beauty, then resume our boasting about our own power and achievement, forgetting the mysterious, incalculable power of a leafy tree.

The Little Lilies *May 22*

Because his lady likes them, the countryman goes out to the flower garden and picks a bunch of lilies of the valley while the dew is still on the grass. He puts them in a glass beside the kitchen sink, the way a man does such things, hoping to surprise and please her. Then he goes out again and cuts across the meadow to the hillside woods, knowing the Mayflowers must be in bloom.

Some call them wild lilies of the valley, which is true enough since the two are cousins, and some, being more precise, call them Canada Mayflowers. In any case, there they are, carpeting the shade beneath the birches and the maples, deep, dew-wet green in leaf, sparkling white in tiny, four-petaled blossom. At most, they grow six inches high, and few stems have as many as a dozen flowers. But they, too, have the sweetness of May in their fragrance, though it is somewhat wilder and less insistent. You have to open your nose to smell it, and by the time the dew is dried you probably can't smell it at all.

But there they are, in the young hours of the morning, among the least of the lilies, frosty white and sparkling in the dappled shade. And the countryman looks and smells and knows he has come to see and sense not only a cousin flower but a cousin morning, a woodsy morning as well as a dooryard morning. A man needs to know them both to know his world, to know himself.

The Persistent Mustards   *May 23*

Wild mustard blooms now at the roadside and in the meadow, yellow as buttercups, bright as a goldfinch. A nuisance to the farmer and the gardener, it delights the unprejudiced eye, for the color is one of May's delights. It is a weed only because it grows so plentifully and so persistently where it is unwanted.

The family name, Crucifera, comes from the Latin for "cross." The four petals of the mustard flower form the arms of a simple cross. The family includes the cresses, the peppergrass, and even horseradish, the largest member of all. Table mustard, the common condiment, is made from the ground seeds of domesticated cousins of those mustards now gone wild. The four common varieties of wild mustard—hedge mustard, field mustard, black mustard and white mustard—all were brought from Europe as field or garden crops originally. They liked our soil and climate and soon took off on their own. Even watercress will wander off down the brookside or across the lowland if given half a chance.

The mustards persist not only because of their adaptability but also because their seeds are so persistent of life. Black mustard and peppergrass seed will sprout and grow after lying dormant for forty years. Any countryman will vouch for this. He may fight mustard in his fields all his life, and still the yellow flowers will be there each May to taunt him. And to delight the eye of those who never tried to rid a field of mustard. But don't try to tell a farmer that mustard is beautiful. Not to him, it isn't.

A Tall Tree   *May 24*

Every garden should have a tree nearby. A tall tree with broad bole and spreading branches, preferably with branches that start well down the trunk or with a low crotch from which a boy might climb. A tree which spreads its roots where it springs from the earth, firm based and strong against the storms.

This is a tree for man as well as boy, the man who has climbed his trees and now can sit beneath them in understanding. For him those branches offer shade and hospitality when the sun has seared his neck and the garden is only half weeded. He can rest his back against that broad bole in Spring, when the spading is half done. Weeding and spading that younger hands once hastened through.

There is reassurance at the foot of such a tree, as well as rest. The years have added to its strength and stature. The wind, the rain, the ice and the blistering sun have all gone into the toughness of its fiber. Its roots strike deep into the soil and find sustenance in the old, old hills.

Youngsters must climb trees, to look out across a world that is misty with adventure. New horizons can be seen from tall trees when one is young. But the time comes when one can sit at the foot of such a tree and see even further than the eye could reach from its highest branch. There are times when one can see all the way to Tarawa and Anzio and Guadalcanal and Cassino.

🌼 For readers too young to remember, Tarawa, Anzio, Guadalcanal, and Cassino were particularly bloody battlegrounds in World War II.

Firebird   *May 25*

Among the local and regional names for the scarlet tanager are "black-winged redbird" and "firebird." Both are vividly descriptive. The tanager's scarlet is as fiery as a glowing bed of hardwood coals on the hearth, and the jet black of his wings makes a startling contrast. Nobody ever forgets a scarlet tanager, once he has seen one. Beside the tanager, the cardinal's deep red seems a little dull and the flash of ruby at the throat of a hummingbird is only a flash. In the tanager, that rich scarlet is breath-taking.

Only the male birds are so clothed, however, and then only in Summer. The females wear yellowish olive-green where the males wear scarlet, and the females' wings are a brownish-gray. Come Fall, and the males moult their scarlet and spend the Winter in much the same garb as the females wear the year around. Happily, they spend most of the days of their scarlet phase here in the Northeast.

Some say that the tanager is not a particularly intelligent bird, and others have reservations about the quality of his song. True, his voice tends to hoarseness. And he isn't as clever as, say, the catbird. But maybe that is only a matter of compensation. The tanager makes out, makes himself heard, and doesn't need to be clever. Let the catbird do his tricks, and let the thrushes sing. Most of us will settle for the scarlet tanager just as he is, a spectacular flash of one of the most vivid colors in all birddom.

Black-winged redbird, redbird, firebird, or tanager—the name doesn't matter. There he is, a gorgeous fellow, simply spectacular. And he is there right now, just down the street, or in that patch of woods, somewhere around. We watch for him. We celebrate him.

May's Golden Dust

If the air of May seems to have golden glint, particularly in the woodland, it is not only because the sunlight has its own aura. The air itself is dusted with the substance of life, the incredibly extravagant pollen crop of the trees. The hickories, the oaks, the walnuts and all the conifers are in blossom and spreading veritable clouds of sulphur-yellow pollen from their stamens in one of the oldest fertility rites on earth. Some of that pollen will reach the female flowers and produce the seeds that keep this a green and hospitable planet.

This golden dust of life, so minute that it dances in the sunbeams that filter through the woodland, hangs most heavily over the pines and spruces now, for they are most generous of all the sylvan producers. It forms a yellow film on rain pools and makes them look like molten gold. It dusts the leaves of the underbrush. It filters into nearby houses and mists polished tabletops. It feels fine as talc between the fingers.

Yet this tree pollen is so nearly indestructible that deposits of it in old peat bogs can be identified centuries later; layers of prehistoric pollen show which trees grew there thousands of years ago. It is the very breath of beginnings. Yet each year, each flowery May, is still misted with this infinitesimal golden dust of life. We probe and search and speculate, and all around us is life itself, finer than dust, insistent as time and eternity, simple as pollen.

The Dainty Season

When one reaches for a word to characterize late May, this time of apple blossom and lilac, this time between new leaf and full foliage, anemone and rose, the best word at hand is "dainty." Seen in the large, which is the only way to see this green and freshly flowering world just now, it is as dainty as fine lace, as fragile looking as dewdrops on a spider web at dawn.

True, an apple blossom is no more fragile or dainty than a rose. But a whole treefull of apple blossoms, pink and white and trimmed with young green and seen against the deep blue sky of May, is magnificently dainty. And it is so fragile that a breeze that barely kisses the cheek will soon bring down those petals in a snowy shower. One bunch of lilacs can look almost gross in the hand, but a big bush of lilacs is like a bold filigree of purple and green. Lilacs and apple trees in the same dooryard can be breathtaking in their beauty and amazing in their daintiness.

And if apple blossoms and lilacs are seen against a hillside of trees in young leaf, the whole world is perfection in daintiness. All new leaves are lacy, from a little distance. They have that translucence of fine jade, and they come in every shade of green. The birches are one shade, the maples another, the ash trees and the poplars still different shades. They dance in the air and the sun gleams through them, warm and golden, full of late May, promising early June. Those leaves will thicken with chlorophyll, of course, and the apple trees will shed their petals and settle down to fruiting, and this moment will be gone. But for a brief time there is this fragile, dainty season of new and wondrous beauty on the bough.

Buttercups   *May 28*

The buttercups are out, a golden frost on the meadows and in the damp uplands. Their petals gleam as though they were waxed and polished especially to reflect the sun, the golden sun of May. And their rosettes of yellow stamens are an open invitation to bees and lesser butterflies to pause and rest a while and feed at leisure.

The buttercups belong to the crowfoot family, so named, it seems, from the shape of the leaves, and are in botanical terms known as Ranunculaceae. They have cousins all over the place, ranging from the lovely little wood anemones of fragile white blossom to the long-spurred columbines and even to the baneberries, red and white. One of the most beautiful of all the buttercup's close kin, however, is the marsh marigold, which not long ago was spreading its deep golden petals along the moist margins of more remote woodland streams.

But the buttercup is a congenial flower. It likes the sun and the open meadow, where it blooms in profusion. It has no particular fragrance; nor does it need any. Its friends have no trouble finding it as it is. Half its beauty is in its simplicity, though its color is hard to match and its bright gleam is seldom surpassed. Were it as rare as the arbutus, say, it would be highly treasured. Instead, it is accepted as just another of May's minor beauties, a meadow wildling of generous nature.

But now and then even the casual passer-by is caught by the sight of a full-flowered clump of buttercup against the sunny side of a lichen-dappled stone wall and understands how magnificent can be such humble flowering.

The Sunrise Hour   *May 29*

The day starts early now, and with its own exultance. Soon after first light the birds begin to celebrate the dawn, and those who would know bird song at its best are awake and listening. But the dawn chorus of the birds is only a part of this jubilation, as those know who are up and outdoors while the day is young and damp with dew.

Trees shimmer in the freshest of new leaves. Roadside grass is lush, hurrying toward June's ripeness. Buttercups gleam gold and wild geraniums turn pink faces toward the sunrise. The roadside meadow is frosty with great patches of bluets. At the first rocky ledge dew drips from the blue-green foliage of wild columbines and their crimson and gold bloom nods, heavy with trapped moisture. Ferns stand tall and brilliant green, fronds still showing a trace of the fiddlehead's curl. Chokecherries are hung with fat white tassels that in another hour will be loud with hungry bees.

Wisps of silver mist hug the hollows, memories of cool midnight. The busyness of the day hasn't yet intruded. You can even hear the breeze whispering in the treetops. Maybe that is what the robins are celebrating, this leisured hour, the robins, the orioles, the tanagers, the grosbeaks, even the doves. This is the sunrise hour, the day's beginnings, when all who know another dimension of time can, for a little while, participate in genesis itself.

The Baltimore Bird   *May 30*

Fortunate is the householder, suburban or rural, with a tall tree and a Baltimore oriole. The two go together invariably, for the remarkable nest must be hung high, and the colorful male oriole seeks a high perch from which to sing by the hour while his mate weaves the nest, lays the eggs and broods the hatch.

Despite the name, this oriole owes no debt to the Maryland metropolis. True, Baltimore has its orioles, but not as many as Hartford, say, or Albany, or New York City, or almost any area of the Northeast. The name comes from the orange and black which makes the male oriole spectacular. They were the family colors of the Calverts, of which one member, the second Baron Baltimore, was the patron of Maryland. When Linnaeus named this particular species he chose to honor Lord Baltimore, and thus the name still stands.

The oriole is a remarkable bird on several counts. Its nest is unique, a woven pouch suspended from a high, thin branch, often in an elm, sometimes in a sycamore or a maple. The female weaves this nest, and her skill at weaving has amazed man for generations. No other bird contrives to weave anything like such a fabric, or fashion such a safe and useful nest.

The male bird is no weaver. He may help gather material, but his special mission in life seems to be to make music. Hour after hour he sings, with one of the richest voices and from an infinitely varied repertoire. Between songs he displays his colorful plumage. There really isn't another bird like him. May and June would be drab indeed without the orioles.

We call them June bugs, and folk to the south of us call them May bugs, which proves only that these big, blundering beetles respond to the season wherever they are. They appear at dusk and linger in darkness, buzzing at a porch light or a lighted window, where they bang and buffet with a clatter almost mechanical. Indeed, with their chitin-armored bodies and stiff wings, they might have come from some whimsical workshop instead of from soft, white grubs in the soil.

The scientific name is Phyllophaga, and it means "leaf eater." Shakespeare spoke of its kind as the "shard-born beetle with its drowsy hum," and among its close cousins is the scarab beetle of Egypt. In our own West another cousin is known as the tumble bug. All are big, in insect terms, and all are awkward in any terms. They fuss and blunder and they lumber so in the air that one wonders how they ever accomplish flight at all. If one gets into a room it eventually bangs itself against a wall and falls to the floor, where it usually lies helpless on its back, looking like some tiny mechanical toy overturned and slowly running down.

Yet this particular family of beetles consists of more than 20,000 species, and several hundred new species are listed each year. No matter what man may think of them, they seem to be a success in nature's terms. Butterflies are more beautiful, and dragonflies are more graceful. Wasps and bees are far more industrious. But the June bugs persist, and mere man doesn't know why. They don't even carry their own lights, as fireflies do. They just buzz and batter their inadequate heads at the door and window.

 JUNE

Predictable as Sunrise   *June 1*

June comes with its own tranquillity, predictable as sunrise, reassuring as the coolness of dusk. The grass grows toward maturity, ready for the haymaker. Trees cast the same cool shade they have cast since the hills were young. Brooks make their way to rivers, and rivers follow their deliberate course to the sea. There is a certainty, an undiminished truth, in sunlight and rain and the fertility of the seed. The fundamentals persist.

Nature has no object lessons, but June and Summer bring the undeniable truth of growth and continuity. Each Summer since time first achieved a green leaf has been another link in the chain of verity that is there for understanding. Every field, every meadow, every roadside is now rich with the proof of sustaining abundance, evidence that the earth is essentially a hospitable place no matter what follies man may commit. June invites man to know these things, to know sun and rain and grass and trees and growing fields. It is a season for repairing the perspective, for admitting, however privately, that there are forces and rhythms that transcend man's particular and transient plans.

June is March and April brought to the enduring truth of

Summer. It is the whole sustaining principle of life and growth, from seed to stem and leaf, from blossom to seed again. That is the eternal rhythm. That is June, and that is Summer.

June Moon   *June 2*

Now come some of the pleasantest nights of our year, nights when you can almost hear the grass growing and the rosebuds straining at their seams. There's a moon almost at the full to gleam on the sumac and the young-leafed sycamores which stand in whitewashed ghostliness. Flowering dogwood, now past its dazzling prime by daylight, glows in fresh beauty again under the flattering moonlight. The fragrance of lilies of the valley floats like a sweet mist over the lower end of the garden.

The brook talks softly, and even the frogs are not as loud as they were a month ago; one croaks throatily, and waits for a higher-pitched answer, and seems to clear his throat before he croaks again. Down where the maples cast deep shadows a whip-poorwill starts his interminable three-note whistling, and you try to count but lose track when he stammers, catches his breath and goes on, and on, and on.

There is a wisp of mist, gleaming like gossamer, hung across the valley, clear in the moonlight against the dark mass of woods on the far hills. You can almost make out the various greens of the trees there, the lighter green of the ash and the elm, the deeper green of the maple; then distinctions vanish in the shadows or a faint breeze moves the leaves and the moonlight gleams, for a moment, on the silvery underside of the whole treetop.

The world has a green, growing fragrance, a hundred odors mingled into one. A late Spring rushes into full leaf and opening bud, and June comes over the hills in the moonlight.

Rediscovery

We seldom remember in April how tall the grass at the roadside and in the meadows will be by June. Or that daisies will frost the fence row and buttercups gild the meadow. We forget, most of us, that chokecherries are now in bloom with their sharp-tanged flowers, and that June is other things than roses.

June is really a time of relative quiet, serenity after the rush of sprouting and leafing and before the fierce heat that drives toward maturity and seed. June's very air can be as sweet as the wild strawberries that grace its middle weeks, sweet as clover, sweet as honeysuckle. A sweetness that could be cloying, but somehow isn't, perhaps because it is still a new sweetness.

Birds still sing, at their best, and not only at morn and at evening but most of the day. The oriole, the robin and the tanager can make a June day fairly vibrate with song, and a part of the song is there in the air before the birds utter a single note. June is that way. The rasping that is July and August, the scraping of cicadas and all their kin, is yet in abeyance. June doesn't assault your ears. It flatters them, then softens the sound of frog and whippoorwill, and is a joy.

These things we know each June. We learn them all over again in the first week, and we wonder how we ever could have forgotten them. For June is peonies as well as roses. June is the first early kitchen-garden produce as well as flower beds. June is a happy memory rediscovered and lived again.

Live Waters

Springs are the live waters of this earth, full of cool sweetness and babbling with the pent-up energy of elemental forces. They ooze or flow or gush from the stony hillsides, following an earth fault to its open end and emerging to form a rivulet or a brook. They water the land, and the course of their flow is marked by the greenest green that grows. Brookside grass achieves a peculiar lushness, and a brookside meadow is something to look upon, particularly when the heat of Summer has begun to crisp the springless hillsides.

Springs feed the rivers of the land and keep them flowing. Follow them to their beginnings and you climb to the source of the brooks. You come at last to the springs where the reservoirs of the earth dole out their waters. The snows, the glaciers and the periodic rains fill and flood the channels, but the steady flow is from those sweet earth-waters that wash the rocks and hesitate in leisurely pools before leaping down the hillsides toward the distant seas.

A spring marked a homesite, in the days when man was making the land his own. Spring waters quenched his thirst and served his flocks and turned his mill, and in the valleys where springs turned brooks to streams there was good soil for his crops. He could contend with stones and stumps, but unless he had water, live water, he faced odds too great to master.

The springs still flow, and their waters are still sweet. The grass stands lush beside their pools, and in the evening there is still the song of live waters making their beneficent way to the sea.

The Flags of June   *June 5*

The iris comes to blossom, the iris named for the rainbow that once spanned a Springtime in Greece. The yellow iris, sometimes called corn flag, and the purple iris, sometimes called blue flag, and all the other early irises that have been dear to the hearts of country folk for generations. And in the meadows and pastures, and down along the brooks, the wild irises, large and small, come into their own, from the big blue fleur-de-lis to the miniature blue-eyed grass, which is probably the least of all the irises and one of the daintiest.

It's a venerable flower, the iris. Some say it was the "hyacinth" of ancient mythology. The Saracens long ago grew it in their cemeteries as a symbol of their grief. In early French art the white iris was an emblem of the Virgin. It supplied the pattern for France's heraldic fleur-de-lis. For more than five centuries the iris was a part of the royal emblem of England.

Several species are native to America, including a few which were used by the Indians as a foodstuff. Orrisroot comes from the iris, for the perfumer and the pharmacist. And the bees love all the irises that bloom.

But for most of us the irises are garden flowers, simple and old-fashioned or hybridized and complex and exotically beautiful. They grow beside old garden walls and along old dooryard fences and in special beds of their own. To an older generation the simple ones were always "flags," and they bloomed when the tulips began to fade. Flags and lilacs and "pineys" all belonged to early June.

The Prelude   *June 6*

Early Spring or late, cool May or warm, by June the days are alive with sound. It comes so gradually, increasing day by day from the cold silence of March, that we are scarcely aware of it. We must force our ears to listen. But there it is, in suburb and countryside, even in a city park, the buzz of the bumblebee, the low stridulation of the lesser cricket at the grassroot, the scratch and rattle of the brash-winged grasshopper, the harsh rustle of the beetle in flight on stiff, inadequate wings. The insect sounds.

This is the lesser chorus, and it goes with daisies in the meadows and wild roses along the pasture margins. Not one of the sounds is really insistent, even when one listens closely; but in sum they are the voice of early June, untold millions of little hummings and buzzings and rustlings that set the long daylight hours to vibrating.

There is no true silence now, for the world is alive and teeming. What we hear is the urgency of life, the insistence of the insignificant which by its very numbers becomes of ultimate significance. Only the pollen of the trees and the spores of ferns and fungi outnumber the insect eggs, and all those eggs are hatching. Hatched, they must proclaim life, mate, lay more eggs, perpetuate life. Later will come the high-pitched shrill of the cicada, the clamor of the katydid. But they await hot noontimes and warm evenings. They are the Summer itself. Now we hear the tune-up and the prelude. This, when we listen closely, is the voice of Summer still approaching.

June

June is the year at the altar, a bride with a bouquet of roses and forget-me-nots, veiled with morning mist and jeweled with dew, gowned with sunrise and romantic as a full moon. June is corn-flower blue and day-lily gold and white lace of daisies in the field. June is bridal wreath and mock orange and the scent of sweet peas on the garden fence.

June is time settling down to the business at hand, which is growth and maturity after the lush preparations when all the trees were leafing out and all the meadows were full of fine new grass and spring beauties and bluets. The rush is past. Now comes the more leisurely time, the June pause to catch up, before the drive of July urges seeding and podding and fruiting. June even has time to think about such matters, if one is not a farmer whose hay must be cut and mowed away.

June is strawberries, red and juiceful and tantalizing to man and bird. June is peas in the garden, late June, for the favored gardener. June is first lettuce and baby beets, and string beans in blossom and susceptible to both beetle and blight. June is corn, both sweet and field varieties, pushing green bayonets toward the sun. June is scallions.

June is a wren outside the window, bursting with song at 5 A.M. June is the flash of an oriole's wing, the throb of his song in midmorning. June is a wood thrush at evening, the sweetest contralto of them all.

June is a peony and a lazy bumblebee and a thunderstorm and a small boy chasing a butterfly. June is soft laughter in the silken dusk and soft starlight over a world where life is good.

The Essence   *June 8*

The man who mows the lawn gave us the season's first whiff of that sweet, green fragrance of fresh-cut grass; but now come the haymakers, and the whole countryside takes on a fragrance as characteristic of June as the fragrance of lilacs is of May. The mowers clatter, the tall grass falls in windrows, and the haymaking is on.

June haymaking used to be a hazardous necessity because of June rain. But not any more. Ingenious technicians got to work and turned out hay choppers and hay driers and a lot of other equipment. Nowadays the farmers stow their early hay green, chopped and fresh, in silos. There it undergoes a process known as ensilage, a fermentation which preserves and even enhances the nourishment and flavor of growing things—for a cow, at least. The mowers start in the hayfields right after breakfast, the rakes soon follow, the chopper follows the rakes, the trucks follow the chopper, and before dusk the hay is in the silo.

Or, if the farmer insists on dry hay from his first crop, he can dry it a bit on the ground, bale it and stow it in a loft equipped with a drier which will cure it safely even in the midst of a wet spell. Dry hay, however, usually comes from a later cutting.

Whatever the ultimate purpose, now the mowers go to work in the hayfields. The brome, the timothy, the clover, the alfalfa are cut, and the sweetness pervades the valleys. Not a hay smell; just a fresh-cut green smell. The hay smell is a further distillation, with sunshine in it, and dew, and a touch of wild mint, and just a trace of buttercup. The essence not only of hay, but of June. A Summer smell if there ever was one.

Why?

June days are just the right length to include a little time to sit and wonder about some of the questions that never make headlines. Why, just to pick at random, are the mosquitoes more numerous and more vicious this year than usual? And why so early? Are they precocious this year, or are they just reminding us that there are other problems than the conquest of outer space?

What has happened to the dandelion? It used to be a lawn weed, a rival of nurtured bluegrass; now it has become a field pest in many places. Some rural pastures are overrun by dandelions. Why? Its spread seems to have coincided with the development of weed-killing sprays, which is ironic indeed. What are we doing, killing the other weeds just to make way for more dandelions?

More brown thrashers than usual, and few bluebirds, are being seen and heard out beyond the pavements. DDT sprays seem to poison the food of robins and bluebirds and decimate their numbers, even to make them infertile. Doesn't the stuff have the same effect on brown thrashers? Why not? Incidentally, why do we keep on spraying our birds to death instead of cherishing and encouraging them? Birds are the best check we have on insects. And they do their work for no pay at all, all for free.

Why does the phoebe flirt its tail and its cousin, the wood peewee, not flirt its tail? How does a hummingbird stow so much energy in so small a body? Why is the house wren called "jenny"? It's the male who does all the singing, makes June vibrate with song. It doesn't matter, but one does wonder why.

Prodigal Gill

If gill-over-the-ground, commonly miscalled ground ivy, were not so plentiful, and hence so much of a weed, it would rate as a choice ground cover with a modest but beautiful display of small violet-blue flowers. It is in full bloom now, growing almost everywhere, along stone walls, in damp shade on the lawn, invading garden borders. A creeper, it trails across the ground like true ivy, but it is actually a mint, one of the many mints that grow wild here but are native to Europe. Its small, scalloped, heart-shaped leaves have the mint tang and its flowers follow the mint pattern.

Gill, like many other mints, came from England. Only one of our wild mints is certainly native, and it has no other common name than simply wild mint. Bee balm and all the other bergamots, most colorful of the tribe, are also from Europe, as are catnip, pennyroyal, spearmint, hyssop and all those aromatic ones. Most of them were brought here for their leaves, but gill was brought for its blossoms.

Gill's blossoms are tiny, seldom more than half an inch long, but they grow in clusters and make a warm display, particularly in Spring. Here they bloom well into Summer, but in England the gill is an April flower, the English equivalent, in a way, of our trailing arbutus. Those who brought it here wanted to remember April in England, and they had no notion that their gill would run away as it did, leap their garden walls and take to the fields. But that's what happened. And now gill is one of the wildlings, a fugitive trying tirelessly to get back into the garden. A prodigal, perhaps, but an independent prodigal, and a prosperous one.

The Wheelbarrow   *June 11*

Consider the wheelbarrow. It may lack the grace of an airplane, the speed of an automobile, the initial capacity of a freight car, but its humble wheel marked out the path of what civilization we still have. Particularly that phase of civilization which leads down Main Street, through the front gate, around the house and into the back garden. It also led the way up Broadway, across State Street and even through Piccadilly Circus; but that's another story.

The story we prefer is a simpler one. It deals with rocks and roots and hunks of sod and bags of lime. It includes dead leaves and lively onions, old compost and new potatoes, seedling flats and spades and rakes, squash and pumpkins and outsize heads of cabbage. And two hardwood handles, two callused hands. It makes the rounds of March mud and May rains, July sun and August thunderstorms, October harvest and November frost. It goes places without ever getting far from home.

Like faith, the wheelbarrow can move mountains. A few drops of oil can silence its loudest complaint. In Spring it is a thing of beauty, particularly if it is both new and red. In Summer it is a challenge to human endurance. In Fall it is—sometimes—a cornucopia. Always it is there, needing only human companionship and cooperation to get things done.

Best of all, it is shaped to its purpose. When the sun is at its height, the garden bench is far away and human energy has dwindled to the very neap, the wheelbarrow waits with welcoming arms and recumbent seat. No rock, no bag of lime, no harvest from the fertile earth ever fitted the contours of the wheelbarrow as well as the weary frame of its owner.

Starlight   *June 12*

How good it is to step forth into the night after a day of rain and see that the sky is clear, the stars are gleaming in their accustomed places. A sky that clears by daylight is full of radiance, but when it clears in darkness there is glittering promise in every winking ray of starlight. There is reassurance in such stars, hung in a night sky washed clean and made ready for clear days to come.

Work is done by sunlight; but it is under the stars that great dreams are dreamed. There is warmth and life in the day's sunshine; but it is the stars that lure man's mind to the endless immensity of a universe so broad that tangible reality can never span it.

No night is so dark as a starless night, nor is any life more drab than that of one who has never known the thrill of starlight after storm, the comfort of it and the soothing reassurance of stars once more in order. Give a sailor a star to steer by and he will come home to port. Give an airman the company of a star shining clear and you have given him both certainty and direction. Give any man a star on which to fix his eye and he can reach as far as his imagination points the way.

The rains come, and the dark days of a perverse season; and the sky clears at evening. There is a sweet smell to the darkness, the fresh fragrance of a rain-washed world. And there is the brilliance of a thousand galaxies overhead, starlight in a clear night sky.

The Bumblebee   *June 13*

Behold the bumblebee, that big, improbable black and gold insect that shouldn't be able to fly but does, that could be a model of industry but isn't, and that is neither meek nor mild though Englishmen call it the humblebee. It is a hummer and bumbler, noisy as a locust, colorful as a butterfly, and as much a part of the sunny June day as a pasture rose or a wild strawberry.

The bumblebee is an exponent of the easy life and an example of moderation in most matters. Like most bees, it has social instincts, but not to excess; its communities are mere villages, so to speak. Not liking to waste energy, it often nests in field-mouse dens in or near clover fields. Able to make wax, it sometimes fills small waxen jugs with honey for a rainy day or two, but it doesn't seem to think the world will end if it fails to hoard honey by the bucketful. Armed like a whiteface hornet, it seldom goes looking for trouble. Its kind has been here on earth a long, long time.

Bumblebees tolerate man, up to a point, but they refuse to be domesticated. They eat when hungry, rest when tired, and are neither thieves nor killers. They even sleep at night—which is more than be said for some insects—often sweetly couched in an aster blossom or a zinnia. They aren't as improvident as grasshoppers, but they don't work themselves to death in six weeks, either, as honeybees do. Man could do worse than ponder the bumblebees, especially on a sunny June afternoon.

The Lessons of the Land *June 14*

Things even out, after a fashion. Six months ago the countryman's day had only a little over nine hours of sunlight. Now it has fifteen hours when the sun is above the horizon, and what we call the year's longest day is just ahead. Back in December the countryman's daily chores were at the year's minimum, barn chores mostly. Now everything needs doing at once. The corn needs plowing, the hay needs cutting, the garden needs hoeing, and the daily barn chores are still there besides. Longer daylight, but more work to be done. He now pays for his Winter leisure, what there was of it.

It's an old maxim that we pay for Summer by enduring Winter. But it works the other way round in the country. You pay for Winter and its lightened labor by working from dawn till dusk when Summer comes. There will be times, before Fall comes with its relaxation, when the countryman works sixteen hours a day just to keep up with things. All growing things are working overtime now, too.

That's one of the lessons a man can't avoid if he lives close to the land. It is as old as the time of man, and it is embedded in the ancient knowledge. "For everything there is a season—a time to plant, and a time to pluck up that which is planted." All things, even rest, have their price; especially a full barn and an ample pantry. Nobody has ever yet repealed that law, and nobody ever will. Not as long as Summer follows Spring and Winter follows Fall. That's another of the lessons.

"Pineys" *June 15*

Some of us used to smile when Grandmother called them "pineys," smile in imagined superior knowledge. They were peonies, of course—huge blossoms that summoned the June bees and colored the whole garden and made sweet the dusk, and finally fell in a

profligate showering of petals. Peonies, magnificent flowers that belonged in Grandmother's garden.

What we didn't know was that Grandmother was as right as anybody else; for peony is "piney," and it was *paeonia* in the old Latin, and a close approximation of that in solid back-country English. Grandmother was even more old-fashioned than she knew; but she was right.

And she was right when she dug up her pineys and packed them in a box of New England soil and stowed them in the Conestoga wagon when she went West. Those pineys took root in the rich bottomlands of the Ohio Valley, on the prairies beyond the Mississippi, on the High Plains, in the stony soil of the deserts, on the warm western slope of the Sierras. They meant home to her, in June, wherever she might be.

They still mean home. Home in June. Sweet peas are lovely, and roses are superb; rhododendron is breath-taking, and columbines are simply beautiful. But peonies are homely, and friendly, and generous beyond belief. Give them half a chance and they are yours for a lifetime; yours in magnificent color and abundance when June is at its peak.

The Foreverness of June   *June 16*

Mid-June, no matter what the year, is a kind of summary of all the Junes that ever were. It is a remembering, a knowing and a recalling, a time that was and is and always will be, a timeless time. The daisies that whiten the roadside are remembered daisies, and the bird songs are all songs that have sung in the human heart since hearts first sang. Mid-June is hoped-for truth and longed-for beauty and hoped-for happiness, dreams that could come true five minutes from now.

Wild strawberries ripen, remembered perfection with the taste of yesterday's youth. Pasture roses bloom with the simplicity of beauty as new as the night's dew and as old as time itself. The sun approaches the solstice and there are fifteen hours and more of daylight, within a few seconds of the year's longest span. The rains have eased the drouth, the remembered sweet rains of June. Shade lies cool and deep beneath the long-known maples. Fireflies wink in the long dusk. Brooks have not yet languished into July's torpor. Venus is the morning star, and Mars is the star of evening.

The bee hum of mid-June bids one look for yesterday, and find it, in the lush meadows. Butterfly wings lead one down the hillside with other Junes. A dragonfly bids one to the water's edge, there to see mirrored the face of yesterday's June vagabond. And all around, overhead, underfoot, in the very air, is the remembering, the knowing, the very being of June and the possession by it, the partaking and the foreverness, the sweet foreverness of mid-June.

This Green World   *June 17*

For those who deal with the soil there's little time now to sit back and worry about complexities. The farmer uses every hour of daylight to do such simple things as get in his early hay, cultivate the early weeds out of his corn, keep up with his pastures and keep the kitchen garden from getting completely out of hand. The vegetable gardener is weeding, planting, transplanting, watching the early peas and lettuce, fending the birds from his strawberry patch, trying to keep up with the frantic growth of his lawn. The flower gardener is lost in peonies and roses, guarding his delphinium, filling the blank spots with annuals, taking up early bulbs, putting in late ones, debudding, debugging, spraying, dusting, picking.

And anyone who talks, or even thinks, in terms of scarcity seems rather silly now. Everything that grows is both beautiful and abundant, lavish and luxuriant. If there ever comes a time to take five minutes at the end of a long day and consider the teeming generosity of this earth, this must be it. All man has to do is cooperate with the big forces, the sun, the rain, the growing urge.

Seeds sprout, stems grow, leaves spread in the sunlight. Man plants, weeds, cultivates, and harvests.

It sounds simple, and it is simple, with the simplicity of all great truths. The confusions and complexities are alien to the plow and the hoe. They are essentially man-to-man, not man-to-earth, and, whether the hoeman or plowman stops to think about them or not, he knows how to classify them. This is a simple, busy time when man should be more concerned with his relationship to his environment than with anything else. If his feet are on the ground, literally, that's what he is concerned with, too.

Knee-Deep in June   *June 18*

We are knee-deep in June, as James Whitcomb Riley put it. A good many birds are still singing, at least morning and evening, and the drone of the cicadas is yet to come. Bees do the droning now, bees in clover. And farmers with their tractors, at work in the hayfields. June is haytime, and anyone with a nose to smell can tell you that if he has been out in the country. There's no other smell in the world quite like fresh-cut hay seasoning in the June sun.

Knee-deep in June, which means roses both in the garden and along the fence rows. The pasture roses didn't winterkill, as so many of the garden roses did, and they are pink as dawn just now, flushed and sweet and almost as much a lure to the bees as is the clover. June without roses, all kinds of roses, just wouldn't be June.

And strawberries, of which Riley also spoke in celebrating June. Strawberries, also both wild and tame, come to their ripeness now. And in those berries is the sweetness of early Summer, June's own concentrate. The wild ones hide in the meadow grass, but the tame ones are there in the garden for anyone, preferably the owner, to savor, sun-warm and full of juice. Raspberries approach ripeness now, too, including the little wild blackcaps, which are a treasure to anyone abroad in June. But give the blackcaps another week to sweeten.

Knee-deep in June. A wonderful time to be alive and sentient. A time of richness, of early ripeness, of Summer at its very best.

The Turn   *June 19*

The days grow long. The solstice approaches and the urgent growth of Spring has run its first course. The growing things have spread their tissue of chlorophyll to catch the maximum of sunlight, and from now on they will be strengthening limb and twig, fattening fruit, building toward the season's maturity. First things come first, the leaves and then the blossoms, and after that the sturdy stems and the ripening fruit.

The heat and drought have brought the roses to quick and hurried bloom; but in their wake comes the honeysuckle, sweetening every roadside with an overabundance of fragrance that makes the season seem later than it is. Buttercups are overwhelmed by daisies, and black-eyed Susans flash their rouged gold along the hillsides. Blackberries were lush with bloom and hasten now toward fruit, ahead of schedule. Elderberries have hurried into blossom and nod in the warm wind with the aspect of July.

Summer comes not by the calendar any more than snow waits for a definite date in December. Summer comes from the root and the sun and the feel of the air. And Summer is here. You can feel it of an evening, when the tree-lined roads are like dark tunnels with starlight in the distance and the breeze whispers among the leaves. You can feel it in the early morning, when thin mist hangs over the dry valleys, the earth still warm and the leaves eager for any cooling touch. You can feel it at high noon, when the first of the cicadas sets the air to quivering. Seed heads ripen on the meadow grass. July rocks show dry and hot in the June brook. The solstice will be late this year, because the Summer turn came early.

Few birds are more seldom seen or better known by call and reputation than the whippoorwill here in the Northeast. The bird's call is fascinating to the uninitiate; it is also one of the most insistently repetitious birdcalls ever uttered, and two whippoorwills challenging each other vocally can disrupt sleep for hours. Yet those who heard the whippoorwill's call in youth will go miles to hear it again. It isn't a song; it is a memory, a legend.

Even in name the whippoorwill is a legend. It belongs to the scientific family called Caprimulgidae, and *caprimulgus* is Latin for "goatsucker." Because members of the family haunted herds of goats at dusk, they long ago were believed to milk the goats and live on milk. Later it was learned that they lived on flying insects and followed the goats because they attracted such insects. But the name persisted, finally outranked the English common name, nightjar, which at least had truth to back it up, for if any bird can jar and jolt the night, this one can. But the family name is goatsucker, even to ornithologists.

There are other members of the family in the South, chuckwill's-widow and poorwill, and there is the nighthawk, the least vocal one of all. But we know best and remember longest the whippoorwill, which comes north in mid-Spring, summers here, and goes south again for the Winter. It builds no nest worthy of the name, it hatches two eggs on a pile of dead leaves, and it sleeps all day. It is seldom seen. But its call, which sometimes is repeated several hundred times almost without pause, is seldom forgotten. Old men who haven't heard a whippoorwill in years will smile with remembering at the very name—whippoorwill—and wish to hear it again.

❧ The whippoorwills sometimes arrive in my area as early as mid-April, often within a day or two of the first barn swallows, and I have heard them calling as late as the second week in October. Those on my own hillside keep a rigid evening schedule apparently keyed to the time of sunset. In May they begin calling at 8:40 P.M., in mid-June they start at 9:15, in late July they start at 8:45; and from then on their calls begin progressively earlier but consistently about half an hour after sunset. They also have the unhappy habit of calling loudly at about 3 A.M., a habit I deplore. The clock times I mention here are Eastern Daylight Saving Time, one hour ahead of Eastern Standard Time.

Summer   *June 21*

Summer comes officially tomorrow morning, signaled by the solstice; we are well on our way toward July and August. But Summer is considerably more than a solstice and the slow diminishing of daylight's span in the annual march from Spring to Fall.

Summer is misted dawns and searing afternoons, hot days, warm nights, thunderstorms cracking their writhing whips. Summer is shirt sleeves, sunburn, bathing suits, tall cold drinks, dazzling beaches and shimmering lakes. Summer is the green countryside, the cool fragrance of mountain pines.

Summer is the house wren bubbling over with morning song. It is the long afternoon aquiver with the sibilance of the cicada. It is slow dusk freckled with fireflies—and prickly with mosquitoes. Summer is a meadowful of daisies, a field of corn reaching for the sun, a straw hat, a hoe and a garden.

Summer is the fresh garden pea, new lettuce crisp in the salad bowl, snap beans, sun-ripe raspberries on the bush and chilled strawberries in a bowl of cream. Summer is the weed, the gnawing insect, the foraging woodchuck, the nibbling rabbit. Summer is sweat.

Summer is April and May grown into June and July, the green world working almost eighteen hours a day. It is a lazy river and a languishing brook. It is a vacation dreamed of, realized, too soon over and done, too soon a memory.

Summer is a promissory note signed in June, its long days spent and gone before you know it, and due to be repaid next January.

SUMMER

 JUNE

Solstice *June 22*

Solstice, we call it, the Summer solstice, when the earth begins to swing back on its trunnions and the longest day of the year is at hand and daylight begins its creeping abbreviation once more. Solstice, and Summer, and bee drone in the clover field; first fledglings out of the nest, corn almost knee-high, another Spring complete.

Taken literally, solstice means that the sun stands still. But that's an illusion. There is no standing still in any season. The earth turns, and the year turns, and sunrise changes, and sunset alters, day by day. And neither man nor his affairs stand still. Change is the only constant. Trees grow, corn ripens and man must grow and ripen with them, even as the sun goes through its cycle. To plant, to harvest, to learn, to know—that is the law of time. The solstice is the year's meridian, not its resting place.

To stop time, to make the sun stand still—that has been the dream of many dreamers. To decide and act, and have the chance to redecide and act anew on the same problem. But no problem is ever the same twice, as no day or year is like any other. The seed sprouts and grows, and there's the harvest. Summer comes, with its elusive and passing solstice, and we move on, webbed in time and change.

There is no stopping, no turning back. The solstice, and then the equinox, and Winter again, and the round renewed. The corn grows tall, the bee drones, the berry ripens. Another Summer.

The Day's Eye   *June 23*

Summer wouldn't really be Summer without daisies, even though the common field daisy, known to almost every man, woman and child, is sometimes called farmer's curse. Any farmer can tell you why. Daisies populate roadsides, but they invade pastures, meadows and all kinds of cultivated fields, and the invasion is en masse. So while most farmers smile at picnicking youngsters who gather fistfuls of daisies, they frown in utter bafflement at Summer visitors who actually pick daisies and arrange them in vases.

The daisy is kin to the chrysanthemum and a member of the big and varied composite family. The flower's golden center consists of a mass of botanically perfect miniature blossoms, each complete with stamens and pistil. The white petals are actually rays, each the single petal of a miniature pistillate flower. When the petals wither and the flower head ripens, it produces a whole packet of seeds. These seeds have vigorous vitality; hence the persistence of the daisy.

The daisy's name comes from "day's eye" and refers to the yellow center, which in folklore represented the sun. Sometimes the common field daisy is called the oxeye daisy, for which there is little reason since most oxen's eyes are brown, not yellow. But the name daisy is loosely applied to black-eyed Susans and even to asters, by some, so the name doesn't really matter. Daisies grow in vacant lots and even in the city's concrete gutters, if they can find a crack. They are tough as urchins, persistent as beggars. And to the unbiased eye they are beautiful, even in a meadow. Unless you happen to be a farmer.

The Urgency

If man is ever going to admit that he belongs to the earth, not the other way round, it probably will be in late June. Then it is that life surpasses man's affairs with incredible urgency and outreaches him in every direction. Even the farmer, on whom we all depend for the substance of existence, knows then that the best he can do is cooperate with wind and weather, soil and seed. The incalculable energy of chlorophyll, the green leaf itself, dominates the earth, and the root in the soil is the inescapable fact. Even the roadside weed ignores man's legislation.

The urgency is everywhere. Grass blankets the earth, reaching for the sun, spreads its roots, flowers and comes to seed. The forest widens its canopy, strengthens its boles, nurtures its seedlings, ripens its perpetuating nuts. The birds nest and hatch their fledglings. The beetle and the bee are busy at the grassroot and the blossom, and the butterfly lays eggs that will hatch and crawl and eat and pupate and take to the air once more. Fish spawn and meadow voles harvest the wild meadows, and owls and foxes feed their young. Dragonflies and swallows and nighthawks seine the air where the minute winged creatures flit out their minute life spans.

And man, who glibly calls the earth his own, neither powers the leaf nor energizes the fragile wing. Man participates, but his dominance is limited. It is the urgency of life, of growth, that rules. Late June and early Summer are the ultimate, unarguable proof.

Rubythroat

Seen in sunlight, it is a blur of wings, an iridescent flash of bronzed green and a touch of ruby red. At dusk it may be mistaken for a hovering sphinx moth. Actually, it is the hummer, the ruby-throated hummingbird, the smallest bird we have and one of the most remarkable. We see it now in the flower gardens, on high terraces in the city, in side yards in the suburbs, at the old-fashioned flowers in the country dooryard.

There are only a few varieties of hummingbirds, all native to the Western Hemisphere, and the only one we know here in the Northeast is the rubythroat. All the dimensions of its life except its migratory flight are on a miniature scale. Its body is not much bigger than a bumblebee, its nest is the size of half a walnut shell, and its eggs are no bigger than fat garden peas. It lives on nectar and miniature insects. But it can run away from a hurrying bee, it can outmaneuver a swallow, and on its annual migration to Mexico it crosses the Gulf of Mexico, flying some 500 miles nonstop.

This brilliant little atom of bird life, however, is full of everyday energy and self-confidence that sometimes amounts to truculence. It seems to fear nothing on wings. It will attack a hawk, a crow, even a rambunctious kingbird, and put any one of them to flight. A strange bundle of paradoxes, this little winged jewel. It loves flowers, couldn't live without them. Its chief competitors are bees and moths. But bird it is, every milligram of it, and soon it will be haunting the bergamot and the jewelweed, a gem on wings, a little demon dressed like a miniature dandy.

❦ The rubythroat sometimes migrates all the way to Panama, though nobody yet knows how it stores enough energy for such a flight in its tiny body—a full-grown ruby-throated hummingbird weighs less than the nickel you spend to mail a letter.

Fishing   *June 26*

There is a common and accepted fiction that fishermen go fishing to catch fish. Some do, of course; but more don't. The fish caught are only a lesser part of the catch. The greater part is the day in the open, the little things that feed the eyes, the ears, and the soul, though we are so perverse and so practical that we seldom talk about them.

How many of us would get up to see an early Summer dawn without the excuse that fish bite better then? Yet it's really the dawn world that a man goes out to see, a sunrise full of the golden green of trees spangled with brand new leaves, full of robin song, full of mist from the lake or river, full of the strange, thin echoes of man's world just coming awake. It's the sudden flight of a nesting duck, startled into whirring wings and beaten water and gleaming light on swift ripples. It's the sight of wild geranium bowing under the weight of dew, and the red and gold and blue-silver leaf of wild columbine. It's the smell of wood smoke from a farmhouse chimney, and the taste of vacuum coffee on a sunlit bank or sand bar.

It's the fishing, yes. The way a fly follows a riffle, the way a plug plops, the way a wormed hook goes down into a deep pool. The strike, the rush, the play of line, the sound of reel, the catch, or the lost fish. But it's also the gleam of a dragonfly, the rattling cry of a kingfisher, the stark awkwardness verging on grace and beauty of a heron. It's the slow climb of the sun, the slow travel of the shadows, the drift of a cloud.

Fish? Oh, yes, one must have a reason and the day must have a purpose. But it's the fishing, really, the dawn and the morning and the day, and man's knowing that it's still there, still real.

The Primroses   *June 27*

Some of the most beautiful yellows to be found anywhere are now to be found in the evening primroses, the primrose itself and the lesser members of the family called sundrops. They are hot-weather flowers, and they are so adaptable that they grow almost anywhere, in fields and at roadsides, east of the Rocky Mountains.

These primroses are not to be confused with the primulas, to which they are no kin whatever. These are members of the botanical family Oenothera, and they are native to America. Some varieties have been tamed and taken over by the gardeners to brighten the garden spectrum; but we speak here of the wildlings.

The evening primrose is the largest of the group, a sturdy plant which on occasion grows six feet high. It bears a handful of flowers toward the tip on short stems rising from the bases of the upper leaves. Those flowers are sometimes two inches across. They shun full sunlight, opening toward dusk; and their opening is a marvel of blossoming, for they can unfurl completely in a minute or two. They are host to the evening moths, which do the pollinating.

The sundrops are somewhat smaller, both in plant and flower, but otherwise they are much the same as the tall primroses. And they too have that magnificent color, one of the purest yellows found in any flower. Beside the primrose, the buttercup seems tinged with orange and the dandelion with green.

In the plains country of the Southwest there is still another variety, smaller in plant but larger in flower. This primrose is often four inches across, truly magnificent. But everywhere the primrose grows it lends color to the countryside and sweetens the evening. It's as Summery as sweet clover, and twice as beautiful.

Corn   *June 28*

Whenever modern man gets to thinking too much of himself, he would do well to go out in the garden and look around. And if he thinks of himself as the sum of all intelligence, he should take a particularly long look at the stalks of corn growing there. That corn is a plant developed by men whose name and origin are lost in the misty past. But those simple men knew, somehow, how to hybridize plants. In a method we have still to learn, and over a period of time we cannot even calculate, they developed corn as we know it from a wild grass.

Look at the stalk, sturdy, economical, efficient. It stands braced on its roots. It is of quick growth. Its long, broad leaves are so arranged that they catch rain and dew and funnel it down where it is needed. As a plant, it is very near to perfection. It silks out, as we say, with vastly more silk than is needed, just so each kernel on the incipient ear can be properly fertilized. It tassels out, with a pollen-bearing apparatus that is ideal for its purpose.

And it concentrates its yield, a big quantity of useful grain in compact form. It ripens and is an almost perfect storage crop. It is packed with nutriment for man or beast. It comes in varieties which suit almost all climates and long or short seasons.

Look at the corn, and pause for a moment and wonder how it was evolved, and by what simple men. We are wise, and we have improved the corn we inherited, but nobody has yet found out how to evolve a corn plant in the first place. That was done before man became "civilized."

Living Starlight   *June 29*

These are firefly nights, when one can look out over a moist meadow or even a suburban lawn and see flecks of living starlight winking in the darkness. Entomologists call the small, soft beetles who make those blinking lights Lampyridae, reaching back to the Greek word for a torch. Man has known them for centuries, scientists have investigated them, and they still remain a comfort to those iconoclasts who believe that nature should have a few enduring mysteries.

The actual light of the firefly is no longer a mystery. It is produced by slow, practically heatless oxidation of a substance called luciferin in the insect's body. The process is quite marvelous, but it is known to science. But why the insect produces its light is still a baffling question. Half a dozen theories have been advanced, and none proven. Among the most persuasive has been the idea that the light had some mating purpose, some lure, some sexual significance. But when the flashes have been timed and checked, the investigators come up against the fact that the insect's immature larvae and even the unhatched eggs are often luminous. Others have suggested that the light is a warning to nocturnal birds, a survival instrument. But other insects, without lights, survive the night birds.

The theories fall, and the firefly goes right on flashing in the Summer night. And nobody knows why. There it is, one of those minor mysteries that keep this complex world from being reduced to a chemical formula or a mathematical equation. It could be that the firefly's winking light has no purpose at all except to check man's impulse toward the arrogance of total knowledge.

The Lilies of the Field   *June 30*

The wood lilies and the meadow lilies are about to bloom, both of them wildlings and both sometimes called tiger lilies. The true tiger lily is a garden flower of Asiatic origin, but only the devoted botanist would object too much to such a use of the common name. And the botanist probably would call the wood lily *Lilium philadelphicum* and the meadow lily *Lilium canadensis*.

There is a clear difference between the two wild lilies, however. The wood lily prefers the edge of the woodland, its stem and leaves are a bright light green and its flowers open upward, loose cups facing the sun. Even the word "cups" is too generous, for the six petals, each a warm orange-scarlet spotted with purplish-brown, narrow almost to stems at the base so that they seem to stand apart.

The meadow lily's stem and leaves are a lighter green. In both species the leaves form whorls about the stem. The meadow lily's blossom, however, droops from its stem and faces downward, and the petals are joined at the base in a funnel shape. Some call it the Turk's cap. Its color is more yellow than that of the wood lily, but it too is spotted with purplish-brown.

Why any spotted lily should be called a tiger lily rather than a leopard lily is one of those mysteries of nomenclature that reach far back into the mists of time. Back, indeed, to a time when few people knew a tiger from a leopard, but nearly everyone knew the flowers of the fields. By any name, however, these two wild lilies happily persist and make late June and July colorful.

 JULY

July

July is the year at high noon, a young matron with hazel eyes, sun-bleached golden hair and a cloud-filmy red, white and blue scarf with spangles. July is festival and celebration and long-remembered holiday as well as full moon and fireflies and smell of sweet clover at the roadside.

July is gray-green of oat fields turning to gold. July is meadows frosted with Queen Anne's lace and daisies, and night hawks in the evening sky, and fledgling robins, and half-grown rabbits eating the lettuce in the garden. July is lightning and thunderstorms that jolt the hills, rain like silver threads hung from the high, dark clouds. It is field corn reaching for the sun and glistening with the morning dew and thrusting its gold-hung spire of tassel up for the dry winds to kiss and bless and make fertile the sprouting young ears beneath.

July is weeds grown lush, horseweed in the waste place, and milkweed and nettle and forbidding thistle; and pigweed and purslane and rough-leafed German weed in the garden. It is string beans prolific, and bean beetles; it is squash flowers, venerable symbol of fertility, and squash beetles; it is tomatoes coming to fruit and horned tomato worms which turn into sphinx moths.

July is get-up-and-go, vacation time, the shore, the lake, the country, anywhere but home. July is hot afternoons and sultry nights, and mornings when it's a joy just to be alive. It's fresh cherry pie. It's the first sweet corn. It's baby beets, well buttered, please. July is a picnic and a red canoe and a sunburned neck and a softball game and ice tinkling in a tall glass. July is a blind date with Summer.

Yarrow   *July 2*

Yarrow spreads its fine foliage along the country roadside now, and its grayish-yellow flower heads are bright with bees and butterflies. Walk through a patch of it and the peculiar pungence of its crushed leaves and stems will tweak at your remembering nose. You've known that flavor before.

Yarrow: a name that goes back to the old Anglo-Saxon. Some call it milfoil, which refers to the leaves and has a Latin source. If you care for the botanist's designation, it is *Achillea millefolium,* which echoes the legend that Achilles, the Greek, first discovered the plant's medicinal virtues. But forgot them, apparently, when he most needed them.

Yarrow is an herb right out of the old yarb doctor's lists. It is still used in Scotland and in back-country Europe as a healing agent, a treatment for wounds, a folk tonic. Thus it came by such common names as sanguinary, nosebleed, soldiers-woundwort. And today it has a respected place in more formal medicine, its essence providing a powerful tonic and stimulant as well as a flavoring for other mixtures. Hence the familiarity with which your nose tweaks when you have crushed a handful of yarrow leaves. You must have known the taste of yarrow in one of those dark-brown prescriptions of your childhood. Most of us did.

But along the roadsides it is just another wildling, a weed among weeds. Individually, its flowers are inconspicuous. Look at them closely, however, and they have minute beauty. And their clusters demand a place in a wild bouquet, where the yarrow foliage adds peculiar grace. And pungence, don't forget. In a very different way than that of rosemary, yarrow too is for remembrance.

Cities of Flowers   *July 3*

The elderberries come to bloom with their big, flat-topped, spice-scented heads of blossom, strikingly white against the warm green foliage. At a glance, the heads look like big, fluffy flowers, but if one looks closely they will be seen as floral communities, masses of tiny individual florets. Nearby are the heads of red clover, sweet in their own honeyed way, and at the road's edge are wild daisies nodding in the sun. They, too, are communities of blossoms, every clover head and every daisy flower. In a sense, they are among the ant colonies of the flower kingdom, flowers that have their own villages and small cities.

Look closely at a head of clover and you see a deftly contrived bouquet of miniature individual blooms, each like a tiny sweet pea. And the daisy flower is essentially a mass of yellow florets ringed with florets that have long, single white petals, the "petals" of the daisy itself. The despised dandelion of the front lawn is a community of tiny blossoms, each of which eventually makes its own silk-tufted seed. So is the thistle of neglected field and roadside. So is the blue blossom of the wild chicory. Composites, the botanists call them, tucking a whole definition into one word.

The elderberries are the most spectacular of the community flowers just now, but the lesser ones are blooming in every field. Man isn't the only living thing that is essentially gregarious. Man just goes out from his villages and cities to look at the country, and there he sees, often without recognizing them, whole cities of flowers.

Independence

Maybe it was coincidence that this country's independence was proclaimed in early July, but the countryman now has ample reason to doubt it. This is the time of year when anything less than freedom seems intolerable. The land itself won't be fettered, and it invites a man to work for and achieve the only kind of independence that endures, that which is paid for in sweat and hard work.

July is abundance on the land. Its long days seem specially shaped for a man to tend and harvest, to prepare for his own tomorrow. There is a richness and a beauty of natural growth that challenges a man to stand up and proclaim his own manhood. The countryman now hasn't much time to argue about petty matters, because the big problems are out there in the hayfield and on the cropland. Weather and weeds are more important that ideologies.

Sometimes it seems that the further man gets from the soil, the less he understands about fundamental independence, which is a way of living as well as a way of thinking. You can't argue a bushel of wheat or a bale of hay into being, and you can't legislate an improvident man into affluence. No court has yet altered the march of the seasons. About all man can do is protect his own freedom to work and live with the world around him. Those who proclaimed this country's independence still lived close enough to the land to know this. Every July provides a reminder, if we will only pause long enough to recognize it.

Basswood

The basswood will soon be in blossom; it is in fat bud now. And the bees will be gathering, so that the clumps of basswood will be loud as well as sweet, and the honeycomb will be full of some of the sweetest honey ever made.

The basswood is a linden, and our native basswood is close kin of the famous European shade tree. The name "bass" comes from "bast," or fiber, the reference being to the tough inner bark of the tree, which was long used in making cordage and nets. The wood itself is soft, fine-grained and easily worked into woodenware, occasionally into furniture.

The strangest thing about the basswood, however, is its flower and fruit. The flowers, small and creamy white and so full of nectar that it literally drips from them, grow on a pendant stem that springs from the center of a leaflike wing. This wing, long and slender and a lighter green than the tree's true leaves, eventually provides a glider for the seed, and thus are new groves of basswood started.

Travel the streams of the hill country and you see the basswoods now, full-leafed and lush and about to open flower. They hug the streambanks, and they make deep, cool shade. Indians once made dugout canoes from big basswood trunks. Now we make paper pulp from them. Or chopping bowls.

But in July the basswood along the streams is a tree of flowers and fragrance, and we ask no more of it. Dozens of other trees make better timber and better firewood, but where's another tree that smells as sweet at this time of year?

The Spice of July   *July 6*

Walk the meadows now, and the margins of the woodlands, and your path will soon be sharply fragrant with the tang of mint. For the mints grow wild all over the northern half of this country, and most encounters with them release their characteristic sweetly peppered oils. Brush the tousle-headed bee balm, crush the creeping gill-over-the-ground underfoot, or merely walk through a clump of catnip or spearmint and your clothes will carry the fragrance for hours. Grasp a nettle by mistake, however, and you probably will be distracted from its scent by the acid of its sting.

Of all the mints, only the nettles are really unfriendly; and even among the nettles there is one which yields a cordage fiber known as Kentucky hemp. Even in their wild state, most of the other mints will yield aromatic oils that we use one way or another every day—spearmint, peppermint, horehound, bergamot, catnip, pennyroyal. That's one reason they are here, for of all the mints we have only one that is a native of America. Ironically, that one, *Mentha arvensis,* has no common name except wild mint. But it is a rich-scented plant and it grows from coast to coast, sometimes as a garden captive, more often beside a brook or at a pasture's edge.

Of all the mints, only bee balm and wild bergamot have blossoms of consequence except to the bees. They are not showy. Their virtues are for the nose and the palate, not the eye. But one can seldom walk far in the fields without being aware of them. They are the spice of July, the tang that heightens the sweetness of honeysuckle and clover.

The Succulent Bean   *July 7*

The bean is a strange vegetable. It provides food for man and beast and, like all members of the legume family, it enriches the soil in which it grows. It is edible both green and dried. Just now it comes to the table in green form, the snap bean fresh from the garden. Properly cooked and buttered, it is one of the most satisfying of all early garden yield. Later it will be a challenge to every gardener alive—every neighbor, every week-ender, every casual visitor, will be begged to take beans, just to be rid of them. But that's for later. Just now it is a treasure and a gustatory delight.

The bean is such a simple thing to grow, and it can be such a trial to the gardener! It sprouts easily—unless cold, wet weather attends the planting. It grows quickly—unless cutworms attack. Or unless rabbits or woodchucks find it. Or unless any of a dozen voracious beetles descend. Or unless mildew attacks. It blossoms profusely, and the blossoms turn into pods overnight—unless blight sets in on a damp, chill day. It thrives with pampering, with weeding, with hoeing. Yet on occasion a stray bean will grow like mad despite total neglect in the midst of a weed patch. The bean is unpredictable. But satisfying.

The bean has been grown since prehistoric times. Indians grew it here long before the white man came. It probably will be grown as long as man grows anything. But if it grows another ten thousand years, it will never taste better than it does right now, young and green and tender. It won't taste half as good in August. And in October it will be just another shelled bean. But right now— well, right now the bean is a wonderful achievement.

Honeysuckle   *July 8*

You don't need to be a bumblebee to appreciate honeysuckle— but it might help. Then you could taste it as well as see and smell it. You can taste it, of course, if you still have small-boy instincts and know how to get at the nectar sac; but most of us are content to revel in its fragrance.

For honeysuckle is one of the major sensory delights among the less ostentatious of Summer's roadside flowers. All it asks is a hospitable rootbed and its share of rain and sun. Give it a fence to climb on and it waves its creamy blossoms at every passer-by. Give it a fence row of bushes and it leaps right over their heads with its own sweet display. On a bank it sprawls eagerly in all directions. Of course, it is the honeysuckle vine, not the bush, that we are speaking of, the humble twiner full of fragrant blossoms that perfume the countryside from mid-June till mid-July.

Look closely at the flowers and you find that they are eccentric trumpets with bipetaled lips. One petal is little more than a narrow strap; but the other is broad and four-lobed. In fact, the larger petal might serve as a pattern for a small white glove for one of Disney's four-fingered gnomes. And the long, slender stamens are like a tuft of white gnomish hair.

It is the flower's fragrance, however, not its individual beauty, that one remembers. There's nothing quite like it on a Summer's evening when the cool of night creeps through the valleys and a new moon hangs in the western sky.

Beyond the Fact July 9

Relentless, inquiring man has factual answers to a multitude of matters, but there are countless others that seem, especially on a Summer morning, to transcend cold fact and invite the warmth of understanding. Yet how can their meaning, which is something felt and sensed, be translated into the language of our common speech?

We see the mist rising from a lake or river, like incense to the creation of a new day. We hear the throb of a wood thrush's song in the distance. We see the glint of first sunlight on a lawn still wet with dew, the amazing whiteness of a daisy petal and the sharp orange contrast of a tawny hawkweed bloom. We smell the incredible sweetness of a milkweed's brownish-lavender blossom tuft. We hear the crisp, secret rustle of a whispering breeze in a cornfield and catch one swift glimpse of a scarlet tanager against the clear, clean blue of the sky.

We see the way a bindweed's twining stem climbs, and the way its blossom twists out of its bud and becomes a white trumpet. We listen to the scolding of a mother robin and the remote, sad call of a mourning dove. We smell a hayfield, watch a barn swallow in flight, hear a bumblebee humming in search of breakfast. We feel the sting of a nettle on an unwary hand reaching to pick a few seedy, tanged-sweet blackcap berries. We sense the day, the pungent, busy morning world that needs no human hand to shape it. And we know that factual answers are not enough.

Jewelweed July 10

Give it half a chance and jewelweed will take over almost any damp, woodsy spot. Its tall, bright green stems and leaves almost translucent in the sunlight, it makes a small jungle; but walk through it and you leave a clear path, for those stems have all the brittle frailty of any succulent plant. Break them and they ooze a juice which country boys declare is a cure for poison ivy.

Seen in the morning sunlight, a patch of jewelweed seems to gleam with orange-yellow spangles. Look more closely and you find the flowers which give the plant its common name. Strange flowers with a deep saclike base and the petals joined in a bell-shaped form with divided lobes, the whole a rich golden yellow, almost a bronze, and speckled as a robin's egg, the speckles a browning red. The flowers are small and fragile, and they hang from slender stems. Bees seek them out, and now and then a hummingbird comes to explore their depths.

Touch-me-not, the plant is sometimes called, because when the flowers are gone and the seed pods ripen, some inner tension is established which pops those seeds as from a miniature catapult if any passer-by should brush against them. Thus does the jewelweed spread so swiftly—it hurls its seeds in all directions, profligate and persistent. Botanically the plant belongs to the family called Balsaminaceae, and it is close kin to the cultivated flower known as balsam or, erroneously, lady's slipper, which adds its fragrance and varicolored beauty to the old-fashioned garden. But jewelweed is no cutting flower, even for those who would bring the wildlings indoors. It is largely foliage anyway. Its jewels are small and are best seen in the damp woodland by those who are willing to go there before the morning dew has dried.

Purslane   *July 11*

In the flower garden we plant portulaca and cherish it for its gay flowers. But just across the way, where the vegetables grow, we wage endless war with portulaca's first cousin, purslane.

Purslane is a weed. It is a pesky weed despite the fact that in France it is sometimes plucked for salad and that our grandmothers called it pussley and cooked it as a green. Neither fact alters its flavor or character. Cooked, it is gelatinous. Raw, it is merely green and without much flavor. The humble peppergrass has more taste. The best that can be said for it is that its taste is not unpleasant. Which is too bad—if it were more tasty it would not be a weed.

But weed it is, and one of the most pestiferous in the garden. It starts out with little hint of trouble. The first few leaves look almost harmless. But turn your back on it for a few days, particularly a few warm, damp days, and it takes the whole place. Go to work with a hoe and it reveals its true character. Hoe it out in the afternoon and by morning half of it has taken root again. Hoe it out in the morning, and unless the day is blistering it lies half wilted until the cool of evening and then crawls back to where it grew and starts all over again. Root it out completely and haul it away, and within a week a whole new crop has replaced it.

You can fight purslane all through July and August, and into September, and still not win. It will be back next year, lush as ever. There are bigger weeds, and more flagrant ones, but few are more persistent. And if anyone tells you that purslane grows only on fertile soil, thus engaging in a kind of backhanded flattery, laugh at him. Purslane grows anywhere except on the granite tops of the highest mountains. And it doesn't even have a pretty flower.

The Battle of the Weeds *July 12*

Now come the days when you can tell the real gardener by the hoe in his hand and the ache in his back. You don't even have to look at his garden; just look at him. He is doing battle with the weeds.

Perhaps it is academic, but now and then the gardener and his blood brother, the farmer, wonder what is a weed and why. Simmer all the definitions, and you come down to the fact that any plant becomes a weed when it insists on growing where it isn't wanted. Grass that graces a lawn becomes a weed in the garden. Mustard that makes good pot greens and a tasty condiment becomes a pesky weed in the hayfield. The asters that glorify the roadsides, and that in tamed and domesticated form are cherished in the flower bed, are to be rooted out among the tomatoes or the corn. Chicory, in some places a cultivated flower and root, is a weed among the cabbages. Even the onion and the radish are weeds in the rose bed.

So now the man with the hoe is out there in the sun, making his own definitions, and enforcing them. It was easy enough to plant, back in April and early May. He was master of the soil, chooser of the seed. But now the harvest is at stake. Hence the hoe. Hence that aching back. He denominates the weeds, wields the blade, pulls the root. He wants carrots, not Queen Anne's lace; beans, not bugleweed. He wants corn, squash and tomatoes. Now he demonstrates the aching difference between the mere planter and the gardener.

The Flying Dragon   *July 13*

Strange tales and mistaken legends are hinted at in such names as devil's darning needle, horse-stinger and snake-feeder; but all such names are libels on the dragonfly which now haunts ponds and streams and nearby meadows. The dragonfly neither stings nor consorts with snakes. It is, in fact, one of the most skillful fishermen of the air-ocean, catching gnats, midges and mosquitoes in a kind of seine it forms with its legs. It is strong in flight and keen of vision. Its eyes probably are the best any insect ever developed, and its long, iridescent wings are near perfection.

The dragonfly has a long history. Fossil dragonflies at least 35,000,000 years old have been found, and such fossils prove that the dragonfly early achieved its present form. Long ago there were dragonflies with a wingspread of two feet. Today the largest of them are seldom more than seven inches across the wings. Otherwise, time seems to have changed them little. The ancient ones looked as fierce as those of today, and no doubt their flight was as skillful as the flight of today's misnamed dragon of the air. Whether the prehistoric ones had metallic color and sheen to their wings cannot be said.

But here they are, in mid-Summer, all over the lowlands, busy as bees and ten times as curious. Still-fishermen know them well, for they must investigate all fish lines, it seems. And their iridescent flight catches the eye. Small wonder that terrible tales still cling to them. They invite superstition. They look like holdovers from the age of dragons, though the largest thing they would harm is smaller than a housefly.

Elderberries   *July 14*

The elderberry bushes are in bloom, and seeing them from the roadside one thinks that they deserve a better fate than to be regarded as weeds and grubbed out. Many a cherished lawn shrub isn't much prettier than an elderberry bush in full bloom.

Time was when the elderberry was respected. The white flower head which now covers the bush and is a lure for bees by the hundred matures into a lush pannicle of purplish-black berries. Those berries are full of sweet juice, so sweet it refuses to turn into jelly without the help of apples or some other pectin-rich components. But that juice, when properly handled, makes elderberry wine. There was a time when most rural cellars included at least a jug and often a keg of elderberry wine. Elderberry wine had certain indisputable medicinal qualities, as well as a kick and a tongue-tantalizing flavor. It was surprising how many countrymen felt a bit puny as long as the elderberry wine lasted, puny enough to need a glass of it every day. But where can you find real, homemade elderberry wine today, no matter how puny you feel?

Elderberries also made many a tasty pie in country kitchens. In upstate New York the elderberry pie was so much esteemed that the berries were gathered and dried at the height of the season for pie making during the Winter. But who today dries elderberries, and who but those with long memories even makes fresh elderberry pies?

So today the elderberry bushes bloom, and they bow with their load of fruit, and the birds flock to them with delight. And all the old pleasure that sprang from those humble bushes in the past is little more than a memory. But while they bloom they are a delight to the eye. And, as we say, the bees love them.

Height of Summer   *July 15*

Now comes the height of Summer when, although the sun is already inclining toward Autumn by celestial measurement, our latitude has weather fit for the tropics and vegetation almost to match. The trees stand lush and listless, their great canopies of chlorophyll working magic with sun and air and moisture, their April growth solidifying itself, their roots atingle with life in the warm earth. Uncut meadows stand high with ripening grass. Cherries redden, berries fatten on the thorny canes, apples begin to weight the boughs. Streams run low and ponds thicken with algae that soon will scum them with dog-days green. Buttercups are past their prime. Daisies gleam.

There is an anachronism in all our Summers, or at least a seeming one, that stems from our arbitrary calendar. The longest day of sunlight, by such a system, comes at the beginning of Summer rather than in its midst. In consequence, all Summer long we are inclining toward Summer's end instead of building to a climax and then tapering off. Logic rejects such a system, even as it shakes its head at a Winter whose depth of darkness comes at its very beginning. But there they stand, each season somewhat out of gear; and the deft explanation of the lag is excuse for a calculation.

Explain it as one may, a solstice remains an arbitrary date, an invisible line never seen on a leaf or in a bud or petal. Despite the calculators, the trees, the grass, the lilies of the field all say the calendar nay. The solstice is well behind, and here, in mid-July, we come to the middle of Summer; and logic has nothing to do, beyond cold mathematics, with arbitrary dates and seasons.

Matin Song to a Garden *July 16*

Early morning is the best time of day to work in a garden. You can really appreciate a garden then, when the sun is not too high or too hot, when the dew is still on the lettuce leaves and the bean beetles haven't begun their midday forays. You're full of energy then, too, and persistent purslane doesn't seem to be a major enemy.

You have to leave the beans alone, of course. They have a phobia about being disturbed before their leaves have dried off. They are definitely antisocial in the early morning; they sulk and get attacks of mildew. So you concentrate on the carrots and the corn and the tomatoes and all the cabbage family. And the weeds. Why doesn't somebody cross weeds with beans and produce pests which curl up and die because of matutinal disturbance?

If you get there early enough, you probably will have company in the garden shortly after dawn. Rabbits also like the early morning; peas and beans and cabbages must taste much better to a rabbit at that time of day. Why don't the dear little Easter bunnies like purslane and lamb's-quarters? That's another of those mysteries. Before you get morbid about it, you greet your long-eared little neighbors with a barrage of stones. And then you get down to business.

You weed, you cultivate, you gloat over your fine, straight rows. You congratulate yourself and think what a splendid world it is, after all. You decide to pick beans a little later. And you listen to the robins and feel full of contentment. Then the sun gets high enough to scorch the back of your neck, and gardening is just another chore. That's why you get at it early—it's fun, then.

Mid-July *July 17*

By mid-July the season has begun to assert itself. The earliest of the wild asters come to bloom while the black-eyed Susans still

possess the neglected meadow. Tiny blackcaps ripen on the wild raspberry's thorny stems. Rank-grown sweet clover is in bloom and chicory begins to show blue flowers on gray-green stems at the roadside. Elderberry bushes nod with a swelling freight of berries, still green as leaves but with promise of the purple fruit that will bow the bushes in a few more weeks. Wild parsnip goes to seed and wild carrot comes to bloom, the ruby-studded head of Queen Anne's lace.

Cornfields begin to tassel out, not yet hazed with pollen and still reaching for the sun. Hayfields, cut and mowed away only a few weeks ago, are green again with the urgency of grass and clover. Apple trees which only yesterday, it seems, were giant bouquets now begin to make their obeisance to the earth that nourishes their weighting fruit. The garden bean is full of pods and the Summer squash is ready for the pot. The garden weed grows overnight, knowing no truce with the man who wields the hoe. July is the month of decision, with D day in the garden marked by every sunrise.

July is April's hope, May's promise and June's growth pushing toward completion. July is mid-Summer, a season in itself. The bee and the ant now put man to shame as a sluggard. The quiet chlorophyll in the leaf makes man's fissioned atom a puny force. The silent urgency of root and flower and leaf are manifest now, in mid-July, the power and the glory of the green earth itself.

Susan's Eyes   *July 18*

Black-eyed Susan's eyes aren't really black at all. They are a purplish-brown, as anyone can see who takes the trouble to look for more than a passing glance at the Susans which are so profuse now at the roadside and in the meadows. *Rudbeckia hirta* is the official name, the botanical name, and it is a biennial flower that came out of the West along with commercial clover seed. Once in the East, it took to the soil and climate with vigor and pertinacity. Now its dark-eyed yellow flowers are common from Maine southward, wherever it finds a foothold. And it is particularly adaptable to almost any foothold available.

The yellow petals have a peculiarly rich golden color. They are full of sunlight. Like so many of the Compositae, its petals vary in number—thirteen on this flower, fifteen on another of the same plant, fourteen on the next flower. And they curl and twist, sometimes fray out at the tips for no obvious reason. The flower's sepals, the green "petals" that encase the bud and later form a supporting background for the flower, outnumber the petals, sometimes as much as two to one. And there are countless florets encircling the disk, Susan's eye; they open their tiny blossoms in succession and ring the disk with still another halo of golden yellow, the ripened pollen.

Bees and butterflies love the Susans, and so do most country youngsters. Weeds they certainly are when they invade the garden, but at the roadside they are bright and jaunty and full of the Summer sun. And they don't discourage easily, as many a gardener knows. Cut them or pull them up—they'll be back, as surely as the July sunshine, to which they belong.

Clover   _July 19_

Roadsides are sweet now with honeysuckle and clover, the warm, sweet fragrance of Summer at its peak. Honeysuckle begins to pass its prime, though there will be blossom and lesser sweetness till the asters bloom. But clover blooms all Summer long, a delight to the bees, a friend to the soil and a pleasure to anyone who pauses to look.

One thing about clover: it takes the soil as it finds it, sends down eager roots, spends the whole season at a complex chemical job and gives a new supply of fresh nitrates to the soil it occupies. Clover rebuilds the soil, and is constantly reaching for new soil to reclaim. Give it half a chance and it will take over a gravelly roadside or a worn-out field where few other plants will grow, and in a few seasons the clover has given it new life. And all the while the clover will cloak that soil in cool green, brighten the landscape with its miniature sweet pea blossoms, and feed every bee within range.

The one thing clover needs to thrive is cooperation of the bees. Take away the bee and the clover won't outlast the season, as Australia learned long ago, for the bees fertilize the clover blooms and thus enable it to reseed itself. On the other hand, take away the clover and the bees would be hard put to fill their hives. Clover honey outweighs all other varieties, year after year.

It would be a dull and less fragrant Summer without clover, and a drab and diminishing world without the cooperation of bees and clover. Together they help keep the planet green and sweet, with no thanks asked.

The Legendary Milkweed   *July 20*

The milkweeds are in bloom and their fragrance, like a blend of tuberose and honeysuckle, is heavy at the roadside and along the damp pond margin. The most colorful member of the family, the lovely butterfly weed, even carries the word *tuberosa* in its Latin name. But the common milkweed, a less showy but more abundant member of the family and the one which produces the big silvery-green pods, seems to have more fragrance, perhaps only because it is more plentiful and has more bloom to scent the air.

The milkweeds are known botanically as Asclepias, and ancient lore clusters around them. Asclepius, their namesake, was the legendary god of healing. His first teacher was Chiron, a centaur. Asclepius became so skillful that he could revive the dead, and Zeus, in a fit of jealousy, killed him. The serpent was sacred to Asclepius, and the serpent-twined staff of Mercury, one of the symbols of modern medicine, can be traced to him. Whether Asclepius used milkweed juice in his potions or not, folk healers have cherished the plant for treating respiratory illness. In fact, another common name for butterfly weed is pleurisy root. Though a weed, the plant is not without distinction.

We know it chiefly as a roadside weed whose seed fluff should, but doesn't, substitute for silk, and whose juice might, but doesn't, compete with natural rubber. Country folk often eat the young milkweed shoots like asparagus. Bees love milkweed pollen, and often die entrapped in the blossoms. But in mid-Summer the milkweed is chiefly a fragrance, one of the sweetest of all the flowers at the roadside.

Perfection   *July 21*

The great mulleins stand majestic in the pastures and along the roadsides, gray-green and in lonely grandeur. They are weeds and of no consequence as flowering plants, not half as pretty as a thistle, for instance. But there is a classic beauty in their symmetry and their tall, straight stems and carefully graduated leaves. They have a smaller cousin, the moth mullein, with very different leaves and pretty white or yellow flowers in a loose head. But the moth mullein is only a flower. The great mullein is a kind of apotheosis of simple plant perfection.

Back in January the great mulleins could be seen, even on cold and snowy days, in pastures or open woodland. The tall stalk had fallen, but there on the ground lay the mat of basal leaves, gray-green as they are now and only somewhat crisped and browned at the edges. Usually they lay in a snow-free circle, as though they somehow generated a few degrees of warmth; and they looked ready to resume growth at any moment. They waited, however, until May, then sent up the first new leaves and the beginning of the stalk.

Now they stand with the central stalk as tall as a man and two inches through at the base. The base leaves are little changed, but up the stem, regular as though calibrated, are the long, acute-tipped leaves, clasping the stem and graduated from eight or ten inches long to only an inch or so at the top, where the flower head rises. The flower head is a long cluster of gray-green buds, a knobby kind of upthrust thumb. But it blooms as it grows, at leisure and with a kind of deliberation. Only two or three flowers open at a time, bright yellow in color but quite without ostentation. It is no flowering beauty, this plant. It is simply a plant grown to the kind of simple perfection a sculptor might have dreamed in thinking of line and leaf and symmetry.

Sumac Plumes   *July 22*

Sumac comes to fruit, its spikes or berries already forecasting the war paint that will mark the leaves by September. Look close, however, and you will see that those berries are still green—odd little green seeds covered with maroon hair and clustered in characteristic spikes. And the shrub's leaves are still as green as any leaf in the woodland, green plumes reaching for their share of sunlight.

We usually think of sumac as a weed, a shrub or small tree that invades the waste places and is of no real value, is not actually dangerous. For there is one poisonous variety, as vicious as poison ivy. The poison sumac, however, has no red berries. Its berries are gray-green and they hang in loose clusters. No sumac with red-headed berries in an upright spike is dangerous.

In earlier days our own forefathers gathered sumac leaves and bark and even roots to use in tanning and dyeing. European sumac is still used along the Mediterranean in that way. And in Asia there is a sumac that yields a seed oil that can be made into candles and a juice that makes a natural varnish for lacquer work. If sumac were less common here, if it demanded care and pampering, it probably would be cherished and admired simply for its own beauty. It decks the woods and the waysides now. Autumn without its early color would lack an element of beauty, for its reds, its yellows and oranges are unique among the early Autumn leaves.

Just now the sumac's fruit can be spectacular. Its frondlike leaves can be supremely graceful. And by moonlight and in a breeze it can be eerily beautiful, twinkling with reflected moonlight that has a green shimmer like nothing else in the woodland.

The Cicada   *July 23*

There are two schools of thought about the cicada and its sounds.
One school calls the cicada the twanging of a taut and ragged
nerve at the peak of a galling Summer day, a quiver so painful
that you wince a quarter of a mile away. A wounded lion, such
people say, can make more noise for a little while, and a bull elk
trumpeting for a mate can make more noise for quite a while; but,
they point out, wounded lions are relatively scarce and bull elk
are common only in Wyoming. Millions of cicadas live here.

There are, this school admits, two types of local cicadas, the
periodic ones, sometimes called seventeen-year locusts, and the
dog-day harvest flies. The periodic ones spend the better part of
seventeen years in silence and underground between noisy, adult
generations. The harvest flies spend only two years in such silent
anonymity. But, they also point out, both species somehow contrive to have a noisy adult generation on hand every Summer.
How this came about, nobody knows.

The cicada authorities also say that mosquitoes buzz, crickets
chirp, but cicadas shrill. Only the males make noise, but the
male's whole body vibrates with the resonance but not the melody
of a violin. And, they point out, the fact that the cicada's name is
accented on the second syllable makes no difference at all—his
noise is also loudest and shrillest in the middle.

The other school in this matter thinks that cicadas make a
drowsy sound. Besides, they say, cicadas are silent at night, when
people like to sleep. They are the kind of people who think that
katydids make music. Katydids, by the way, will be along in another week or two.

Sundial of the Seasons   *July 24*

Dusk comes somewhat earlier now, the Summer solstice already a
month behind us and the daylight slowly diminishing. Time's

dimensions are unchanged, but the landmarks shift even as the familiar star patterns shift in the night skies. Summer passes.

You see the change in the way the shadows fall. You see it in the trees, the subtle difference in the color of their leaves, in the ripening seed heads of the wild grasses, in young acorns on the oaks. Pasture roses fade. Black-eyed Susan and bouncing Bet flourish at the roadside. Queen Anne's lace is frothy white where daisies frosted the fence row a few weeks ago. Milkweed blossoms fade.

You hear the change in the bird calls, with fewer songs of ecstasy and more parental scolding. The wood thrush, the dove and the whippoorwill dominate the dusk. You hear it most decisively, when you pause to listen, in the insect sounds, for time has special dimensions for chitin-clad life that is granted only one Summer's duration. Bees are busier, wasps are more truculent, harvest flies more sibilant in the heat of the afternoon. Beetles click in haste, ants scurry, dragonflies dart on rattling wings.

And in the dusk, when the sphinx moths haunt the flower garden, crickets stridulate, mosquitoes hum, late lunas and other light-mad moths bang the window screens. August and katydids are just over the horizon, and Autumn is not far behind them. The shadow of time moves slowly but surely across the sundial of the seasons.

Mid-Summer Thrush   *July 25*

Most bird songs thin away as July lengthens, even the morning chorus having only a fraction of the volume it had in June; but even a sultry evening in late July does not silence the wood thrush. Early dusk comes and the clear, contralto notes ring through the woods or across the open fields, as fine an evening call as one might ask. The wood thrush, which some call the song thrush, the swamp robin or the bell bird, has no fine, intricate melody, but the simple song it sings has a deep, liquid sweetness with the quality of a flute in its lower ranges.

In habit, the wood thrush is midway between its cousins, the robin and the hermit thrush; it is not a lawn bird, though it occasionally nests in a tree near a country or suburban house, and it is no hermit completely shunning human habitations. A sleek bird dressed in rich browns, even to the polka dots on its white chest and belly, it is about the size of the robin. Some call the wood thrush the handsomest of all thrushes.

It is perhaps a tribute to the bird that some observers have likened its simple song to phrases in various classical compositions, to Weber's "Invitation to the Dance," to a part of Handel's "Largo," and to an aria from Gounod's "Faust." The literal accuracy of such comparisons is less important than the fact that musicians find reason for comparison. The bird has a voice; that's the sum of it. The bird can sing and its song is a reminder of good music.

Apparently the wood thrush, too, knows music. It sings, of a Summer evening, well into the dusk. Then a whippoorwill begins to cry. And the wood thrush stops singing. Of what use is music when a whippoorwill begins to make the night echo?

Sweet Corn   *July 26*

Sweet corn now begins to come to the pot, and if there is a more satisfying garden crop few countrymen can name it. Lettuce is good for the blood and the appetite, snap beans are a fine, fresh taste for a few weeks, and garden-ripe tomatoes are really something. But when the first corn comes to the table, steaming, savory and ready for the customers, you can push everything else aside. Everything. Corn needs no appetizer, no accompaniment but a dash of salt, a trace of pepper, and plenty of butter. And let the cobs fall where they may.

Perhaps there are a few people, here and there, who don't appreciate sweet corn. If so, the chances are that they've known it only from a distance, so to speak. Perfection demands that corn proceed from stalk to cooking pot as fast as a man can walk, and from pot to plate with even greater dispatch. Any delays, any way stations, rob it of some degree of flavor. And the cook who doesn't know to the second when it should come from the pot should never be trusted with it. How do you know? Well, it's a matter of instinct, mostly, fortified with a keen sense of smell. Those who would time it by the clock are rank amateurs. It simply smells done, looks done, and is done. Country cooks usually know.

Hurry it to the pot, watch it like a hawk, dash it to the table. Then eat. And ceremony is forgotten. So is conversation, for the first few ears, at least. After that you catch your breath and thank the Indians. Then you start all over again.

❧ I have been told, firmly and authoritatively, by women I respect as good cooks otherwise, that sweet corn should always be cooked by the clock. But even they disagree on exactly how long to cook it and whether to steam it or boil it. Until such advisers get together on their advice, this household will continue to ignore the clock and cook corn by smell; and I shall not alter the words above by one degree or one second.

Migrant Man   *July 27*

Spring and Fall are the logical times for migration, but man, with his genius for doing things differently, has made mid-Summer his migratory time. He might have done worse, for this land, this America, is a broad and generous land to see in full Summer lushness.

It's a green land. That is the first impression as you head west from this Atlantic shore. A green and fertile land full of fruit and grain and all the foodstuffs for a nation. Living with cities, we forget how lost are cities in the vast green that reaches the length and breadth of America. Technological our economy may be, but still the great factory is the green leaf, the blade of grass or corn, the leaf of tree.

You drive and drive and drive, and all round you is the lushness of the open country. And the small towns, so many that they make the city almost unique. We talk of our urbanity, our steady move to the larger towns and cities, but it has only a little lessened the expanse of the fields and woodlands. It is the people who have moved; the land is still there, the green and wooded land with all its streams and rivers and mountains and plains; and the cities have merely grown a little larger, a bigger statistic in the national total.

Space, that is the outstanding fact which strikes the eye and then the mind. A hilltop where you can see half across a state, and not a city in sight. A ridge that reaches all the way to the horizon, and the only sign of a factory is a smudge of smoke in a distant valley. A river that flows for miles between wooded banks. And the farms outnumber the villages and the cities on the riverbank are a rarity. Space, room, expanse—that is America; green space, fertile land; and man, migrant man, only the traveler there.

❦ This traveler's report was written in a motel in Davenport, Iowa.

Why?   *July 28*

The answers don't come easily at midday, in late July, but in the evening, with a full moon and whatever cool comes with sunset, the questions call for pondering. Don't mosquitoes ever suffer from heat prostration? Why are there so many female mosquitoes, equipped with "stingers," and so few males, which don't bite? Why does "succession" corn succeed in coming to ear all at the same time? Why does a packet of scarlet annual poppy seed contain so many sickly pink ones and so few deep red ones? When does a whippoorwill get time to catch all the insects it needs to survive? It sleeps all day and calls all night.

If fish don't bite during a hot spell—and they don't—how do they survive? Why do road builders pick the hottest day of the year to retar a road? Is there a more poignant monument to a vanished woman than hollyhocks blooming beside an old cellar hole on a back road? Who ever thinks, when he eats raspberries, that the "rasp" comes from an antique word for roughness, which comes down to us elsewhere in the name of a coarse file? Why are starlings, which eat Japanese beetles, so plentiful in the cities and so few in the country at Jap beetle time?

Who named the mourning dove so aptly? Is there a more plaintive call in all birddom than that of the dove at evening? Where does a house wren get all its energy? Maybe someone should examine its thyroid. And why doesn't a robin, four times as big, sing half as much as a wren? What happened to those fine old rural craftsmen, the expert hay stackers, when the hay baler was invented? Did you ever use a snath? Or did you know it as a snathe or a snead?

The Light of Summer   *July 29*

The light has already begun to change. You see it at midday as well as at dusk, and if you are an early riser you see it clearly at dawn. It's still the light of Summer. Even without a calendar, one would never mistake it for Spring light, or the light of Fall. But the shadows lie a little differently now than they did a month ago. The distance has a feel, if not an actual look, of gathering haze. August is in the offing. Sunset loses its June clarity, tends now toward brassy color. The dazzle of rain-washed air is more pronounced now after a shower.

Each season has its own light and almost each hour of the day. Spring dawns sparkle with clarity, and May's midday light is tinged with green, subtle as the green of new leaves. Fall days are golden, reflecting not so much the color of the turning leaves as the Fall haze. Winter light is silvered and frosted, and the Winter dawns and dusks are full of blue light and purple. Winter's shadows are long shadows, no matter what the time of day, for the sun we see is off there to the south, slanting at us.

But the light of July and August is the day's dazzle, hot light, with the season's dust slowly accumulating and making the sky we see a giant silvered reflector. In Spring the sky was a bowl of blue, and in Fall it will be a turquoise dome. Now it is a shimmering tent, ripped in vast gashes from time to time by an afternoon thunderstorm, briefly clean and blue, then that smothering tent again. Late July, tending toward August; hot Summer, tending toward Autumn. You see it even in the shadows—warm, gray-green shadows.

The Sphinx *July 30*

The sphinx moths are busy over the flower gardens these late July evenings. Some call them hawk moths and others know them as hummingbird moths. They may be mistaken for hummingbirds in the dusk, for at a glance they seem about the same size and they haunt the deep-throated flowers, the petunias, the bergamots, all the trumpet flowers, much as does the daytime hummer. But they are moths, not birds, and at one stage of their lives they were hungry caterpillars eating the heart out of a ripening tomato.

Now, however, these creatures of the dusk are winged ones, patterned with a quiet beauty in dark tones of gray and brown and olive green. And each one has a long proboscis, a sucking tube, coiled like a spring beneath its head. As it prepares to feed, it uncoils this tube and thrusts it deep into the nectar pockets of the chosen flower. Thus it eats, thus it lives out its life, this one phase of it.

For all its nectar supping, the sphinx is no flibbertigibbet, as are some moths and butterflies. It is seldom drawn to a lighted window to beat its wings to shreds against the screen. It doesn't flit from flower to flower, whimsical, tasting here, tasting there. It feeds, it goes about its business clothed in quiet beauty. It lays its eggs and its purpose is fulfilled. The eggs hatch into green hornworms that have no resemblance at all to a sphinx moth. Wings and beauty come later, in another Summer of warm dusks and deep-throated flowers. The worm eats the tomato, but the moth must live on nectar.

Like a good many other wildlings, roadside chicory is too abundant for the good of its own reputation. If it were a rarer plant, the beauty of its blossoms and the clean, clear quality of their blue would be more often noted and admired. For the chicory blossom is an example of one of the best blues in the floral spectrum, blue as the innocent eyes of a six-year-old blonde. Only the flowers of the flax plant can compete with it in color.

But chicory grows along the dry and gravelly roadsides, ubiquitous as ragweed. It grows where little else can find a foothold, and it persists in heat and drought. Come mid-July and it rears its slim stalks and opens its flowers, like a baby-blue mist; and if the season is particularly dry it seems to thrive as few other plants do, thrive and bloom in profusion. Not even the yellow evening primroses, which also make the most of the waste places, can make so much of so little encouragement.

One reason for the chicory's colorful persistence is the long, vigorous root from which it springs. And that root is the reason chicory was first brought to America from its native Europe. For generations, Europeans have harvested the chicory root, dried and roasted it and used it as a substitute and adulterant for coffee. Early Americans used chicory in the same way and grew their own supply. They also used its young leaves for salad. Thus it got its foothold here, escaping from fields and gardens. Now it is a weed and in poorly tended fields it can be a nuisance. But it is also a touch of roadside beauty, a handsome flower whose chief offense is that it is so common and so persistent.

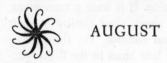 AUGUST

August

August is the year at early harvest, a farm wife with a baby napping in the crib, a preserving kettle on the stove, fryers in the freezer, new potatoes in the pot, and a husband in the hayfield baling the second cutting. August is tomatoes ripening and the insistent note of the cicada punctuating the heat of midafternoon. August is the smell of corn pollen, and the taste of roasting ears, and the stain of blackberry juice on the fingers.

August is the flame of phlox in the dooryard and hollyhocks down by the roadside blooming now up at their tips. August is Summer squash by the bushel, and Winter squash swelling beneath the broad parasol of trailing leaves. August is ripe oats. August is a languid river and a springhouse brook reduced to a trickle.

August is a few impatient asters trying to compete with late daisies; it is day lilies all through blooming and looking ragged and outworn; it is the first sprays of goldenrod in the uncut fence row. August is baby rabbits almost grown, and pilfering in the garden; it is fledglings all feathered and on the wing; it is a cow, her Spring calf forgotten, chewing a leisurely cud in the shade of a tired elm tree at the side of the meadow.

August is the heavy grapes in the vineyard, and the lacy leaf where the Japanese beetle feasted in metallic glitter; it is wild grapes festooned on the trees at the riverbank; it is algae on the pond and the fat green thumbs of cattails in the swamp, and ironweed purpling, and vervain in full bloom. August is a hastening sun, earlier to bed and later to rise. August is Summer thinking of the cut and color of her Autumn costume.

August Harvest   *August 2*

The August ripeness creeps across the land, somewhat hastened by the heat but forever typical of the season. Forerunner of the later total harvest, it is a reminder, too, that no harvest is a brief and isolated completion in any year. Harvest is a continuing event, from the first hay through the oats, the wheat, the barley and rye to that amazing abundance which is corn and Autumn.

Traveling west you see August harvest in all its stages; and the seeing is a fresh reminder of this country's scope, its variety, its ever-amazing bounty. The corn everywhere, from the patchy little fields of the East to the vastness of Illinois and Iowa cornfields which scent whole counties with the smell of corn pollen. The deep, rich green of soybeans, all but unknown a few decades ago and now almost typical of much of the Midwest. The oat fields, and the rye and barley and wheat fields, all now clipped and thrashed of their grain, now golden stubble quartered and halved and striped by brown or black furrows of fresh plowing. And, as one approaches the Western mountains, the endless, ordered fields of sugar beets, garden fresh and tended.

And the hay. Hay everywhere, timothy and clover and alfalfa and native grass. The clover in red bloom, the alfalfa in purple bloom, and both honey sweet. Hay in bloom, and hay cut and baled, and hay in fresh windrows curing in the sun. Stacks of hay, bales of hay, millions of tons of hay; for this land of ours, while it has its special hay lands, has hayfields and mowings and meadows and pasture lands everywhere. Ours is an essentially grassy land,

and even where the hot winds and the swirling dust have blighted the Plains the grass still struggles for its native foothold between the dunes of dust momentarily at rest.

You travel, and you see this creeping harvest, this ripeness of August building toward the ripeness of Autumn, the vast harvest yet to come, and you know again the reality of statistics. For here is the diet, the nutrition, the plenty which statistics can only hint at in dry terms of mathematics. Here is the storehouse, here is the grain bin, here is the plenty of a nation ripening in the August sunlight.

❦ This traveler's report was written in Denver, Colo.

The Worts   *August 3*

Ragwort still shows its rather dusty yellow flowers at the roadside, and soapwort makes a display of pink in the waste places. They are only two of the dozens of worts that thrive and bloom without particular notice or acclaim, since the old-time gatherers of wild herbs have largely vanished. For the worts were among the prime items on the "yarb" list. The very fact that the syllable "wort" is incorporated in the common name is testimony to their past. "Wort" goes back to the Gothic word for root, and to the Anglo-Saxon *wyrt,* meaning "herb."

Any casual list of worts will run to at least a hundred and fifty plants, running the alphabetic scale from adderwort to yellowwort. Go through such a list and you will find the whole range of human ailments set forth, or at least so much of the range as was known and denominated a hundred years ago. Take cankerwort. Go on down to gutwort, which might have lacked elegance but probably reduced many an ache. Nettlewort may have assuaged the sting of the nettle, and if so it surely was potent. Quinzywort certainly was used as a hot infusion for a very sore throat.

There was even a rupturewort. We still recognize soapwort, mentioned above, which is nothing more than bouncing Bet, a pleasant flower with a root that can substitute for soap. And there is toothwort, there is navelwort, there is sneezewort, there is the generic woundwort, and there is wartwort. The worts, the persistent herbs of the old back-country apothecary, constitute a kind of folk poetry of human ills and aches, of pain and hope and trust, and inevitably of occasional cure.

Phlox Flame   *August 4*

Phlox means "flame" in the original Greek, and it flames now in gardens all over America. Perhaps it is because the season is slow this year, but the phlox seems more than usually brilliant up through central New England, up Connecticut Valley way and into the old mountains that rise from the Berkshires north. It flames in almost every dooryard.

But the brightest flame of all is beside old stone walls and clapboards weathered gray through generations of time. On back roads, where too many houses stand with vacant windows and sagging roofs, you find such phlox, now and then, where vanished hands once tended herbs and flowers between more urgent household tasks.

It is commonly said that phlox untended reverts to the dull magenta color. It needs tending and cutting to hold its beauty. Yet somehow banks of crimson and cherry red and white persist in a few of those forgotten gardens. The grass grows tall, the steeple bush encroaches, even the stones from the wall have tumbled into the flower bed; but there persist the strong colors. One wonders if the cows have cropped it at a proper time, or if some passer-by came, year after year, to cut choice heads.

However it happened, there stands the phlox, aflame with beauty as it must have flamed when some forgotten woman set it there and watched it come to bloom and paused to smell its fragrance before she went back to the canning kettle. There it is, persistent monument to one who could sing at her work seeing the phlox in the dooryard, aflame when August came this way.

Those who fish for bass and trout loftily ignore the existence of the catfish, and perhaps properly so; he is not for them. But the countryman, the man who knows a channel cat from a mud cat or a bullhead, knows that there's fun as well as food in catfish water. You fish for cats either day or night, but country boys, and men too, like to go in the evening. There's something about a deepening night on a pond or a streambank that gets into a country fisherman's emotions and settles there most pleasantly. For such an evening you take a lantern, a can of worms, a light pole and, if you are fishing from a boat, a hand line. And take a congenial companion, a quiet conversationalist, not a chatterer.

Once on the water, or beside it, bait the hook generously with worms. Night crawlers, the big fellows that abound in soft earth at the edge of the barnyard, are best of all. Let the bait sink in promising water and keep an attentive finger on the line. If catfish are there, one will find your worm; and if he is of respectable size you will know it, particularly if you fish with light tackle. But you'll soon bring him in. Experienced hands know how to handle him, how to avoid the sharp horns with which he is armed, how to disengage the hook; inexperienced hands soon learn—or decide catfishing is not for them.

Dusk deepens and soon the night is there to enjoy. This is what you came for, as much as the fish themselves—the starlight, the wind in the willows, the night call of a heron, the gleaming wake of a muskrat in the water. But you don't talk much about these things, not to outsiders. You tell them, if they ask, that you had a mess of catfish by midnight, that you skinned them, soaked them in salt water and had them fried for breakfast. Good? Well, a catfish fisherman enjoys them. That's about all you can say—to an outsider.

Roadside Renegades

We call them weeds and grant them only renegade status, and the farmer and the gardener are at war with them every year. Few of them have even a degree of floral beauty to give them status. But there they are, in our dooryards, at our roadsides and in our fields and gardens, notable chiefly because they help to keep the unlikely places of this earth green, important because of their incredible insistence. They are ripening seeds now with a prodigality that makes our own huge harvests seem puny by comparison.

Consider the hedge mustard, for instance, that straggly roadside weed which musters only a few tiny yellow blossoms at a time and yet matures half a million seeds per plant in a single season. Consider common pigweed, rank, fat-stemmed and topped by a bristly green mass of rudimentary blossoms. One pigweed plant will produce 200,000 seeds. Consider purslane, the sprawling, red-stemmed garden weed whose blossoms are like tiny yellow dewdrops. One purslane plant ripens 200,000 seeds in a season. Consider fleabane, which does have the virtue of small, white asterlike flowers. One fleabane plant will scatter a quarter of a million seed hostages to the future in one Summer.

They and scores of others are, in man's lexicon, the outcasts and the renegades of the plant world. Some are hosts to bees and butterflies, some provide wild forage, some help feed the Winter birds. Man has no use for them, but nature obviously does. Scorned and warred upon, they still persist, remarkable examples of the way life refuses to be defeated.

The Urgency

Goldenrod has been in bloom along back-country roads for several weeks, somewhat earlier than usual. Milkweed is in fat pod, here and there. Small-headed Canada thistles, more numerous than usual in hillside pastures this year, are going to seed. More sumac than usual is showing early color. On rocky hillsides an occasional birch or ash begins to show September yellow. The Summer's drought begins to catch up with the season, bringing the face of Autumn ahead of schedule.

The seasons are not fixed, except on the calendar, for growing things make their own schedules. They lean with the wind and they hurry or delay their seasons with the rain and the sunlight. Their purpose is growth and self-perpetuation, and everything from first sprouting to scattering of ripe seeds is keyed to that purpose. Blossoms appear at a proper time for fertilization of the species by the wind, the bees, the moths or whatever is the chosen agency. Seed heads mature in a natural course, deliberately if the weather invites deliberation, in haste if haste is called for. And that is what is happening now—the maturing process has been speeded up, the plant's strength is going into seeding and the future.

Summer is not yet over. Autumn and full ripeness still lie ahead. But there is an urgency for plants that must be obeyed, the urgency of survival. They have survived other droughts, and they will survive this one by obeying that urgency. So they now prepare for next year, they ripen early, they finish the season's job while the hoarded juices of life remain in their stems.

Askutasquash   *August 8*

The Indians of the Southwest had an eye for beauty as well as meaning when they chose the squash blossom as a symbol of fertility and plenty. It has a generous grace of form as well as a richness of color ranging from golden orange to sun yellow. In some plants the bloom is a hand's breadth across, so big it is almost rank. Yet the petal texture is tissue thin, easily crushed by a careless touch.

The modern botanist speaks of the family as Cucurbita and includes in it the gardener's pumpkin, his muskmelon, his cucumber and his squashes of various shapes and sizes. The Indian called it *askutasquash* and contributed the syllable that we have applied to one branch of the family. The Indian's *askutasquash* were primarily the tough-shelled pumpkins and the tough-skinned squash that mature late and keep well into the Winter. He usually grew them in the same field with his corn; the squash blossom and the corn tassel were twin symbols of fertility in many of the old Indian ceremonies.

Look at a classic Navaho silver necklace and you will find the squash blossom, symbolized in the white metal, the open petals and the round fertile ovary beneath, for it is the female flower. In silver it is conventionalized to a fine simplicity; but there it is, the August blossom of the squash vine which crept along the sandy soil and opened its petals to the sun, the rain, and the four-winged bee. Look at the garden today and there it is in live color, still open to sun and rain and bees, Cucurbita or *askutasquash* as you will, symbol of the soil's fertile plenty.

The Perseids   *August 9*

This is the time of the Perseids, those meteors that come swarming into our earthly view every August. If anyone still indulges in the old incantation "Money, money, money!" when one sees a falling star, this is the time to put in that bid for a fortune. Between sixty and seventy meteors an hour can be seen at the height of the Perseid shower, tonight and tomorrow night. They come from the constellation Perseus, which rises in the northeast rather late in the evening, but they can be seen all night long.

Meteors are stray bits of matter that go whipping through the cosmos, and we know them best when they reach the earth's atmosphere and flare into streaks of light from friction with the rarefied air. If one of them survives the flame and reaches the earth, we call it a meteorite, a messenger from outer space. Its message is that the earth is not alone in the universe, that the stars we see are more than sparks on that vast blue blanket of night. There is substance out there, reality, other celestial bodies composed of substantially the same materials as this earth.

So if you glance at the northeastern sky tomorrow night and see a falling star, don't mistake the message. That is stardust, proof of the twin fires of creation and dissolution, and it has been wandering through the universe for more years than mankind has known. Time is of no human consequence to those meteors. And even while they flame and die the universe continues in its appointed rounds. The Perseids may be the fiery flecks of a dead comet, but thousands of living stars and planets are still there, the outposts of a universe that goes on and on.

A Time for All Things   *August 10*

Bouncing Bet blooms at the roadside, blackberries ripen and goldenrod begins to show color. It takes no calendar to tell root and stem that the calm days of mid-August are here. Sweet corn is ready for the pot, early tomatoes ripen and lettuce sends up its seed head. Last Spring's sprouted seed comes to fruit.

None of these things depends on a calendar of the days and months. They are their own calendar, marks on a span of time that reaches far back into the shadows of the past. The mark is there for all to see, in every field and meadow and treetop, as it was last year and ten years ago and when the centuries were young.

Smartweed and dock, wild cousins of the buckwheat, come to seed. Wild carrot whitens the fence row, its early blooms already cupped to that shape which prompts some to call them bird's nests. The great mullein, its tall spike at full height, puts forth scattered bloom, sparingly as though with great effort and from far away and long ago. Their season is upon them, mysteriously calculated by their juice and fiber from the time of last snow, first warm rain and hot sun.

The time is here. This is that point in the great continuity when these things happen, and will continue to happen year after year. Any Summer arrives at this point, only to lead on to the next and the next, and so to Summer again. These things we can count on; these things will happen again and again, so long as the earth turns.

Cicadas sing at high noon, as cicadas have sung for eons. In the cool of evening bull-lunged frogs croak as they have croaked since swamps first rose from the seas. Tomorrow, or next week, katydids will shrill that they, too, are a part of the continuity.

Katydid   *August 11*

The katydid is a green grasshopper with a built-in fiddle that can play only one monotonous three-note tune. But nature so managed matters that the katydid has a reputation as a prophet, a reputation actually about as dubious as that of the woodchuck or the woolly bear caterpillar. In fact, whoever wrote the lyrics for the katydid's tune missed a bet by not using the words, "Frost is near," or "Six more weeks." Obviously, the prophet's mantle fell late on the katydid's green wings.

As an insect, the katydid has few distinctions. It hatches from an egg that looks something like a miniature lentil. It has no wings to begin with, hence no "voice," since it creates its characteristic sound as a cricket does, by rubbing its wings together. It eats leaves but is not the voracious type and does no lasting damage to the trees it patronizes. By August it reaches the winged stage and begins to make itself heard. The male does. The female is a silent partner. If she disputes her mate, human ears never hear her. Her ears, by the way, are near her knees, which may make the sound feel like sciatica.

Sometimes it frosts six weeks after the first katydid is heard, but more often it doesn't in this area. Our katydids miss the mark by two weeks, at least. But there is no doubt that when the katydid begins to scratch the night the bloom is fading from the rose of Summer. Their clocks may be fast, but they are personally shaping the season, filing the echoing edges of the night, scraping them, rasping them, fitting August to September, to Autumn.

The Mountains *August 12*

There's something about a mountain that engraves itself upon a man's emotions. Any mountain does it, whether it is the old and weathered uplift of the Berkshires, the more rugged upthrust of the Alleghenies, the singular oak-clad Ozarks, or the majestic Rockies. And all mountains gain stature and emotional impact with their approach and surroundings, for no mountain stands alone and isolated in time or place.

That is perhaps the reason the Rockies are such awesome mountains. One approaches them across a vast upland plain so that they rise out of the distance with an almost mystic, mirage-like unreality. Yet there they stand, once they have emerged from the blue haze of distance, the venerable barrier to travel which blocked and diverted the way west in the days when the great tides of migration all turned their backs on the sunrise. And, for all the change and shifting of the tides, they remain, the Great Barrier.

One approaches them and senses the presence of great forces. Forces beyond man's easy comprehension. It is all well enough to think of such an upthrust as wrinkles on the earth's old forehead, but even as wrinkles they are stupendous. In their presence man is inconsequential. And there is a strange reality, for man the insignificant rises in the mountains' presence to a kind of magnificence of his own. It is essentially emotional and not often conscious, but who can stand in the presence of such a thing as a mountain and remain unchanged?

We rationalize our mountains, almost all of us. We love them because of their cool air, their pines and spruces, their white-water streams; we go to them to find change, or isolation, or grandeur. And yet it is what happens to us, inside, it is the emotional and even the spiritual surge, that draws us back to those mountains again and again. It was not altogether a matter of mysticism which prompted the ancients to the belief that their gods dwelt in the high places of this earth. Those gods, by whatever name we know them, still dwell there, and we would from time to time draw near unto them, that we may know them, and ourselves, more intimately.

❦ Written in Boulder, Colo.

The Pond   *August 13*

The quiet ponds are scummed over now and full of algae; and one gets the feeling that anything could happen in such waters, any kind of life arise from them. Here, in the dead heat of late Summer, is the marshy margin and the primordial ooze with cattails growing in it, and he who approaches it might be walking backward in time toward remote beginnings.

Even the pond creatures and those along its margins belong to another time than the present. Of the reptiles, the snapping turtle is one of the ancients, armored like a creature of the Silurian Age and eyeing the world as from the midst of a tree-fern jungle. The frogs are primitives, tadpoles which have shed gills and tails and crept up onto land in the venerable cycle of living things from the ooze to the rocks. The water snakes are still slithering through the vanished age when pterodactyls had not yet grown wings. And in the air drift and dart such dragonflies as can be found as fossils in rocks older than coal.

Even the birds that haunt the pond have an otherworldly air, the gaunt herons with their beady eyes and darting beaks, the bobtailed kingfishers, which have neither grace nor particular beauty, for all their quick, spectacular efficiency. They, too, might be creatures of the in-between time, when the land was still rising from the swamps.

The water is green with algae, tepid with mud warmth, a kind of protoplasmic soup full of strange and struggling uncertainties. But the hills look down, and the hills are certainty itself, for they are the land risen from the muck, the rock, the soil, the maturity of an age reflected briefly in the stagnant pond.

The Queen's Lace   *August 14*

It's the wild carrot which frills the fence rows with white, lacy heads now, and its fine-cut, bright green foliage is almost the color of that of the tame carrots in the garden. The root, however, is very different, tough and bitter and not at all tasty. Some call the flower Queen Anne's lace, paying tribute to the flat-topped heads of florets, dainty as fine lace and pretty enough to deck a queen. And some call it bird's nest, because as the flower heads ripen into seeds the stems curl upward and form a cup-shaped basket much like a bird's nest.

In the center of most wild carrot flower clusters one finds a single purple floret, the jewel or amethyst, as it is often called. Some casual observers use this purple floret as their means of differentiating between the wild carrot and the somewhat similar flower head of the yarrow, but it is an unreliable index. Some wild carrots have no "jewel." And the yarrow heads are looser and the bloom has a grayish tinge, while the wild carrot is clear white. And the foliage of the two plants is quite different.

The wild carrot is a weed, but it carries a royal name. Which Anne it was named for seems doubtful. Anne of Brittany was Queen of France, Anne of Denmark became the wife of James I of England, Anne of Austria became the wife of France's Louis XIII and James II's daughter Anne married Prince George of Denmark and became Britain's queen. All wore lace, of course, the finest lace of their time, and to have been named for any of them would have been high tribute. But a queen's lace now decorates the roadside and the queen herself is forgotten. "Vanity of vanities . . . all is vanity."

Fat, green pods mark the milkweeds, pods tightly packed with silk-flossed seeds that will shimmer in the September air like the morning mists that now rise from the waters on whose margin the milkweed flourishes. In boggy slews the fat, green thumbs of the cattails turn warm reddish brown, ripening to compact cylinders of fluff that await bird and breeze to spread over the marshland in a thin fog of air-borne seed. In the unkempt meadow the thistles turn from lavender and purple to gray, ripening tufts of fluff that will be loosened by goldfinches and caught by the Autumn air in a glistening flight to new seedbeds.

The far travelers of the plant world, the original sailors of the air in the plant kingdom, prepare their hostages to the wind. The gossamer parachutes, each with its germ of life, approach their time of departure. The winds of Autumn will bring down the leaves, but they will also carry a fragile freight of next year's green and urgent life. Who can count the fluff-borne seeds that will fill the late September air?

Burs hitchhike. Nuts are carried and planted by the squirrels. Pod plants often fling their seed. Maples and ash trees equip their seeds with vanes on which to glide a little way. But the fluffy ones, the down-clad seeds that ride the air, are the far travelers. Their baggage is light but potent, and their multitude is beyond numbers. And Autumn is their element, the restless Autumn air. Just now they are preparing for departure, ripening, drying their wings, getting ready to go when the wind beckons.

Down the Long Hill *August 16*

Sunrise comes later, now, and dusk creeps over the hills earlier in the evening. Reckoned from late June, when the solstice marked the year's longest day, we have already lost an hour and a half of sunlight. Another month and the Autumn equinox will be here and daylight will equal darkness, briefly. The year has turned, noticeably, and Summer is walking down the long hill toward Autumn and the Winter beyond.

On a scorching August day such a change seems to run counter to the season as we now know it. Now, we feel, as the hot humidity lies heavy upon us, is the Summer's peak. If the season is already moving downhill, why do the temperatures remain here on the summit? The reason is that it takes the earth a time to warm up, and that it does not cool off in a moment. Any housewife knows that if she is going to cook a roast or bake a pie she must give her oven a time to get hot; and that even though the oven is turned off before the cooking is done it will retain the heat long enough to crust the roast or scorch the pie. So with the earth. It took from June to August for it to warm up, and it will take till late September for it to cool off again.

But the trees show the true season, and so do the grass in the meadow and the tall weeds at the roadside. Early apples begin to ripen. Daisies fade and goldenrod shows impatient yellow. New growth is slow; seed pods fatten; the soft growth of May hardens toward maturity. Dog days are virtually over. Another Summer seeps away as dusk settles in the valleys a few minutes earlier one day after another.

August Moon   *August 17*

There's warmth to an August moon, and the fullness of mid-Summer. It isn't a harvest moon that seems about to fill the sky when it first climbs over the horizon; but it is a generous moon that lights the green hills with a kind of ripening-apple glow. There is a mellowness about a moonlit night in August that is a sweet antidote for the cicada heat and the dusty glare of an August afternoon.

An October moon is a moon of maturity and harvest, taking to itself something of the crisp corn yellow of the fields and the deepening crimson of the maple hilltops. But an August moon is a moon of growing plenty still upon the vine. In it you can see the richness of that venerable symbol of fertility, the squash blossom; and the sweet golden kernel of new corn, the pollen fragrance, is in August moonlight. There is a sense of completion, of earth bounty come to its mid-August peak.

Katydids scratch the night, but there is also the silent beat of moth wings. And on a distant hill is the tentative bark of a fox, testing the air for some faint hint of Autumn. Summer it still is; but Summer passing the peak, reluctantly starting the long, leisurely glide toward frost and November. Early windfalls scent the breeze from the orchard, not quite a cider tang but the promise of cider to come.

And there is the August moon rising in the east, a late midyear moon over a northern hemisphere of mid-Summer plenty and mid-Summer peace.

The Night Criers   *August 18*

These August nights are the noisiest nights of the year. The insect fiddlers by now have mustered virtually their full chorus, and most of them are nocturnal. The last major section to join the chorus is the harshest of all, the katydids, who can and do make the whole night vibrate.

Nearly all these night criers are wing-scratchers. Only an entomologist can list them accurately and completely, for they include both true and false katydids, several varieties of crickets, certain grasshoppers, and lesser-known kin of them all. They have two things in common: They love the night, and they have "files" or "scratchers" with which to vibrate their wings and make their night sounds.

Some of them have been with us for weeks, but the great chorus does not really begin until the hot, humid nights of August. We heard the early arrivals without listening, for the ear can ignore a slowly growing chorus until it becomes a din. The katydids make it a din, and now the ear is fully aware of every theme and variation. We had no such a chorus in April, but it requires the August clamor to make us fully aware of that.

We shall not have silent night again until the heavy frosts have come. But there is silence now, if one lies sleepless long enough. In the thin hour when dawn is almost here the night criers rest their noisy wings, and the quiet is like a vacuum. You listen, and briefly it is as though November had come with its silence. Then another day breaks and it is August and Summer, vibrant, pulsing with small, winged life once more.

Powerful Pollen   *August 19*

The winds of August are particularly painful to some people, not because they are winds but because they are laden with pollen. To those susceptible to hay fever such winds are poisonous, literally so. The pollen they carry, pollen of ragweed and grass and plantain and certain trees, is in a minor way as poisonous as a snake's venom. Wind-blown pollens contain proteins that have a serious effect on the human system, and certain of those pollens are capable of penetrating the mucous membranes. To susceptible persons, a few breaths of pollen-laden air are viciously harmful.

The likeness to snake venom is not farfetched. Venom is a concentrated form of lethal protein, with other ingredients. All pollen has a large amount of protein, too. But the pollen of many plants contains protein not so readily absorbed by the human membranes and therefore not so poisonous. And a good deal of the pollen is not wind-blown, being too heavy or designed, in the peculiar scheme of plant life, for more direct transportation, such as that provided by bees.

Generally speaking, no plant with conspicuous flowers or strong fragrance will cause trouble for hay fever sufferers. Such plants have pollen designed to be carried by insects, and the petals of showy flowers, or their fragrance, is proof of it. The lesser ones which depend on the wind for pollination are the villains.

So August winds, even cool winds, have their unwelcome aspects, from which neither city nor country escapes. They are laden with pollen, and the person with a pollen allergy is at their mercy. And all because some plants, in the mysterious process of evolution, never got around to petaling their flowers and making friends with the bees.

Joe Pye   *August 20*

If the shade of old Joe Pye isn't out in the morning mists of late August surveying the crop of wild herbs at the pasture margin and down by the cattail swamp, he is missing the chance of his afterlife. His namesake plant, which the botanists call *Eupatorium purpureum,* is now in full bloom in the lowlands, magenta-red and eye catching. Near by are its cousins, boneset and thorough-wort, and over in the edge of the woodland is the snow-white froth of snakeroot, still another cousin, in a special richness of blossom.

Joe Pye was a "yarb man," an Indian with special skills who made the rounds of rural New England years ago and seems to have been a specialist at reducing fevers. Beyond that, little is known about him; even his dates appear to be lost. But he is one of the few herb doctors who ever had a plant named after him. We still call it joe-pye weed. It has no other common name.

So if the morning mist over some back pasture seems in-habited, it could be that Joe Pye is there, at least looking over the situation and appraising the season's yield. Looking at the bee balm, perhaps, and the wood sage. Examining the horehound and the catnip. Finding the pleurisy root and the wild licorice and the feverfew and the tansy. Undoubtedly smiling at the banks of bouncing Bet, thinking of it as soapwort and wondering how many women still use its roots for a shampoo. And certainly cast-ing a special look at the *Eupatorium purpureum,* his own plant.

❧ A tavern ledger kept by Capt. Isaac Marsh in Stockbridge, Mass., during the late 1700's shows several charges against one Joe Pye for rum, a typical one being: "7-26-1775, 1 qt. rum, 1 s. 6 p." A 1782 entry in the same ledger credits Joe Pye with "1 hat and 1 bu. wheat," and a list of debtors to Capt. Marsh dated 1789 includes the name of Joe Pye. Old Joe may or may not have been a Stockbridge Indian, but the name Pye persisted in the tribe even after it moved from the Berkshires. If this was our Joe Pye, the yarb man, it is quite possible that some of the rum he bought went into his potent medicines. Better-known tonic makers than Joe Pye became famous and affluent selling herb-flavored rum as an elixir.

The Roads   *August 21*

The roads of America, particularly the roads of the West, are the paths of history. West of the Mississippi the traveler is, more often than not, going the way of the great migrations, following the ox teams and the mule trains that hauled the Conestoga wagons into a new land. The years lie lightly on those roads.

The old ruts are gone, for the most part, but the memories remain. For it is only a century since the great trails to California, to Oregon, to Utah, to Denver, to Santa Fe were the roads of hope and hurt, of dream and disappointment, dusted with persistence and watered with blood and tears and sweat. A people were on the move, going places, moving into a new land. And it is less than a century since the great north-south trails were carved out by the hooves of cattle and cow ponies following the paths of the vanishing buffalo from old land to new.

The trails are highways now, and the miles of little consequence. Distance has become relative, measured in hours and days rather than in weeks and months. But still the major trails remain, the great routes which follow the watercourses, the easy grades, the lower mountain passes. For man has always carried his cargoes, whether of hope or of dreams or of the freight of today's factories, by the easier routes. And water has always known the gentler slopes.

So we travel up the Missouri, or up the Platte, or the Arkansas or the Republican to cross the vast distances. And we travel with history, the lesser known history, the history of men, the individuals, the hopers, the dreamers. The difficult, peaceful roads that led to the peaceful conquest of settlement.

❦ This report was written near Wichita, Kans., close by the old Chisholm Trail over which Texas longhorn steers were trailed from San Antonio to Abilene in the late 1860's and '70's.

Tomatoes   *August 22*

Tomatoes ripen, and there is rejoicing among those who know good garden food when they taste it. There is private celebration, which might very well be made public. If it were, perhaps we would be able, once and for all, to scotch that nonsense about tomatoes being long considered poisonous. Every now and then the old tale comes up. Not long ago a radio announcer said they were considered poisonous fifty years ago. Why, fifty years ago tomatoes were sold all over America, canned and succulent the year around! One encyclopedia says they weren't considered edible until "well within the last century." That also is nonsense.

The tomato is a native American. It was grown and eaten by Aztecs and Incas when the white man first arrived. The name comes from the Aztec word *tomatl*. The Spaniards took tomato seeds back to Spain early in the sixteenth century, and the tomato has been grown, eaten and improved there ever since. Gardeners in England knew and grew the tomato in the seventeenth century. The tomato was grown here in the colonies before 1750, from seed imported from England and Spain.

Thomas Jefferson grew tomatoes. Among his garden records is mention of the "Spanish tomato (very much larger than the common kind)," which indicates that there was a "common kind."

Jefferson grew them in his salad garden, and they were neither exotic nor a curiosity. In fact, they were on sale in the Washington markets long, long ago, by Jefferson's own account. So let's be through with the "poisonous tomato" nonsense.

Why? *August 23*

August hurries toward September, but there is still time to wonder about some of the questions that Summer poses. Why do the wild flowers vary in number so much from year to year? One year the milkweed is everywhere, another year chicory seems to possess the roadsides, and still another Summer is all daisies or black-eyed Susans. This year some areas are all twined and festooned with climbing wild cucumber, the star-leafed vine with clusters of tiny six-pointed white star flowers. It seems to be a wild cucumber year. Why?

Are there more goldfinches than usual? And fewer robins and more brown thrashers? Here and there the goldfinches appear in flocks, and certainly with no idea of migrating. Soon they will be busy, and beautiful, at the ripening thistle heads. Why has it been such a good season for butterflies, particularly the whites and yellows? They still twinkle over wild meadows, dozens of them at a time, in the hot afternoon sun.

Why does the occasional sumac, even one shrub in a whole green clump, call it a day in mid-August and put on its Autumn war paint? Does it grow tired and sleepy, or has it finished its season's work early? Is the showy goldenrod more vigorous than usual, or does one just forget from year to year? And isn't there more ironweed than usual, too? Jewelweed outgrew and outflowered itself, to the delight of the hummingbirds. Why all this lushness? A perfect growing season, of course, for a number of plants. And does this mean an early Fall, or a late one? Now *that's* a question to ponder!

Morning Mist

As August slowly cools away toward Autumn, dawns become misty as with a foretaste of the chill ahead. Over the ponds and streams the mist is like smoke, curling and wreathing in the sunrise air as the mysterious little currents of breeze play tag; white smoke, the incense of fading Summer, which vanishes as the sun reaches higher above the horizon.

This is not the haze of high humidity which clouds the hills on a sultry mid-Summer morning. This is the shimmery gauze of the changing season, the dew which washes the dust from the Summer-weary leaves along the streams and keeps green the valleys beyond the season's prime. This is the blown breath of Autumn long before there is even a hint of frost in the air.

It comes on a morning with a clear sky and a clean horizon, a brilliant morning full of blue and green and the long shadows of sunrise. It is not a gray mist; it is white, white as daisy petals, whiter than cumulus clouds, shimmery white and so thin it shimmers of silver as the sun strikes through it. It is like spider web jeweled with dew, and even less tangible. Wave a hand and there is a swirl and a quick gleam of sun in mistless air.

Indian Summer will come, and the thin, far haze on the hill-tops; but this is even less substantial. The haze of Indian Summer will be day-long; this is morning mist, sunrise magic which vanishes even while you watch. It is a curl of shimmer, the very essence of impermanence, a swift glimpse of Autumn already round the bend of the river and waiting there beyond the hills.

Crab Apples

Crab apples are ripe. They hang like scarlet jewels in the late August sun on a thousand hills and in the dooryards and along the green borders; and beneath the trees the windfalls are like a froth of red and green bubbles in the grass. And on ten thousand shelves are glasses of fresh honey-amber crab apple jelly.

The crab is a venerable fruit still full of the tang of the wild. It is the native apple of the north, sturdy and persistent, and it still represents a concentration of elementally sturdy qualities. The fruit itself is small, for quick growth and ripening. The flesh is firm and crisp and full of juice. The flavor has something of late frost and stony hillsides, a concentration that has a kind of acid independence; it has enough flavor for an apple three times its size.

It's that flavor which makes crab apple jelly so well worth the making. Jelly made from the juice of the crab's big cousins may have the same body, the same general color, but never the same taste. Who ever distinguishes by name among jellies made from winesaps or russets or northern spies? And who ever fails to give crab apple jelly its full title?

Crabs also make a rather special cider, though you'll almost never find it in the market. Only those with their own trees and their own press ever make it and then only if they have a discerning palate and the patience to gather a few bushels of crabs at a proper time and put them through the mill.

You'll find that tang, too, in Springtime, when the crab tree is in bloom. But the blossom fragrance is only a promise; here's performance, here's the fruit itself in full red ripeness on the bough.

The Insistence of the Seed   *August 26*

The miracle of the seed now declares itself in every field and garden in the land. It waits for late August only because the enduring wonder is more than a sprouting or a blossoming or a leafing, but consists ultimately of the seed again, the means of reproduction and endless repetition. The rooting and the leafing are only means toward the achievement itself, and the blossoming is but a step in the process, though we pay proper obeisance and cherish the beauty as an end in itself. But the purpose and the persistent reason is life that will somehow endure beyond this one season. And now that purpose manifests itself.

Everywhere you turn you see it. The uncut grass comes to head and ripens its seed. Pods begin to form where the milkweed hung its sweet lavender bloom so recently. The sweet clover at the roadside is not half so fragrant now that its blossom has gone to seed. The pasture rose has green haws where the petals spread themselves in June. Cattails lift green thumbs of packed seeds to ripen in the southing sun. Thistle heads begin to turn to fat tufts of floss which delight the goldfinches.

Garden beans grow too tough to eat, hastening the seed toward ripeness. Lettuce bolts, sending up its seed heads overnight. Sweet corn, ready for the pot today, will be too ripe by day after tomorrow. Tomatoes load the vines, full of seed already yellow with maturity. It is a race now between the succulent prime and the too-ripe seeding, a race the gardener inevitably loses in the end for the seeding is inevitable. This is the miracle itself, the insistence of the seed, the persistence of the mysterious germ that is life.

Zinnias   *August 27*

One thing about the zinnia: It doesn't need pampering. Give it a rootbed, sunlight and a start, and it will make its own way. It responds to care and cultivation, but it makes few demands. And with half a chance a bed of zinnias will brighten the end of August as few other flowers. Zinnias will brighten the forepart of August too, but there is more competition then.

The zinnia's colors are strong, old-fashioned colors with little subtlety. Botanists and breeders have done things to its shape, twisting its petals and quilling and even fringing them, but it remains a zinnia for all that. Not even the specialist can alter its zinnia scent, which an old-fashioned gardener can recognize in the dark of the moon. And its generosity is magnificent; cut one bloom and two will take its place.

Some call it a rank and weedy plant and liken it to the sunflower. But no matter. There's a relationship, all right; there's kinship, too, with the big daisies and, in lesser degree, with the asters. But the zinnia needs no apologies. It holds its bright head high, in the garden or in the decorator's bowl, and speaks for itself.

Its name is touched with German, in honor of the German botanist Zinn. But it is as native to this continent as the pumpkin. Mexico and our own Southwest cradled it and the early Aztecs honored its beauty. Cortez found it flourishing in the legendary gardens of Montezuma when he captured the City of Mexico. It still has the glow of the southern sun on its petals. Particularly in late August.

❧ Reference books speak of Johann Gottfried Zinn as a botanist, but one of his descendants tells me that botany was his avocation. His profession was medicine. He was summoned from Germany to be personal physician to Catherine, wife of England's King George III. A pioneer eye and brain specialist, he gave his name to a part of the brain still known as the Zone of Zinn.

Landmarks   *August 28*

A man must pause now and then, when the storms of human passion have filled the sky with the dust of emotions, pause and wonder if the old landmarks are still there. So, when the heat of the day is past and evening comes, a man steps outdoors to look, to feel, to sense the world around him.

These late August evenings, a moon well into its first quarter hangs high in the west, where it has been at this phase ever since there was a moon. North, as the dusk deepens, stands the pole-star, and beneath it and to the west a few degrees hangs the Big Dipper, just where it has always been on a late August evening. To the east is the Great Square of Pegasus, old and fixed in the firmament when the Greeks first knew it. And overhead flies Cygnus, the swan.

A man listens, and the scratchy stridulation of a katydid rasps at the dusk. There is an answer, then another, and soon there is a chorus. As always, in late Summer; as it was before man was here to listen. And the crickets chirp and trill in the meadow grass, as they have chirped and trilled for several eons. From the edge of the woodland comes the call of the whippoorwill, over and over, repetitious as the years but reminding man that birds were here and flying before man came and walked on two feet.

A breeze moves down the valley, and the leaves whisper in the treetops. Trees that count the centuries, a breeze that curled around this earth when the hills were mountains. The leaves whisper, and a man listens, and he knows that there still are landmarks.

Homecoming *August 29*

More than half the pleasure of going is in the return, as any traveler knows. To go, to see the far place, the place beyond the horizon, is exciting; but to return is satisfying as few other things can ever be. To know after absence the familiar street and road and village and house is to know again the satisfaction of home.

Few of us are that kind of traveler who can be at home forever away from home. The new, the strange and the different have their lure, but one needs a place to call his own. One needs to belong somewhere, to feel the roots, however tenuous, of identity with place. Home, we call it, whether it be a room or a house or an apartment, a farm or a plot of grass or a well-known street or park. Home, where one can feel and touch and see and find comfort in familiar things. The place where one belongs.

Man, being man and an ambulatory creature with a degree of restlessness in his blood, must be up and gone from time to time. He must go, if only to assure himself that the horizon has no boundary. He must move from here to yonder, if only to know that he is neither slave nor prisoner. What are hills for, if not to have a farther side? And what is the purpose of that distant rim of sky if not to lure a man beyond his own small orbit? But once one has gone, one must come back.

And that is the final satisfaction of a trip, whether it is a vacation or just a journey—the return itself. The homecoming. The trip back, and the home at the end. To go is good, but to come back is best.

Migrant Monarchs   *August 30*

Of all the Autumn migrants, perhaps the most remarkable are the monarch butterflies, many of which are now emerging from the chrysalis stage on maturing milkweed plants. For a few more weeks we will see the black and orange beauty of their wings at our roadsides and over our meadows, colorful as day lilies. Then, as the nights grow cooler, off they will go, southward.

Incredible as it seems, these big, fragile insects are as successful at migration as most birds. Those from the Northeast go to Florida, those from the Midwest to the Mexican border and those from the Pacific Northwest to California's Monterey Peninsula. Sometimes they travel single file in streams that reach for miles. Sometimes they go in flocks like sunset-colored clouds. At night they rest in trees, chilled and almost dormant; when the next morning's sun has warmed and revived them, they are off again, southward.

They winter in the sun, slowly fatten for the return trip and when Spring flows north again they come with it. Their wings faded and frayed, many of the males fail to complete the return, but most of the females survive, find milkweed plants, lay their eggs and die, their cycle completed. And late Summer brings a new generation of monarchs, each with the urge to migrate.

Why they migrate is a persistent mystery. How they find their way is still unknown. But when we see them now, over our astered meadows, we are seeing one phase of one of the most colorful of the great natural rhythms that mark the year's seasons.

Mountain ash trees are loaded with berries, and if one believes the old lore, that should make this a bad year for evil spirits. The mountain ash, of which there are two native American varieties, is known in England as the rowan tree, and rowans were planted in dooryards and at church gates to ward off eerie mischief makers. Crosses of rowan wood were cherished as charms and amulets. Milkmaids protected their cows from the black elves with rowan boughs. Travelers on lonely roads at night fended off the devil and his cohorts by carrying rowan branches.

Little of this old lore seems to attach to our native mountain ash trees, which thrive in the hills of New England and well down into the Alleghenies. They are modest-sized trees of little commercial value, but they do have beautiful clusters of white bloom in June and generous bunches of pea-size berries in early Autumn, berries that range in color from bittersweet-orange to lacquer-red. The imported rowans usually have more blossoms and more berries, and they have been planted in parks and along many of our major highways, where they are spectacular just now.

The rowans along the highways probably weren't planted to ward off evil spirits; highway landscapers are not notably superstitious. The rowans are beautiful roadside trees, and that suffices. They are a boon to the birds, which is a dividend. The birds aren't superstitious either, but they know an edible berry when they see one. That's why they are busy in the rowans just now.

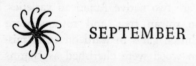 SEPTEMBER

September

September 1

September is the year at the turn, a young mother sending her children off to school and wondering if she can ever catch up with Summer tasks unfinished. It is Autumn at hand and Summer reluctant to leave; it is days loud with cicadas and nights loud with katydids; it is beets for pickling and pears for canning and apples for pies and sauce and cider. It is hot days and cool nights and hurricane and flood and deep hurt and high triumph.

September is both more than a month and less, for it is almost a season in itself. It is flickers in restless flocks, readying for migration; it is goldfinches in thistledown; it is fledglings on the wing, and half-grown rabbits in the garden, and lambs in the feed lot. It is the gleam of goldenrod and the white and lavender and purple of fence row asters, with the bright spangle of bittersweet berries.

September is fog over the river valleys at dawn and the creep of early scarlet among the maples in the swamp. It is sumac in war paint. It is bronze of hillside grass gone to seed. It is walnuts ripening and squirrels busy among the hickories. It is late phlox like a flame in the garden, and zinnias in bold color, and chrysanthemums budding. It is a last gallant flaunt of portulaca and petunias defying time and early frost.

September is the first tang of wood smoke and the smolder of burning leaves. It is bass and perch revitalized in the chilling waters of pond and stream. It is the hunter's dog sniffing the air and quivering to be off to the underbrush. September is time hastening and days shortening, it is the long nights of Autumn closing in with their big stars and glinting moon. September is the wonder and fulfillment and the ever-amazing promise of another Autumn.

❧ Most cicadas have had their shrill say by the end of July, but some years I hear a few of them into late August and early September. Two or three cicadas shrilling on a hot afternoon, at any time, can sound like a whole tribe, and in September they seem to be proclaiming the end of the world; as they probably are—the end of their world, at least.

Royalty among the Asters   *September 2*

Here and there a few of them came to bloom in August, but the big purple roadside asters belong to September, with a measure of overlap into October. They are New England asters, both in common name and in Latin, and although they grow as far south as the Carolinas they are a special Autumn glory of the Northeast. They seem to achieve a maximum of size and color in the hills and valleys of lower New England. Come to a roadside there that is splashed with purple and gold and you have come upon a stand of New England asters at their September best.

There are dozens of native asters, but the big purple one is queen of them all, both in size and color. Others range from tiny whites through medium-sized lavenders, and all are lavish in their offering of bloom. But the New England aster, though it now and then appears in a white phase, is often two inches across, rich with royal color, and sometimes stands six feet tall. Perhaps the blossom center is no more golden than that of any other aster, but with the deep purple of the surrounding rays it looks like a twenty-four-karat coin.

It is so beautiful that gardeners sometimes grow it. It appreciates such care, but never demands it. With root room at any roadside, it asks no favors. Even the crews that neaten the roadsides seldom discourage it; a midsummer mowing may shorten its stems, but September finds it in eye-catching, spectacular bloom. One sometimes thinks it was for this that the whole aster tribe evolved. If there is royalty among the wildflowers, the New England aster is certainly a member.

Color in the Treetops
September 3

The old tales die hard. Year after year one hears that it's the frost that colors the woodlands, though sumac, chokecherry and an occasional maple begin to turn before the temperature on the chilliest nights gets much below 50. Actually, an early frost lessens the color rather than heightens it. If frost strikes before the coloring process is well started, the leaves turn sere rather than gold and orange and crimson. It's the length of daylight that sets off the whole colorful change, not the temperature.

All through the Summer months the leaves have been full of chlorophyll, that green pigment which, powered by sunlight, changes air and moisture into starches and sugars. By September those leaves have accomplished their season's work. Diminishing daylight somehow notifies the trees what time it is, and they begin preparing for Winter. The essential elements begin to withdraw from the leaves into trunk and branch and root. The leaves are expendable. Gradually they are sealed off at the stems.

The chlorophyll, no longer renewed by the tree's circulation, wastes away. As the chlorophyll diminishes, two yellow pigments, carotene and xanthophyll, are revealed. Other pigments called anthocyanins are produced from excess sugar remaining in the leaves. The carotene and xanthophyll predominate in birch leaves and produce the vivid gold. The anthocyanins predominate in many maples, in dogwoods, in cherries, in most oaks; they produce the reds and purples.

This process is already under way. It will be speeded up as the

Autumn equinox approaches. But it's a matter of time and day-light, not the doing of mythical Jack Frost, who never yet has colored a leaf anything but dead, withered brown.

The Voices   *September 4*

We speak of the wind and its voices, but most of the voices are in the trees. And even those voices vary from season to season, almost from month to month. They are speaking now, as the Fall winds rise—the winds, not the gales, which have, beyond denial, voices of their own.

The big oaks speak with a heavy voice, crisp with the crispness of their leaves. And the big maples have a strong voice, with their big leaves rustling, and thousands of them. At first listening one would think there was little difference between the voice of an oak and that of a maple, but stand in an oak grove and listen, then move to a clump of maples. The difference is clear—a softer voice in the maples, with their looser stems and softer leaves.

The whisperers, of course, are the members of the willow family, the poplars in particular. The aspens and the cottonwoods whisper in anything but an absolute calm. Give them a breeze and you can hear them afar, fairly chattering, their heart-shaped leaves on long, limber stems, each leaf dancing against a dozen others. The birches come a close second with their whispers, the small gray birches in particular; and as their leaves crisp with September they, too, almost chatter.

The evergreens, the pines and the spruces, hum rather than speak; and theirs is the closest of all to music. But the music of the pines is best heard at night, and best of all on a Winter night when their deciduous brothers of the woodland stand stark in the moonlight. One has to listen most closely now to hear them at all, but their time's coming.

Lily Berries September 5

The lesser fruits and berries are ripening in the woodland, particularly those of the lily family, whose members are not usually thought of as fruiting plants. But there they are, coloring underfoot and waiting to be discovered.

The fat blue berries of the clintonia are among the most conspicuous on their straight stems above the withering funnel of broad leaves. Clintonia berries are among the few true blues to be found in the woods, and are much more conspicuous than the greenish-white flowers that precede them. The plant, incidentally, was named for the New York governor, De Witt Clinton.

In the same woods with clintonia are sure to be found false spikenard and false Solomon's seal, with the leaves beginning to droop. The berries, however, are like clusters of greenish pearls spattered with tiny flecks of brown, beginnings of the dull red that will cover the berries in another few weeks. True Solomon's seal is also there, its somewhat larger berries hung in a series of twins at each leaf joint; these berries, green to begin with, now start to turn blue-black and look something like small wild grapes. Also nearby will be found the little Canada mayflower, the false lily of the valley, which was so sweet last Spring. The mayflower's berries are much like those of false spikenard, yellow-white, brown speckled, and turning to a translucent ruby-red.

There are also such berries as those of the trillium and the Indian cucumber and the greenbrier, all of them belonging to the lily family. We usually think of lilies only as flowering plants, but the birds know better. The birds know the various lily berries, and will soon be making the most of them.

September's Certainties September 6

There are the certainties of September, a month by grace of the calendar but a season by its own insistence. Now comes the time

of pause and slow transition, a time neither new nor old, growth nor completion, Summer nor Autumn.

There is the certainty of fire in the maples, now evident in the coals and brands of the sumacs. The coinage of October is now being minted in the elms, and the ripeness of the grape is forecast in the big New England asters, purple as amethysts. The certainty of Indian Summer's mists is there in the thistledown and the finespun silk of the milkweed. The frosts to come are foreshadowed in the froth of small white asters at every roadside.

The crows now know the certainty of their own tenure and proclaim it loudly. The jays no longer make any secret of their presence or their coming inheritance. The cricket and the katydid tell the darkness the certainty of time and its implacable demands. The whippoorwill and the owl exchange confidences in the night, reluctant companions in the slowly shifting eternity of starlight.

There is the certainty of sun and evening light, which mark the time of change in the breadth of a shadow, the depth of dawn and dusk. Two more weeks and the compass can set its needle by the morning sun. Yesterday's new moon will wax toward the fullness that will double the certainty of the equinox.

September makes its own commitments, abides by its own inevitabilities in the decisions of time.

The Voices of Change   *September 7*

The trees are talking now of change, and the voices of the leaves are clearly the voices of early Autumn. It's a different wind that blows, a wind that seems to come from far places, and the leaves make a restless sound. Crisping leaves, already with the foretaste of October in them, leaves nearing the end of their season. They rustle, through with Summer's whispering. In a gusty wind they almost chatter.

Before long the leaves will be in color, tides of color on the hills. Then there will be the rush of falling leaves, the swish and crackle of leaves on every breeze, freed from the parent branches. Roadside and gutter will billow with them, and lawns and woodlands will be littered. Frost will come, and that time of leafless calm, that mild second Summer we cherish in the name of the Indians. And after that will come the slow settling of the leaf drifts toward Winter and leaf mold, toward Spring again and another budding, another leafing.

But now, between Summer and Fall, the leaves' purpose fulfilled and yet the time of discard not wholly here, every woodland and every tree-lined street is full of voices. Restless voices, as though it were the sound of a Fall fever of wandering, of need to go, to venture. Or is it the Fall fever of the listener giving tongue to the leaves? Whatever it is, there are the voices, the rustling in every wind. And change is at hand. The year turns. The heart listens and reaches for understanding.

Goldenrod Yellow   *September 8*

Perhaps it only seems that way, but the goldenrod appears to be making more of a show this year than usual. Roadsides and meadow margins glow with the yellow plumes, and on a sunny afternoon the bees are almost as loud as they were at the height of clover bloom. Goldenrod provides a September harvest that adds a special tang to Autumn honey. If it weren't for the goldenrod and the asters, which are also rich in nectar, the bees would soon be out of business for the season.

Most of the goldenrods are native to this country. America has more than a hundred species, all Europe has fewer than ten, Britain has only one. About twenty-five species are commonly found here in the Northeast, ranging from foot-high dwarfs to eight-foot giants. Some species are quite fragrant, such as the anise-scented sweet goldenrod. There is even a white-flowered species, sometimes called silverrod and known botanically as *Solidago bicolor*.

That Latin family name, Solidago, means "to strengthen" and

refers to the plant's reputed herbal qualities. Not many of us have been dosed with an infusion of goldenrod leaves and flowers, but many of our forefathers were. One can be sure than such a brew at least strengthened one's will to be well. The plant also provides a strong yellow dye that the pioneers used to brighten their Winter clothing. Seeing the display it is putting on now, one easily understands why. Goldenrod yellow could brighten even the dark days of dour December.

The Voice of Autumn   *September 9*

The owl has hooted in the evening darkness. The voice of Autumn has echoed across the valley. There is no mistaking it now, for although the green world is still green, it has the gleam of dogwood berries turned scarlet and the shine of goldenrod in the fence corners and the glow of little white asters on the meadow. There is the cider smell of windfall apples in the orchard and the wine tang in the vineyard. You can close your eyes and know what is taking place.

Ripeness is fulfillment, and it comes not at the peak of Summer. It comes when the season begins to ease down the long hill toward Winter and ice, when the days shorten and the stars of night begin to gleam in longer darkness. Ripeness is a summation, of long, hot days and simmering sun and warm rain and the flash of lightning across the Summer sky. It is the beauty of blossom brought to the succulence of fruit, the soft green of new stem toughened to the firm fiber of the reaching twig, the winged seed of the maple now rooted at the grass roots and finding sustenance in the soil. Ripeness is September, warm at midday, chill at dusk and covered with cool dampness at dawn.

The change is more than a matter of sunlight and day length, for there is a rhythm in all growing things, a rest and a resurgence. The seasons belong to that rhythm, as do the day and the night. But so does the apple, and so do the goldenrod and the asters. The peak is past. The wave of the great rhythm now begins to ebb, and the cricket sings, the owl hoots, the crows call querulously. You can hear Autumn from any hillside.

September Night   *September 10*

The Dipper swings low in the north, these evenings, and Cassiopeia is off to the east of the polestar. And east of Cassiopeia, if the evening is clear, stands a moon that soon will be verging on the full and coloring like the pumpkins in the fields. Late in the evening, if you are out where the woods climb the hills, likely as not you will hear the voice of an owl asking its queries of the thickening darkness. And when the owl has hooted, the dogs will set up their clamor, for the night is full of scents that no country dog can ignore. Fox scent, perhaps, or coon scent; a mere man wouldn't know, for all he smells is the September night.

There is the smell of grapes in this night, the sweet, winey smell of a garden vineyard at ripeness, the sharper tang of wild grapes along the wall and climbing on the old wire sheep fence. There is the cidery smell of apples, early apples come down as windfalls and left to soften and ferment a bit in the grass. You miss it, in the daylight; but the cool of night brings it clear and sharp. There is a rank smell of hay from the roadside. Not the sweet fragrance of July hay, but the mint-and-goldenrod smell of high weeds cut and left lie, with the tantalizing fragrance of tall clover mingled in. There is the pond smell, the mucky sourness of the margin ooze where the cattails stand in stiff ranks against the starlight on the horizon.

And there is the sweet wind from the hilltops, slowed down now to a night breeze, the sweetness of September. You smell it, and you feel it, and it seeps into your blood. And you know why the owl hoots and the dogs bark; you almost wish you could, too.

That Cricket

The cricket is a small, black, ambulatory noise surrounded by a sentimental aura. On occasion it lives in the open fields, but its favorite habitat is behind a couch or under a bookcase in a room where somebody is trying to read. It has six legs, which make it an insect; two antennae, which make it a creature of sensitive feelings; two wings that can be scraped together, which make it a nuisance.

Only the male cricket scrapes its wings together to make its characteristic noise—or song, as some insist on calling it. The female has more important matters to attend to. Houses where people wish to read are chiefly inhabited by male crickets. S. H. Scudder, the entomologist, found a good many years ago that the common black cricket's notes are pitched in E natural, two octaves above middle C. We have found that many house crickets are flat, and persistently so. We have also found that while the cricket's customary tempo is eighty beats to the minute, it occasionally skips half a beat. Perhaps it has a bad heart.

Few adult crickets are supposed to survive the Winter in cold climates such as ours. But few adult crickets in this latitude know when Winter begins; they start scratching wing on wing in August and keep at it until the wings are quite worn out. Their wings are very durable. And a new crop of crickets is hatched each Spring.

In China they used to hold cricket fights, pitting cricket against cricket and wagering on the outcome. Or they did until more important fighting engulfed their land. Such a custom had the particular virtue of eliminating one cricket each time a fight was held. The "song" of a Chinese cricket was not considered cozy or sweet or even domestic. The Chinese were wise.

The Stars Lean Closer *September 12*

The stars lean closer now, with Summer's last full moon three weeks past and the night sky arched over the hilltops in early darkness. The Dipper hangs early in the northwest with Cassiopeia's Chair high and beyond the polestar to the east; and Cygnus, the Swan, flies almost overhead. Autumn's gleam is already upon them all.

In the upcountry you feel the threat of frost on clear nights, even as you see it in the stars. But even more clearly you see it before the stars appear, at the long-light time of day just before sunset. Catch a vista of maples in that long light and you see Autumn glowing through the leaves. The deep, lush green is gone. The promise of gold and crimson is there among the branches, though as yet it is achieved on only a stray branch, an impatient limb or an occasional small tree which has not yet learned to time its changes. Or look down a long hillside in that light and you see Autumn full blown for a few minutes, the presunset light bringing out all the gold and russet on the bronzed heads and bronzing stems of the seed-ripe grass.

Frost is not yet on the stars of the maple leaves, not quite; but first frost is not far away. And the stars lean close in the moonless early night, as though to see the windfall pears beneath the backyard tree, themselves like stars in the grass; as though to gauge the turn of the sumac clumps, and the ripeness of the fox grapes twined in the aspens along the river, and the faint touch of purple on the arrowwood leaves in the lowlands.

Autumn on the Doorstep *September 13*

Another week and Summer will be officially at an end, since we demarcate our seasons by the solstices and the equinoxes. We who live in a land of seasonal change will have Autumn on our

doorstep. Even now the sun rises east and sets west, so far as the eye can see; and one hears regret that another Summer is gone.

In a sense, this is so; and yet no season, nor even any year, either stands alone or vanishes completely. Summer is rooted in Spring, and Autumn is essentially Summer's maturity. The apple now reddened on the tree was a fragile blossom, a delight to the eye and a host to the bee, only a few months ago. The honey in the comb was pollen when June was at its height, and rains of April and hot July nights now come to ripeness in the cornfields. Even before the leaves come swirling down, buds are on the bough for another Summer's shade.

Summer ends, and Autumn comes, and he who would have it otherwise would have high tide always and a full moon every night; and thus he would never know the rhythms that are at the heart of life. There is a time of sprouting, a time of growth, and a time of harvest, and all are a part of the greater whole. There comes the time now to savor the harvest, to pause and know another year not yet brought to full finality.

The rhythm of life and thought and change will be close around us now, and the restless energy of Summer will be distilled into the stout brandy of another season. Change is ours to know and accept and build upon, even as the skies of Autumn clear and the leaves begin to fall. Fallen leaves open wider horizons to the seeing eye.

The Silence   *September 14*

Katydids make the lengthening evenings loud, and the midday air still quivers with the crescendo of the cicada. Jays scream at each other, and crows, early and late, renew their unmusical clamor; and there is only an undertone of twitter and brief song from thrush and sparrow. September is full of sound, but it begins to die away with the approach of frost. Unless we listen closely, however, we scarcely note its going until the silence is upon us.

Thus it is with change. Unless it comes all of a sudden, we

tend to overlook it, for gradual change is in the nature of things. But bring silence upon a world filled with sound only a few hours before, and the silence itself is almost painful.

A few weeks ago a particularly vicious hailstorm swept over a small town on the Colorado plains. It passed, and the townsmen surveyed the damage to windows and roofs and trees and gardens. Then they were aware of silence. No bird sang. No insect buzzed. One sweep of hail and theirs was a little world where even the human voice echoed awesomely against the vacancy. The birds lay dead beneath the tattered trees, and even the grasshoppers were gone, stoned to death. And the people said to one another, "How loud the hush! And how lonely!" Then they, too, were quiet.

The hush comes with the deepening of Autumn; but it comes gradually. Our ears are attuned to it, day by quieter day. But even now, if one awakens in the deep darkness of the small hours, one can hear it, a foretaste of Winter silence. It's a little painful now, and a little lonely because it is so strange.

Autumn's Children   *September 15*

The wild asters began to bloom in August, but they are essentially Autumn flowers and their heyday comes about the time of the Autumn equinox. So here they are, along every back road and in all the woodland edges, spilling over into pastures and over the dump heaps, a frothy cloud of blossom. If they weren't so numerous and so ubiquitous, they would be one of our national spectacles, like the laurel or the dogwoods or the October maples in Vermont. Being so common, they are taken for granted. Yet they are a vivid part of the Autumn scene, background to goldenrod and ironweed and the ruddy joe-pye. Blight the asters and you would blight our whole landscape from Labor Day till Columbus Day.

There are more than 250 species of asters, and most of them are native to America. They range in color from white through all the shades of lavender to the deep purple of the vivid New England aster. In size, the blooms vary from true miniatures to the two-inch spread of the showy aster. The petals vary in number from six or eight to forty or fifty, and the leaves range from mere slivers of green to heart-shaped spans as big as a woman's hand. The big, shaggy garden asters are of Oriental origin, remote cousins of our roadside wildlings, tamed and pampered and temperamental.

But the wild ones are tough, insistent and profligate with their bloom. Deep frost eventually does them in, but no glancing blow of early frost can touch them. They are Autumn's children, full of vitality. Some of them will be dancing at the roadside till Thanksgiving, gay as daisies and colorful as an October sunset.

Harvest Moon   *September 16*

This is the week of the harvest moon which, regardless of calendar or equinox, is Autumnal as a corn shock. With reasonably clear skies, it will be a moonlit week, for the harvest moon is not a hasty moon. It comes early and stays late.

There was a time when the harvest moon gave the busy farmer the equivalent of an extra day or two. He could return to the fields after supper and evening milking and continue his harvest by moonlight. That was when corn was cut by hand and husked by hand, when shocks tepeed the fields and fodder was stacked in the barnyard, when the song of the bangboard echoed and the husking peg was familiar to the hand.

But times change, and schedules. Now most of the farmer's long days come at plowing time, or planting, or at haytime. Corn is cut by machine and chopped by machine and stowed in the silo; or it is left standing in the field till a few fine late Fall days, then picked by the mechanical picker, which can outstrip a dozen men.

There's harvesting to be done, of course, but much of it now centers on the kitchen rather than the barns. The last bountiful yield comes from the garden, the late sweet corn, the tomatoes, the root vegetables, the dozen and one kinds of pickles and relishes. The canning, the preserving, the freezing, the kitchen harvest in all its variety, reaches its busy peak, the last rush of the season.

It's still the harvest moon, but the farmer with his field harvest well in hand is looking forward to the next full moon, the one in October. So is his dog. That will be the hunter's moon, and the coons will be busy in the cornfields by then.

❧ Most of the reference books that mention the harvest moon are obviously written by slaves of the almanac. The harvest moon, they say, is the full moon that occurs nearest the Autumnal equinox and can come as early as September 8 and as late as October 6. This is the mathematician's logic and is sheer nonsense. The harvest moon, as any countryman knows, can't occur before mid-September and never occurs in October. Anyone who wants to argue this point can look elsewhere for an opponent; I am not interested in such debate.

Fall Fever   *September 17*

There should be more Fall vacations or, at the least, more Fall week ends. The world is a wonderful place when the heat of Summer is past, the winds are not yet edged with frost, and Winter still lies a comfortable distance ahead. Summer's dust and litter have been washed and blown away, the woodlands are full of wine and gold, and the whole land is at its colorful best.

Once you get out in the open, these Fall days, there is a sense of leisure without lassitude. Spring is all eagerness, Summer is hot laziness or sweaty haste; but Autumn is achievement and a measure of contentment. Autumn is a time when hills wait for climbing, when answers to half-realized questions lie in the thin haze on the horizon. That, at least, is the feeling of Fall. Spring fever makes one wish to lie in the meadow and wait for the answers to seek him out; but Fall fever make one wish to go and find the answers.

Adam ate the apple at this time of year, and this was the season when man first discovered the potentialities in a ripe grape. Things come to fulfillment now. Fledglings are ready to migrate. Young foxes bark in the dusk. Last Spring's fawns come into old orchards to pick and choose among the windfalls. Even the winds are restless.

For the footloose, Fall is the time when one must go. Where? Almost anywhere, on a bright day. A migrant farmhand summed it up when he said, "Every Summer I decide to pick one place and settle down. Then it comes Fall, and I just can't seem to stay where I am. If Fall would just skip a year, maybe I could make up my mind. But Fall never skips."

The Clock of the Stars   *September 18*

Look north on a clear evening now and you see Ursa Major, the Big Dipper, down close to the horizon. The clock of the stars and eternity is pointing time just as it has since there were stars in the sky. The pace of time hasn't altered in eons. Like the seasons themselves, the stellar clock is a constant in a world of change.

It sometimes seems that time, as man knows and lives by it, has been shrinking year by year. What happened, we wonder wistfully, to leisurely days and long Summers? Where are the casual weeks and long-drawn months of the past? Where does time go? Then we look at the stars on a September evening, and, for a little while at least, we know that we, not time, have changed. We have changed our own dimensions. But time goes where it has always gone.

All around us are the old markers, still unchanged—sunrise and sunset, the phases of the moon, the inexorable tides. The pines grow as they have grown forever, the maple's leaves turn and fall, the oak's acorns ripen on their abiding schedule. The squirrel hoards, the woodchuck hibernates, the goose honks high as it flies south, all in the earth's ancient and unchanging time.

This is the season to remember, perhaps to reset the clocks of our own lives. We can never recapture time, but we can know it for what it is. If we only pause long enough to see the eternal wheeling of the stars, we may achieve a degree of patience, perhaps even a degree of tolerance.

Sumac   *September 19*

By the time of the Autumn equinox, the sumacs have put on their ceremonial colors and are ready to lead the parade directly into Indian Summer. They stand like giant Sioux warbonnets along the roadsides and at the edge of the woodlands, brilliant against the yellowing green of the trees and the deepening russet of the fields. Theirs is a clean crimson, one of the most brilliant reds one will see until the maples have come to full flame.

The sumacs are native almost all over the world except near the polar regions, and the name comes almost unchanged from the Old French and even reaches back to the Arabic. Though the wild species are vagrants and even outcasts on much of our land, other places and people have found many uses for them, in tanning, in dyeing, in cabinet work, as condiments, as a varnish base, even as an oil for candles. And everywhere the birds feast on the generous seed heads of the sumac.

Give sumac an inch at the edge of pasture or field and it will take a mile if given time. It is stubborn and persistent. But it does have its beauty, particularly when Autumn turns on the hinge of the equinox. Crimson is not its only color; it also achieves a fine, clean yellow and a rich orange and, at times, almost a purple. Strange that the legend makers never gave it credit for setting an example for the nobler trees of the forest or endowed it with the Autumnal spark which sets the whole woodland ablaze with color. Legendary or not, there it stands now, full of cool Autumn fire, a veritable bed of coals ready to burst into the full flame of Autumn.

Cider

The word "cider" has come down through Greek and Latin from an ancient Hebrew term for strong drink, an intoxicant. We have softened both the word and the substance, and without a hardening adjective the cider we know today is the tanged-sweet juice of the apple, especially in October. True, cider can be potentiated. It can even be distilled, after nature has had her way, and endowed with both fire and lightning. But when caught in its youth and treated kindly, cider is all sunlight and blue skies, spiced with the essence of early Autumn.

Any apple will make cider, of a sort, even the apple that ripens in August. But the cider really worthy of its name needs a touch of frost and an apple that matures its sugar slowly. Its making calls for care in the choice of apples and both skill and understanding at the mill. For the best flavor, it should still be reasonably young, but beyond its childhood. And damnation to him who would stunt its growth with any additive!

Really good cider is as rural as a corn shock. It sings of the golden birch and the crimson maple as well as the bronzing orchard. It twinkles of open skies and a frosty morning on the meadow. It may not be the original nectar of the gods, but it makes a man glad that he is a man. And that apples are apples, with their own inclination. See that golden amber glow in the glass? See those beads of character well slowly up? Taste that distillation of Autumn's wonder? Cider!

A Tree of Your Own

Everybody should own a tree at this time of year. Or a valley full of trees, or a whole hillside. Not legally, in the formal way of "Know all men . . ." and "heirs and assigns" written on a paper; but in the way that one comes to own a tree by seeing it at the turn of the road, or down the sreet, or in a park, and watching it day after day, and seeing color come to its leaves. That way it is your tree whenever you choose to pass that way, and neither fence nor title can take it away from you. And it will be yours as long as you remember.

Red maples are beautiful trees to own that way. They color early and the color steadily deepens. Find one that turns mingled gold and crimson and you have a tree of wonders, for you never know whether another day will bring more gold or more rubies. It will be a great treasure, in any case. And a sour gum is a thrilling tree to own, for its reds and oranges are like those of no other tree that grows. A dogwood, too, is one to consider, for it not only rouges itself with some of the warmest reds in the woodland; it decks itself with berry clusters that outstay the leaves, if the squirrels are not too industrious. Or you may choose the sassafras, and cherish the choice until all the leaves are fallen. For the sassafras is like a golden flame with all the warmth of orange and red and even purple mingled in. No fire that ever leaped on a hearth had the warmth of color that glows in a sassafras on an October hilltop.

Take your choice among these and many others. Make one your own, and know Autumn in a tree that not even the birds can possess more fully. It's yours for the finding, and the keeping in your memory.

AUTUMN

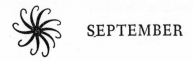 SEPTEMBER

Equinox   *September 22*

Another equinox is tallied off and officially another Summer ends. Autumn comes, on the records by which we divide time and measure life, and the days and the nights for a brief period are almost equal, dark to light, and light to dark. And now the nights will have the smell and touch of frost and the days will have the crisp-leaf rustle of Fall, the brown and yellow of another season's growth come to maturity.

That is the predominant note of Autumn: Maturity. Not death, nor even hibernation. It brings a summing up, a sweetness in the apple and a ripeness in the grain. Spring was a sprouting, an eager reaching for the sun, and Summer was lush growth and blossom and the beginning of fruitfulness. But Autumn is harvest, the maturity toward which the bud, the leaf, the blossom all reached in their time.

No season, of course, is complete in itself. And our arbitrary boundaries of time are more convenient than conclusive. Summer ends and Autumn comes over the land on schedules governed by the land itself, not by either stars or calendars. Travel two hundred miles north or south and you touch the year in another spot. You walk with frost in Maine, and in Virginia you are still in late Summer.

But here, in this particular latitude, you can look out over the hills and see Autumn on the ridge, walking down from the north to these valleys where the mist lies at sunup and the maples begin to flame. And you know that Summer is gone.

Equinoctial Storms   *September 23*

There is a prejudice among weathermen against speaking of the storms which come at this season of the year as equinoctial storms. Their reasoning is simple. The equinox is a matter of astronomical movements, the relative positions of the earth and the sun. Storms are a result of atmospheric conditions, not of astronomical relationships. Therefore, the name "equinoctial storm" is ruled out.

But it just happens that weather disturbances are the rule rather than the exception at this time of year. Things are happening to the atmosphere. Summer is ending; Autumn is beginning. Long, hot days are ended in our northern hemisphere. The earth is beginning to cool off, up here, and there is a new movement of the air. It also happens that these changes are related to the movement of the sun and the position of the earth, for if the sun were not moving southward, as we say, across the celestial equator, there would not be these changes in the temperature and movement of the air currents.

Those factors which make the Autumn equinox also breed the stormy conditions. It is a period of change, and often that change is violent in its stormy nature. The weathermen are willing to call them Autumn storms. It is the equinoctial tag which they reject. And that seems to be in the nature of splitting a hair, for the equinox is the time of seasonal change. Technically it is an astronomical phenomenon; practically it is a date, a particular time of the year. The weather at the time of the equinox tends to be uncertain and often is stormy. In fact, it often expresses itself in an equinoctial storm—and if that be heresy, look at the weather report, then look at the calendar.

He who travels west travels not only with the sun but with history. The flatboats went west with the current, once the forefathers had crossed the Alleghenies, and the ox teams plodded westward all the way. Eastern streams were, relatively, short streams, and eastern land routes paralleled the coast line. But once one started west, one followed traces toward the horizon and streams that flowed across an empire. So one today follows routes that lead all across, to another coast line, across the vast heartland where the generations, not the centuries, are the measure of time.

And already there is the mellowing of time, best seen, perhaps, in the Fall of the year. Then one can see more clearly the outlines of the land and its living, the fields, the harvest, the deep black soil, and the houses and towns and cities men build. The barns, the big barns of a land that glories in its produce. The houses, so like those fine old houses of New England but not so old. The towns, with their center squares inherited from the village greens. And the cities, American as corn and American as codfish though the Midwesterner may deny it.

History came this way, and the younger generations, and made this land their own in a familiar pattern. You are no stranger here. Outlander, perhaps, but of the same blood and breed. And that is the great marvel as you travel, for you belong, you are a part of the vast cornfields, the black soil, the groves of trees, the midlands. You speak the language, and only the inflection varies. Strange rivers, perhaps, and strange flat skyline, but still a familiar land. The midlands, where America first outgrew its colonial status, where New Englanders really became Americans.

❦ This traveler's report was written in a motel near Columbia, Mo.

With the yield in from the garden and most of the crops from the fields, with Summer over and Indian Summer still to come, there's time to ponder the season's questions, with few final answers needed.

Why are the crows so noisy? Are they speeding the migrants on their way so the crows can be kings of the air again? Most of the kingbirds, who harried the crows all Summer, have already gone. Why are there so many berries on the panicle dogwood and the red osier, and so few left on the elderberry bushes?

Why are so many of the roadside flowers in the Fall either purple or gold? The purple asters, for instance, and the remnants of ironweed and joe-pye weed and the big thistles, and the last of the primroses, the persistent sunflowers and the billowing goldenrod. What happens to all the milkweed floss and thistledown? Field mice and chipmunks can't use *all* of it in their Winter quarters. Why are there so many crickets and grasshoppers this year? The crickets have been particularly loud, and so have the katydids, despite the early nipping frost.

Who tells the chickadees when the first quota of sunflower seed is put in the feeding stations? Why do some field mice move indoors, into human habitations, for the Winter? Are they just the shiftless minority in the mouse population? Why are the distant hills so blue? Mist, maybe, but they weren't nearly so blue in the morning mists of June.

Why can't a man take more time to look at a tree or a bird or a flower or a cloud? Autumn isn't the only time of year when they are worth a second look, though it is a rather special time in any year.

Hickory Nuts *September 26*

Hickory nuts are ripening, as every squirrel in the woods knows. Find a shellbark hickory tree and you will find the ground beneath littered with hull fragments marked by squirrel teeth. There will be a few nuts, too, still cased in their four-sectored green hulls, if there has been a stiff wind lately or a heavy rain. Pry the hulls apart and you will find within the yellowish-white nut an inch or so long. Crack the nut on a rock and you will come to the sweet-flavored kernel, still a bit soft but with the promise of that splendid taste the shellbark achieves when fully ripe.

The shellbark is the best of all the hickory nuts. You may run into argument by those who choose to say the butternut belongs to the same family, or by those who hold out for the pecan of more moderate climates. And there will always be the sticklers who say the black walnut is technically of the same family.

But the shellbark partisan will stand by his guns and insist that comparisons be made with the indifferent mockernut and the bitter pignut. The principal problem about shellbarks is beating the squirrels to them. The flavor is at its best when the nuts are left on the trees until frost strikes; but by that time the squirrels have taken title and most of the nuts are stowed elsewhere. So the hickory nut gatherer takes them when he can, early and late, and lets the green hulls loosen indoors. If he is fortunate, he accumulates a peck or two of the hulled nuts, and he hoards them for frosty evenings when the hearth glows and the winesap cider has a proper touch of authority. Then he settles back and clinches, for all time, any argument about which is the sweetest nut in the woods.

Fog   *September 27*

Fog is a unique blend of mood and weather. It is not really weather at all, as rain is, or sunshine. And it is no more palpable than any mood. You feel it on your face and in your hair, as well as in your mind. Yet it creeps in, silently, and it blows away like smoke; and it lies like an emotion over the land. Sun may silver it into brilliance, and shadow may darken it into unwonted desolation. But there it is, fog, atmospheric moisture still uncertain in destination, not quite weather and not altogether mood, yet partaking of both.

The fog of a river valley is like another river, one which lacks the earth moorings of flowing water. It eddies as any river, flows into coves and spills out onto flood plains; but it also creeps up the hillsides, and it has vertical motion. It flouts the laws which govern real rivers.

The fog that creeps across the flatlands is no more than a cloud come down to earth, caressing the fields and touching the trees and the little hills with almost loving fingers. For a time it belongs to the land—or the land to it; certainly it is no strange comer from distant places.

But the fog that rolls in from any ocean and sits on the beach cliffs is the essence of unreality. There it is, and yet the reality of sea and surf are somewhere in its midst. There is no ocean, nor yet any beach or any headland beyond a certain point; there is only land and fog and blue sky and the unreality of waves breaking on a beach that is not there. There is only a mood half realized, and weather that has not yet become reality.

❦ This traveler's report was written somewhere between Astoria and Coos Bay, Ore., where we were fogbound in a small fishing village. Westward the fog seemed to blanket the whole Pacific ocean, but a few miles inland to the east, as we discovered that afternoon, there wasn't so much as a wisp of mist.

Burs   *September 28*

Burs are ripening. Walk along a roadside or across the fields and you will know it all too well. Half an hour's walk can provide half an hour's work getting them off your clothes, to which they cling with hooks and spurs and barbs and spines. But they are worth looking at as you pluck them off, simply as examples of nature's ingenuity.

Undoubtedly there will be tick trefoils, flat little three-cornered green pods covered with barbed bristles. They come from a lesser legume which a month ago had sprays of miniature lilac sweet-pea flowers. Some call them beggar-ticks, but the real beggar-tick is like a small brown sunflower seed with a pair of barbed horns at the top and comes from a relative of the marigold.

There will probably be the tiny brown burs of enchanter's nightshade, too, little balls of hooked bristles that fairly burrow their way into tweeds. They come from an unworthy member of the evening primrose family which is not even remotely related to the nightshade that bears the lovely bittersweet berries.

You may have met burdock, but there will be no mistaking its big, hook-covered burs. Perhaps you will have found a patch of cockleburs, big as a fat thumb and barbarously armed. Or you may have crossed a patch of sandburs, which come in assorted sizes, all high on the list of nuisances, all pointed in their approach.

None of these bur plants, excepting the tick trefoil, is worth a second look when in flower. Their burs should all go into the fire or you will have them for neighbors next year. But they do demonstrate that nature has various ways of getting her seeds around. She has certainly endowed some plants with a lot of stick-to-itiveness.

The Migrants   *September 29*

The birds gather for migration, restless and gregarious, busy but nowhere near so full of song as they were three months ago. In a pasture beside a woodland are at least two dozen flickers, which we do not often think of as flock birds. Down the road is a congregation of robins. High overhead, riding the thermals above the ridges, are half a dozen hawks putting on an aerial display that makes one catch his breath in wonder. Restless, all of them with the inner urge that will soon send them southward.

We know relatively little about migration. We have charted certain flight patterns, and timed the average travel. We know about when each species starts south, and we know roughly how far it goes and how long it stays. Night watchers are now taking a flight census which will probably add new knowledge. But when all the available knowledge is totaled up, great areas of mystery remain. Even such a simple question as why a few robins fail to migrate each year is still unanswered. So is the question of whether the migrants follow food or daylight or temperature.

It could be, of course, that migration itself is nowhere near as complex a matter as we think. Birds are inhabitants of a big world, at home in the air, which has no insurmountable barriers. It may be that a bird's world is like a farmer's farm, except vastly larger. When a farmer's upper pasture thins out, he moves his cows to the lower pasture for a season. It's really not much more complex for a flock of robins to move from New York to Virginia or the Carolinas. They don't have to pack luggage or make reservations or send the dog to a kennel. They just up and go. And a good many of them seem to be making up their minds just now to do just that.

Low Fires   *September 30*

As the chill of September nights reaches over into the daylight hours, there is a quickening of the human pulse. There is new vigor in the air. But in the insect world the fires burn low. The bugs and beetles are nearing the end of their time.

True, if you walk across a meadow in the warmth of early afternoon, swarms of grasshoppers will rise ahead of your footsteps. In the garden, its season all but finished, black field crickets are everywhere, and again the grasshoppers leap ahead of you, pelting the sere corn blades like flung gravel. But they are out in such numbers only to warm themselves in the few hospitable hours of full sun. Go to the garden before nine o'clock in the morning and see how laggard are the ants; at 50 degrees Fahrenheit an ant travels only one-fifteenth as fast as at 100 degrees. You may even find a few small field butterflies, clinging to the weeds, too cold to spread their wings and fly.

The change is even audible, in the evening. A month ago the

snowy tree crickets were making the night vibrate like the E string on a fiddle. They are still rasping out their calls, but at a much slower rate. On a warm August night the tree cricket was fiddling 160 notes a minute; now he is down to 40. And if you are curious about the cricket's temperature sensitivity, count his notes for one minute, divide by 4 and add 40. The result should be a close approximation of the temperature.

The slowdown will continue as the chill deepens. The first sturdy frost will silence most of the insects. A few katydids and crickets will survive, and proclaim their fortune. But by November even they will be silenced. Then will come the long, deep quiet until another Spring, a quiet so intense you can hear a snowflake falling in the night.

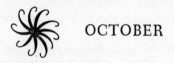 OCTOBER

October   *October 1*

October is the year at rich maturity, a happy woman arrayed in
festival dress and ready for a dance with a giant come down from
the hills attired in a red, red shirt, buckskin pants and moccasins
beaded with frost. October is a brisk wind in the treetops, a whisper among crisp leaves, a breath of apple cider, a gleam from a
jack-o'-lantern, and the echo of laughter under a full moon.

October is bright as a bittersweet berry. October has the high
excitement of a hunting dog's voice on the trail, the day-tang of
walnut hulls and sumac berries, the night call of the owl and the
bark of a restless fox. Geese honk high, in October, and ducks
take off from the river in a shower of diamond drops, southward
bound. The lawn mower's put away for the season, the garden's
sere with frost, and firelight leaps on the hearth at evening. Cider
begins to potentiate and the grape begins to find a heady reason
for ripening.

The pumpkin's in the pie, in October. The corn's in the crib or
the freezer. Pickling's done and thoughts turn to mincemeat.
October is plenty and savor and the hearty meal and time to relax.
October is the year come to harvest, in the barn, in the mow, in
the root cellar, the jam closet, the cold pantry.

October is the long evening and the book beside the fire. It is the blanket-covered night. It is the woodchuck fattening for a long nap, the fat partridge in the hemlock thicket, the deer eating windfalls in the orchard.

October is the power and the glory, to touch, to taste, to hear and to see. October is the splendor and the magnificence.

The Color

Back in the New England hills, at this time of year, one hears talk about "the color." The color is early, the color is late, the color isn't as good as last year, or maybe it's better. But "the color," early or late, good or not so good, doesn't have to be further specified. It means the magnificence of the woodlands in October, the spectacle of the leaves.

Outlanders who cherish the myth of Yankee economy with words may think of this as another example of verbal thrift, but it isn't that at all. If there were words adequate to describe the color, those words would be used. But these people learned long ago that you can't do justice to one swamp maple with words when the color comes, let alone a whole valley of them, or a mountainside of hard maple, hickory and birch, or an oak-clad ridge. Those who try succeed only in drowning themselves in words, none of them really effectual.

Even if you could find the words for one hillside when the color comes, those words would have to be revised from day to day. There's nothing static about the color. It changes hour by hour. It creates its own light. It has its own spectrum, its own boldness and its own subtleties. It challenges the eye, and it defeats the tongue.

But there it is, year after year, predictable as sunrise. It has already started, up the valleys and back in the hills. And the lack of exalting adjectives among those who know it best is the highest tribute they can pay. The color supplies its own superlatives.

Autumn days are tantalizing. They represent a season's summary, a completion that should, in the human lexicon, provide answers to questions that ought to have answers but seldom do. Even a rainy day in October seems right and in order, somehow; and a blue-sky October day is close to perfection. A sugar maple on its way to glory is a kind of golden truth, and a rustling field of ripe corn is both achievement and fulfillment. Autumn days and nights, still closely in balance, should have some inherent verity in the dimensions of life.

Perfection is so rare in the affairs of man, wholly satisfying completion so exceptional, that questions are inevitable. And yet, even now most of the ultimate answers must be taken on faith. Life itself is the enduring mystery, whether it be green with chlorophyll or red with blood. We all partake of it, as we partake of the rhythms, day, night, the seasons, the years, heartbeat after heartbeat. There is truth in a tree; there is also verity in a pulse. There is wonder in a thought as well as in a ripened seed. But answers? Life itself is an answer, perhaps the only answer there is.

It may be that both questions and answers are less important than the incorruptible reality of the turning leaf, the frost-defying aster, the old horizon newly seen. Autumn is neither a puzzle nor a problem; Autumn is for understanding.

Autumn in Your Hand *October 4*

A tree in Autumn is a lovely sight. One tree alone can concentrate the beauty of a whole woodland, leaf by leaf and branch by branch, as one flower can give the essence of a whole garden. The beauty of the turning woods is not alone in the scarlet of a maple grove or the sun-gold glow of a hillside stand of beeches. It is in the subtle change that creeps along the leaves themselves, from point to point and vein to vein. A woodland in full color is awesome as a forest fire, in magnitude at least; but a single tree is like a dancing tongue of flame to warm the heart.

Watch even a single branch outside a certain window, and you are watching the color of change. One morning there is a spot of yellow on a certain leaf, yellow which has not yet quite achieved the glow of gold. Another day and that glow may be there. It spreads. The spot becomes a splash of gold, edged perhaps with a thin line of scarlet. It creeps down the leaf between the veins, and then across the veins; and the scarlet edging widens into a band and then a border. Meanwhile other leaves have begun to turn, some to gold, some to dull bronze, some to blood-red beauty. All on the same branch, yet no two alike either in pattern or coloration. And finally it is a branch as full of color as the whole woodland.

Thus comes Autumn, leaf by leaf and tree by tree; thus the woods become a hooked rug flung across the hills with all its folds and all its colors as they came to hand. But pause beside one tree and look, and you can see Autumn on all the hills. Pick up one leaf of those already cast adrift and you hold Autumn in your hand.

Cargoes   *October 5*

Brooks and rivers now are laden with the Autumn harvest. The watery currents carry a vast armada of leafy colors, a sampling from every bankside tree upstream, and their eddies are like the swirling strokes of a whimsical artist playing with exotic pigments. Watch a stream for ten minutes and you have seen Autumn flowing past, as leisurely as time itself.

But if you would see the dazzle and variety of this seasonal cargo, watch the airy rivers, the winds. See how a breeze invites a milkweed pod to dispatch its silken freight to far places, how it shimmers and dances as the floss spills forth. See the way a wind curls across a meadow, pausing an instant at each thistle head, how it shines with frothy fluff as it goes on. See how a wind in the bogland tests the brown thumbs of the cattails, how it becomes a current of misty silk as the ripe heads release their shimmering lightness, light as fog.

The wind has its common cargo too, the leaves themselves, and it discusses this phase of business in crisp terms in every gutter and at every roadside. It even has its live passengers. A midmorning breeze will pluck a dozen spiderlings from a weed patch, each tiny spider riding a self-made silken strand. A north wind will sometimes be briefly orange with a flight of monarch butterflies on their way south.

It is a varied cargo, this Autumn freight, and it rides every stream that flows on or over the earth.

Why? *October 6*

There are so many questions, and so little time to find the answers. Why does one maple leaf turn half scarlet, the other half clear, golden yellow? Why does a sister maple, not twenty feet away, remain green? Why does a third one show only splashes of color at its branch tips?

Why does the same sassafras turn orange and purple one year, bright yellow the next? Why do some wild grape leaves soften and crinkle to the texture of paper napkins, and others on the same vine turn crisp? Why do gray squirrels go mad over dogwood berries one year and leave them practically untouched the next? What do crows find to caw so much about in October? The weather? Or is there some avian equivalent of the world series?

Where does a woolly bear caterpillar think he is going at this time of year, and why doesn't he hurry? Why is poison ivy so tantalizingly beautiful in the Fall? How in the world does a squirrel get at the meat in a black walnut, and is it worth the bother, the way he has to do it? Why does a white ash turning color look blue or pink in a certain light, when it really is green and yellow? Why do juncos come south so early? To get warm?

Then why don't they keep on going south when it gets really cold?

Why do people pick sumac to take in the house? What's so funny about hard cider? Just how red can a blackberry leaf get? If the woodchuck can whistle, why doesn't he whistle a tune? Why are pokeberry stems red? Don't spiders ever run out of webbing? Why do geese honk in flight, instead of saving their breath? Why don't katydids give up sooner, mate, and be quiet? Why?

To Walk in Beauty   *October 7*

One now walks in Autumn itself, along the suburban street, beside the country road, in every woodland. For Autumn is the time of the fallen leaf, and the leaves are crispness underfoot, brown and red and yellow and sere tan, the leftover of Summer shade, paper-thin jewel flakes that bring the sunlight and the vividness of sunset down to earth.

There was an old Navaho prayer song that said:

> Beauty before me, I return.
> Beauty above me, I return.
> Beauty below me, I return.
> Beauty all around me, with it I return.

It was a song of the Southwest, where the aspens are full of gold now and the scrub oak makes the foothills rich with wine; but we of the Northeastern woodlands should know such a song, when Autumn comes down from the treetops. Beauty, the fragile but abundant beauty of the turning leaves, is before us, above us, below us and all around us.

The birch leaves drift down at midday, a sunny shower. The sugar maples are pure gold when dawn light strikes through them; and beneath them the rustling gold leaf begins to cover the grass. The swamp maples are cherry red, and knee-deep in their own color. The poplars stand naked in pools of tarnished gold, their leaves shed. The beeches are rustling with gilt flakes, to which they will cling for weeks to come. The oaks are leather-clad, russet and oxblood and purple and ruddy brown, brown as acorns, crisp as parchment.

One walks in Autumn, now, beauty above, below and all around.

The Hoarding Days   *October 8*

These are the hoarding days. Not only the traditional ant and bee lay up stores for hungry times ahead but so do the trees and bushes. And the provident ones among the animals come to their busiest season. Field mice have been busy harvesting and stowing away for weeks. Stiff-tailed chipmunks scurry about their tasks, busier than they have been for weeks, filling their winter granaries. The squirrels put even the ants to shame with their industry. And the woodchucks stow their Winter reserves under their own skins; they are gorging now, laying up that body fat which will carry them through the long sleep in Winter-locked dens.

The bees are busy making a last harvest of honey, thanks to late goldenrod and persistent asters. Less provident and shorter-lived insects must do their hoarding in another way, in egg and larva and pupa, hoarding life for another generation. Even the woolly bear caterpillar hurries now to find a shelter, to hoard his precious spark of life which next Spring will emerge as a pink-tinged yellow moth.

The colorful extravagance of the trees just now would seem more like generosity than economy, but it, too, is proof of hoarding among the trees. They have withdrawn sap and other vital substances into stem and root. The expendable leaves, their chlorophyll worn out and not renewed, now reveal sugars, acids and other pigments in the annual glory of color. And even the falling leaves become a kind of hoard of mulch and humus, food for another season's growth. Hoarding is as natural as growth itself.

Twin Fires of Autumn

Now burn the twin fires of Autumn, the smokeless fires of color in the woodland and the leaping flames on the hearth. By day and by night, for a brief span, body and soul are doubly warmed, maple and birch on the hillside, hickory and oak on the fire dogs. And it is one of the season's compensations that as one fire dies the other brightens. The leaves fall and the smoke rises, and Autumn turns toward Winter.

There is an easy symbolism here, of the beauty that fades and the utility that takes its place; but it is too easy to be true. The open fire, the hearth flame, scarcely classifies as utility any more. Ben Franklin, with his open-hearth stove, gave it a lingering utility, but in so doing he was only advancing an idea that became the furnace, which produces heat from a hidden flame at the bidding of an inanimate thermometer. Utility. Efficient heat.

The symbolism fails. The open fire is a thing of beauty, and as profligate, in its small way, as the coloring of the leaves. But there it is, and we cherish it and dream peaceful dreams in its glow. The acrid fragrance of its spiraling smoke is an evening symbol of home and hearthside. Its outdoor counterpart is the curb fire of fallen leaves. But when that sends its pillar of Autumn incense into the dusk, the twin fires have merged, the maples have shivered in the frost and wind and bare branches lift against the stars. And, for another season, the bright flame of the woodlands leaps and gladdens only on the hearth.

Autumn Rain

Fall rain is full of weary leaves and October chill and the feeling of work done and changing season. It has the smell of stubble fields and wood smoke and Autumn plowing, and the feel of frost not far ahead. The roadside streams it raises are littered with the cast-off garb of a Summer gone, and the ponds it fills are brown as the cattails on their marshy margins.

Fall rains come and settle down for a while, as though at one visitation to restore the whole of late Summer's sun-sucked moisture. There is a persistent generosity to an Autumn rain that breeds monotony, and then slow irritation. The earth needs rain; but does it need so much without pause? The wearer of soggy shoes and a constantly dripping raincoat wonders if there isn't some means of distributing the weather, particularly the wet weather. And still it rains.

But there is no sense of malevolence in a Fall rain. It comes, and it continues, and a world whose Summer work is done is cleansed and refreshed and made ready for Winter. This takes time—and rain. No Summer's country boy was ever quite cleansed, particularly if he had roamed the fields barefoot, in one quick scrubbing. And eventually the clouds are rained out and the sun comes back in sight. The world is bright, the skies are clear as a youngster's eyes, and here comes crisp Autumn round the bend.

Let It Frost! *October 11*

The day comes when there's imminent frost in the air, and you take bags and baskets, fork and wheelbarrow, and head for the garden. This is the day. You are tempted to start with the corn, the late sweet corn. You walk down the rows, pluck a few ears; then you put that off till the end. You turn to the squashes, the acorns, the butternuts, the knobbly hubbards. A good many of them are already in, but you gather the rest, heap them beside the path, russet and yellow and deep dark green. Then you heap the pumpkins, yellow-gold and fat as bishops.

Now come the beets, the Winter keepers, and as you dig them you wonder if there's anything like a garden harvest to make one believe in miracles. A handful of beet seeds four months ago has become two barrow loads of fat red beet roots. You turn to the carrots and the sense of miracle increases. Rabbits and wood-chucks ate the carrot tops early and late, but here are those carrots, come to light as you fork the mellow soil, fat and long and crisp, another barrow load from a tablespoon of seeds.

On you go, with that deepening sense of wonder and satisfaction, to the cabbages, the late limas, the last of the broccoli and cauliflower. And when at last you've lined the main path with small mountains of earth bounty, you go back to the corn, knowing that tonight you will eat corn probably for the last time this season. You pick it carefully, ear by choice ear, and you carry it to the kitchen. Then you hitch up your overalls and settle down to the job of stowing the other provender.

Evening comes, and it's all under cover. The Summer's over. The crop is in. Fall's ahead, and Winter. Let it frost!

The Fire   *October 12*

Give a man a free hand and he builds himself a house with running water, several bathrooms, a two-car garage, telephones both upstairs and down, central automatic heat—and a fireplace. He wants no stable, no carriage house, no dug well and old oaken bucket. But he insists on the fireplace. And on October evenings he, personally, arranges the kindling and logs and lights the fire before he settles down to the radio or television.

The hearth fire is as antiquated as the stone arrowhead, yet we cling to it, generation after generation. The further we get from the pains of primitive living, the more we cherish it. Give a man from a heartless apartment a whiff of wood smoke and he will groan in envy. Show him a leaky-roofed cabin forty miles from nowhere, and if it has a fireplace he will buy it in a minute—or try to.

The reasons are all twined in intangibles as thin as wood smoke. Man is a natural fire tender, from ancient times. There is the race pride of the cave man who first caught and tamed fire. There is the instinct to bask safely in the fireglow where a joint of buffalo meat simmers, while the wolves prowl the outer dark.

Such speculation, of course, makes it complicated. But it certainly can't be explained by saying that the man who builds a hearth fire wants to warm his hands. He very seldom does. He wants to see the flames leap, hear the simmering log. Don't ask him why. He doesn't know. And he doesn't care, as long as he has a fireplace, and a fire, and a long, cool evening to sit in front of it and ponder, not too deeply, on the delights of an open fire. Particularly there on his own hearth.

❧ Almost any fruit wood, even chokecherry, makes a fragrant fire. Apple wood is traditionally the most fragrant of all, but I happen to prefer maple on my own hearth, with an oak backlog. I have burned chestnut, cut from standing dead trees self-seasoned for years; it makes a hot fire but tends to be explosive. An old couplet here in the Berkshires says:

> Ash green
> Is wood fit for a queen.

Ash does indeed make a satisfying fire, and as the rhyme implies, it is better when still green than after it has seasoned a year or two. Among the most fragrant hearth smoke I ever smelled was that of the desert country of the Southwest, where they burn piñon pine, a resinous, sooty fuel but pungent as a bowl of chile.

Checking the Draft   *October 13*

Back in the hills some of the farmers are putting Winter bustles on their houses. The process, which is a venerable one, uses the good weather at this time of year and the materials at hand. A low fence, often of mesh wire, is put up two feet or so from the walls all around the house with a gap only for the doorway. Then leaves are packed inside, between the fence and the house walls, those crisp, rustly leaves now coming down in showers with every breeze. The leaves settle, and more leaves are added from time to time. Before the deep frosts strike and the bitter winds blow, the house will be snugged at its footings, the Winter drafts at least mitigated.

There are variants in the process. Sometimes straw is packed instead of leaves. Where there is a sawmill nearby, the fence may be made of slabs and the insulation will be sawdust. And occasionally one will find an old house owned by a real conservative who cuts sod and heaps it around the sills without any fence. Anything to break the force of the wind seeking cracks at floor level. For most of those farmhouses do not have central heat. They are relics of a past way of life; but when they get their Winter bustles, they prove that insulation of a house is not the brand-new idea that we sometimes think.

There were other means of checking the drafts in those old houses. Their builders even pioneered in the "split level" type of construction, raising or lowering the floors of adjoining rooms to break the flow of cold air. Even so, floors were drafty, as any student of antique kitchen chairs must know. Most of them show well-worn front rungs, where Grandmother hooked her heels to keep her feet out of the draft while she sewed or knitted.

Frost Walks the Valleys   *October 14*

First frost has walked through the valleys under the half-moon. You could hear it whispering through the fallen leaves as it hurried down the hillsides in the evening, feel its crisp breath as it passed you on a country road. And at dawn you could see its path, glistening on the goldenrod stems and powdering the purple asters. Midmorning, and the tender gardens in the lowlands had limp and blackened rows of tomato vines to mark its path.

First frost is like a newcomer in a strange country, following the beaten paths of the valleys. It camps in the low meadows, gathering strength and biding its time. First it nips the grasses and the soft creeping plants. Then the bushes, where it curls the leaves and makes the spider webs a gleaming filigree of crystal. Sometimes it may even creep halfway up a swamp maple and then turn back, uncertain of its grip.

Meanwhile, there will be mornings when the valleys are lakes of mist, with the frost there beneath them. There will be noons when the valley air is almost touched with June. There will be evenings when the long light on the hillsides is full of magic.

And there will be nights when the wood smoke wreathes the starlight in the hollows.

But once first frost has passed this way the pattern is set. It will come again on clear, still nights, and with each coming its path will lie higher up the Autumn hillsides. At last it will walk the ridges, leave them, too, shimmering in the dawn. And after that the frost will walk boldly over the land.

Leaf Smoke   *October 15*

There are sound reasons for not burning leaves. Their smoke adds to the urban smog, their smoldering flames create a fire hazard, and unburned leaves make good mulch and compost. Burning them is both wasteful and hazardous, so nowadays enlightened folk either compost Autumn leaves or let the trash men haul them away.

But now and then some suburbanite or villager forgets all these good reasons, or ignores them, and rakes a pile of leaves into some safe place and burns them, for his own good reasons. When he does, other nostalgic people sniff the evening air and remember forgotten Autumns when leaf smoke was the incense of October evenings. Leisurely, uncrowded evenings, uninterrupted by television, unhurried by the delusion of protracted daylight saving time.

It isn't only the leaf smoke, pungent as it is. It is all the other remembered fragrances of the season, the spiced aroma from the pickling kettle in the rural kitchen, the acrid scent of walnut hulls, the smell of roasting chestnuts, the beady tang of apple cider, the savory simmer of mincemeat in the making, the tantalizing smell of pumpkin pie in the oven. It is frosty mornings, and Indian Summer days, and the hearthside smell of wood smoke curling from an evening chimney.

It is wasteful, unwise, in some places illegal leaf smoke. And yet it is October and Autumn evenings and remembered years. If you are middle-aged, don't allow yourself to smell it or you will wonder what happened to those years.

You can travel America for half a lifetime and still get a new thrill of pride and exaltation each time you leave salt water behind and head out across the breadth of the country. It's more than so many miles, or so many days, or so many towns and cities and farms. It is a vast variety of all of them, combined in a strength that can't be appreciated even in one quick survey; the most one gets is the feeling of bigness, and greatness, and underlying power.

Top the Alleghenies and you see the morning shadows stretching west, the streams flowing west, the fields and farms and forests reaching west far beyond the horizon. And you know that the mountain shadows, the streams, the fields, reach only a part of the way ahead. There is a constant beyond, more and more of this America, so lush and bountiful in any Autumn. These streams flow westward, but only to the Mississippi; there they join waters that flow eastward. And the silt of Ohio and Indiana and Illinois mingles with the silt of Nebraska and the Dakotas and Wyoming and Montana, to turn southward through still other parts of this great American whole.

Sycamores fringe the streams, and corn stands russet in the fields and rustling in the shock, and even the cities of this midland are lost in the expanse. Factory smoke rises on the skyline, and soon is lost in the October haze. Highways lattice the countryside, and yet it is the furrowed land, the fields of stubble and new wheat, that dominates. And you know that this America grew out of the land itself, the rolling hills and the fertile valleys, and that it there renews its strength. Seeing its vastness, you understand again, renew your perspective, find faith again in tomorrow and its makers.

❧ This traveler's report was written in Tecumseh, Nebr.

Indian Summer

Of all our seasons, both official and unofficial, Indian Summer is the most indeterminate and subject to most argument. There is general agreement that it consists of a series of warm Autumn days with clear skies, calm air, distant haze, and cool nights. There agreement ends. How many times it may come in a year, when it comes, where the name originated—all are constantly argued.

Not to settle the arguments, but only to cite certain facts, let this be said: Indian Summer can come any time from late September to mid-December. It can come twice or even three times in a season. Nobody knows where the name came from.

As for the name, the Indians themselves had names for their moons or lunar months, but among those names is none that resembles Indian Summer. They used the fine Fall weather to get in the last of their crops, just as rural folk always did and still do. But the name "Indian Summer" does not appear in print or manuscript in this country until 1794, by which time the Indian welcoming committee and their names for local phenomena were largely forgotten.

Indian Summer weather can come as early as late September if it is preceded by an early, hard frost. Otherwise it is just a warm spell in September. It often comes both in October and November. When it comes in early December, nobody calls it Indian Summer. The weather itself is not peculiar to the United States. Germany has its "Old Woman's Summer" and England has "Allhallow Summer" in the Autumn. China and Siam also have such mild Autumn interludes. So do certain parts of the Indian ocean.

And that's about the sum of it. We've just had a spell of Indian Summer in mid-October. We may have another spell of it later. Let those argue who will; we're content to enjoy it.

Dogwood Berries

Dogwood berries gleam in the woodland in lacquer-red clusters, bright as holly at Christmas. There's a big crop of them this Fall, for the dogwoods bloomed magnificently last May, and everywhere there was a blossom there is now a bunch of berries.

Gray squirrels sometimes show a particular fondness for dogwood berries, littering the ground beneath the trees with the bright red outer hulls. What they are after is the kernel. To reach that kernel one has to strip off the fleshy hull, which looks like the flesh of a rose haw but tastes bitter as quinine. Beneath that is a nut, bone hard in shell and only about a quarter of an inch in diameter. Inside this shell is a kernel, a bit of white, oily meat no larger than a radish seed. To the human tongue it has a taste something like the taste of a Brazil nut. Presumably it is a delicacy in the squirrel's diet; certainly it is hard to get at and there's little of it when brought to light.

The quinine taste of the fleshy hull comes from the same tannic principle that is present in the bark of the flowering dogwood. A brew made of the bark has certain quinine properties and has been used as a fairly effective home remedy for fevers. But it is powerfully bitter on the tongue. And the oily quality of the kernel of the nut is no illusion, either. At one time the fruit of a related dogwood, *Cornus sanguinea,* was pressed in France to obtain an oil for soap making.

But to the passer-by or the walker on country roads the dogwood berries are only another item of Autumn beauty which, if left to themselves, will still gleam on the branch well into the Winter.

The River Grape

Most of the fox grapes have ripened and fulfilled their destiny, one way or another; fox grapes ripen in the woods by the first week in October. But along the rivers and brooks the fox grape's smaller cousin, the wild river grape, now comes into its own. And those who cherish a delicacy as rare as wild strawberry jam have been out gathering river grapes, simmering them, jelling their purple-black juice, stowing it carefully away.

The fox grape, with its larger fruit, is the forebear of our concords and catawbas; the river grape has seldom lured the hybridist because its fruit is less than half an inch in diameter, sometimes no larger than the fruit of the elderberry. And it tends to a sharp sourness on the tongue, at least until a light frost has somewhat tempered it. But the river grape is a persistent vine, one that drapes the trees and bushes along a thousand Northeastern streams. That is its final defense, for it is not an easy fruit to pick. Those who would gather river grapes by the pailful had best do it from a boat, working along the shallows where trees overhang and vines drape low.

But for the persistent ones, the river grape is a treasure. Its juice is a bit too sharp for most palates when taken as grape juice, but the wine made from it is something special. You find little river grape wine any more; it is too tedious a job to gather enough grapes even for the small press and the little keg. River grape jelly is more easily made, and it is a special delight with wild duck, venison, most wild game, and with a good, sharp country cheese. You can't buy it, however; you make it, or find someone who does. Now is the time when the wise ones, the ones who know a good thing when they see it, make river grape jelly.

October Wind   *October 20*

We would say a kind word now for the October wind. Not for the gale which brings down a freight of dead limbs in the woodland, and certainly not for the wind that whoops down from shivering Baffinland, but for the wind October knows best, a wind that accompanies clean, blue skies, starry nights, crisp leaves and frost-touched gardens. A sweater-cool wind with a chrysanthemum in its buttonhole and a glass of sweet cider in its hand.

It is a shimmering wind, gleaming with thistledown and silken with milkweed floss. It whispers in the treetops, where sugar-maple gold still persists, and it rustles at the roadside with a scurry of stiff poplar leaves and crisp, brown elm leaves in the gutters. It is rich with the fragrance of ripe orchards on the hillside, and it quivers at evening with the rasping complaint of the late katydid and the worried stridulation of the cricket. It ruffles the mirror of lake and pond and rouses a brown surf in the ripe grass of the uncut meadow. It shakes tomorrow's oaks from the acorn trees, and it strews next September's goldenrod along the roadside.

It is a wind to walk with, out where wood smoke from the evening hearth tangs the air. It brings the high honk of the migrant goose, the Autumn bark of the hunting fox, the treetop caw of the crow who soon will inherit the woodland. There will be other voices soon enough, but now the wind sings an October song written in gold and crimson notes on the crisp, blue sky of Autumn.

The Day's Dimensions   *October 21*

Even as Autumn days shorten, they increase in height and breadth. It is as though there were a constant ratio which keeps the days in balance; and if it seems strange to think of any day in such dimensions, look about you, now that the leaves are thinning out. The eye can reach. New vistas open. The horizon is there just beyond that row of maples from which the morning's breeze has shaken a shower of gold and scarlet. The sun slants in the window where, two weeks ago, the shadow of the elms lay deep.

The hills are no longer remote, and at night you can look up and see the constellations of Andromeda and Pegasus. Even in a land of trees, we no longer are canopied from the sky and walled in from the horizon. Our earth's distances invite the eye. And as the eyes reach, so must the mind stretch to meet these new horizons.

True, they are not new horizons; we have seen them in other Autumns, and they have been there through the succession of Winters. But the very fact that they now seem new, if only because newly seen, is human reason enough for the seasonal succession. We bind our lives and thoughts with too many walls and canopies, at best; it is good to have those barriers thin away, from time to time, and reveal the broader scope. It is good to be reminded that not only the day but life itself is a matter of more than one dimension.

Autumn is the eternal corrective. It is ripeness and color and a time of completion; but it is also breadth, and depth, and distance. What man can stand with Autumn on a hilltop and fail to see the span of his world and the substance of the rolling hills that reach to the far horizon?

Hunter's Moon   *October 22*

Now comes the hunter's moon, the full moon of October, which for night after night is a beacon to man and dog and big buck coon. Cornfields rustle, rabbits lie close, the owl courses the crisp meadow on silent wings. And even a country house is a prison, friendly, but a prison just the same. A man has to get up and go, once the moon has risen. He has to know the night smell of October, the night feel, the night wonder.

The hunt is only an excuse. There's also the country road with its long shadows and its gleam of late goldenrod and aster. There's the tang of black walnuts underfoot, the crispness of russet leaves, the bold silver of white birch boles, moonlit mottle of sycamore, dark whisper of a hemlock grove. And the soft rush and quick flash of doe and fawns startled from the orchard's windfalls.

Soon or late, the dog gives tongue, sharp, sudden, echoing all across the hills, the trail song of a dog born for such an October night. Through the corn field, down through the woods, across the brook, up the hill, back to the stand of maples. Then the sharp yips, the dog cry: "Coon treed!" And if there's to be coon as well as hunt, the tree must be found, the quarry caught.

It doesn't too much matter whether there's a coon caught or only the chase. There's always the night, the companionship, the remembered tales beside a fire. There's man talk, and dog talk, and there's the silence of close friendship with October all around. And if a man gets home late and full of muscle-weariness, that doesn't much matter either, because a man has also filled himself with soul ease and a measure of contentment.

Sky Walker   *October 23*

The sky walker will be abroad tonight. He always walks the moonlight. Autumn moonlight in particular, when the katydids have almost ceased their rasping chorus. No doubt the sky walker strides the land at other times as well, but his presence can best be known when the Autumn quiet lies upon the hills.

Go out in the moonlight and watch the treetops, if you would know the sky walker. The night is silent as a moonbeam, the trees themselves untouched by as much as a wisp of breeze. Then there is a far-off whisper, a crisp sibilance in the distance. It grows, and the leaves of a whole treetop are in motion, crisp Autumn leaves not yet fallen from the branch. Then the next tree is touched, and the next, and a whole path of rustling leaves becomes evident. The sky walker has come striding through those trees, scuffling the leaves ahead of him as a schoolboy scuffles the roadside leaves on his homeward path at sundown. And when he has passed by, there is silence again, the silence of still leaves in October moonlight.

No one ever sees the sky walker, and no one ever will. Sometimes he seems to be there in a wisp of mist; but at best the watcher has seen nothing more than the sky walker's mist-white moccasins, perhaps not even the moccasins but only the momentary scuffle of mist risen dustlike from his footsteps. No one has ever seen him, yet he must be there, making his moonlit rounds when the leaves are brittle with Autumn. We have heard him often as he passed by, particularly when the moon is at the full and we ourselves are full of understanding.

The Migrant Geese   *October 24*

Two sounds of Autumn are unmistakable, the hurrying rustle of crisp leaves blown along the street or road by a gusty wind, and the gabble of a flock of migrating geese. Both are warnings of chill days and crisp nights ahead, fireside and topcoat weather. The leaves have been slow to fall this year, but the geese are on the wing, close to their usual schedule. Cold weather, seasonal weather, has begun to settle in up where the geese spend their Summers.

Most birds migrate in silence, but not the geese. Whether you are walking down a city street, standing in a suburban back yard or working in a rural woodlot, you know when the geese fly over. First you hear the distant gabble, a faint clamor that seems to echo from the whole sky. You search the sky, and the gabble comes closer. Then you see them, flying high, marking a *V* almost like a dotted pencil line. You listen and watch, and the flight is so high it seems almost leisurely. If it is a close *V* in firm formation it probably is Canada geese. If it is a looser *V*, rippling and waving, it is more likely the less common snow geese. Whichever, the flock's gabbling voice is like the voice of restless Autumn, and the flight never wavers. On and on, over the hills and the towns and the city itself, to the far horizon, and still beyond, southward. And only that restless echo, faint and haunting, remains.

They are footloose as the Autumn wind, and they follow the sun. There is something both exhilarating and faintly sad in the echo of their going. Maybe it's the echo of another Summer gone. Maybe it's the freedom song of the skies. Whatever, it haunts the earth-bound heart.

Autumn Is for Understanding

There's deep scuffling of leaves underfoot, and Taurus and the Pleiades can be seen in the eastern sky at evening. Apples are in, somehow symbolic of the whole Summer's yield, and the pressure is relaxed. One can now mend walls and tidy up the fields and garden and snug the place for Winter.

The pace changes. It's not exactly a time for leisure, but there is occasion now to look at the far hills and to think longer thoughts, thoughts not bounded by a cornstalk's height or a pasture's breadth. The big rhythms seep into the soul, the rhythms of the seasons and the years rather than the rhythms of the long days and short, hot nights.

One can look at a white oak now and see the beauty of a stout tree in late October. One can watch an early flight of teal and marvel at the instinct that compasses a duck north or south. One can watch a squirrel at his hoarding and hear the sweet whisperings of the chickadees in the orchard. One can feel the world about him, and see it, and somewhat understand.

Autumn is for understanding, for the longer thoughts and the deeper comprehensions. How well it is that each year should bring such a time, to rest the muscles, yes, from the long Summer tensions, but even more important, to relax the mind and give it time and room to span the valleys of belief. Now a man's mind can reach beyond himself.

October is the fallen leaf, but it is also a wider horizon more clearly seen. It is the distant hills once more in sight, and the enduring constellations above them once again.

The Woolly Bears

Autumn writes its signature in a thousand ways, from the penciled flight of geese against the sky to the gleaming symmetry of a frosted spider web at sunrise. But one of the commonest of all is the looping script traced along suburban sidewalks and across rural dooryards on a sunny afternoon by the woolly bear caterpillars.

The woolly bear is the larval form of the small pinkish-yellow Isabella tiger moth and is somewhat unusual because it hibernates. But it hibernates by degrees, in a sense, sleeping through the first frosty days, then emerging during a warm spell for a last few hours in the sun. Then back it goes, to a leaf pile, a heap of stones, an outbuilding, some shelter where it can curl up for the long sleep. Perhaps it is this sensing of a cold night to come and the consequent haste to find cover that long ago gave the woolly bear a reputation as a weather forecaster. If the black bands at each end of the woolly bear are wider than the reddish-brown central band, the saying goes, it will be a mild Winter.

And what are the woolly bears saying now? Well, as usual, some say yes and some say no. For the fact is that those bands vary from one caterpillar to another every Autumn. They can't even agree among themselves. They are prophets, yes, but . . . They know a warm afternoon when it comes, and they know enough to get in out of the cold on a frosty night. They may not know the coming Winter, but they can spell Autumn unmistakably.

The Larch   *October 27*

The larches, or tamaracks, stand now in the woodland like giant candle flames of yellowish tan, tall and slim and symmetrical. They are preparing to shed their needles, for they are the woodchucks of the pine family, the only cone-bearing trees in our area which "hibernate" for the Winter. Soon now their tufted needles will fall in a yellowish shower and the bright tan of their branches will stand out against the grays and browns of the Winter hillsides.

As a species, the larches are among the oldest trees of the chilly northlands. They have seen ice ages come and go; the earth has wrinkled and convulsed beneath their roots. And in the briefer time of man the larches have given their strength and warmth to his house and fire. Their trunks are long and slim, and their wood is hard and resinous; they resist the rotting of time, and they burn with a long, hot flame. Small wonder that man learned long ago to build on sills of larch and to keel and frame the longboats of venture with timbers of larch.

Those who would personify it call the larch a cautious tree; but it were better described as stoutly individual. Though it belongs to the family of evergreens, it sheds its needles. A conifei, its cones are inconspicuous and its seeds so small they tempt only a very hungry squirrel. A tree of the rocky upland, it occasionally invades the lesser swamp and thrives there. In the Spring it blossoms inconspicuously in March or April, but it takes its time about putting forth new needles. All Summer long it is a beautiful spire of warm green, but by November it turns resolutely deciduous. In Winter it shrugs off snow. Thus it lives to a stout old age.

To Walk with Autumn   *October 28*

There may be other times as good as late October to go out afoot and see the world, but there certainly isn't a better one. To walk with the scuffle of new-fallen leaves, to feel the mild sun and see the Autumn sky, to have the company of busy squirrels in the woods and restless ducks on the river, is to sense the season at first hand. To look at the hills in their true dimensions and see to the end of the valleys whence the frost came creeping down last night is to know a world that has achieved the annual miracle.

Walk the country roads and the open fields now and you are a witness to great events accomplished. The sugar maples stand in deep pools of their own leaf gold. The goldenrod is graceful and gray with ripeness. The milkweed offers a richness of silk and seed to every breeze. The white oaks, still brown and crimson with persistent leaves, have planted tomorrow's groves in their own shade. The jack-in-the-pulpit has summarized its own sermon on immortality in a cluster of lacquer-red berries.

Yesterday is all around you, last Spring's growth and last Summer's maturity and last month's ripeness. But tomorrow is there too, the sprout, the leaf, the blossom, waiting only for another Spring. The ripeness is but a part of the continuity, achievement rather than completion. We think of it as the evening of the year; but after the dusk comes starlight, and dawn, and another day. To walk with Autumn is to be in the presence of forever.

Dressed for Winter   *October 29*

One wouldn't say that birds are exactly fashion conscious, but they have their seasonal attire, as anyone who walks the country roads can see. Even those that don't change the pattern with the season have their change of costume. The crows, for instance, have put on fresh black coats after a Summer in nondescript feathers that had turned a bit rusty by September. No protective coloration for them, however; they seem to glory in the contrast of jet black against the white of Winter. And the blue jays, which looked rather gray all Summer long, now are in fresh blue and white, vivid as the Autumn sky.

The lesser woodpeckers, the hairies and the downies, are in fresh feather, too. It is the familiar pattern, a tweedy kind of black and white, but it is so fresh it might have just come from the cleaners, certainly not the worn and weathered costume they wore all Summer. The robins on the other hand—and quite a few are still here—have changed their brick-red Summer weskits for duller ones. And the starlings now wear well-speckled coats with little of the greenish gloss they had last Spring.

The real changelings, however, are the goldfinches, daffodil yellow all Summer, but now as quietly attired, in browns and grays, as the field sparrows. They even flock with the sparrows in the weed patches at the roadside, recognizable only by jet-black wings and hints of yellow on their shoulders. They leave the gay Winter attire to the cardinals, who are as preened and polished as a holly berry, and almost as Christmasy, even in October.

Wild Clematis   *October 30*

The wild clematis vines now reveal themselves along the roadsides and in odd fence corners, sere and leafless, graying toward Winter. The long, twisting stems are typical of the climbers, reminding of the graceful drapes of dark green leaves that made midsummer more lush, more verdant. And where the flowers bloomed in flat clusters of greenish white, insignificant individually but pleasantly eye catching as a group, now stand the tufts of grayish withered styles which give the plant its Autumn name, Old Man's Beard.

Few plants have seasonal names, and fewer still have common names that so well denote the seasons and the passage of time. Botanically this is *Clematis virginiana*. At the height of its flowering season it is virgin's bower, a name full of fancy and simple poetry. It becomes a bower, decorated with the small blossoms almost virginal in appearance. It is feminine, it is innocent, it is host to brightly colored bees and flies.

October comes, the waning of the year. Leaves crisp and fall. The seed is dispersed. Time has its way. The once green styles of the flowers twist and twine and become the whitening tufts that mark the empty seed capsules. And now it becomes Old Man's Beard, no longer young, no longer virginal, no longer even remotely feminine. It is age and approaching Winter, it is time passing, the year slowly, inevitably turning. Where once was the virgin's bower now is the gnarling ancient, the white beard of the frosty nights and the clear, chill days that shorten into Winter.

When we set the clocks back an hour last night, we told ourselves we were changing time, taking back that hour we spent for longer evenings last April. But the sun rose unchanged this morning, on its own schedule, and the only change was in the position of the hands on those ticking machines by which man meters his own life. We adjusted our own gauge of the hours somewhat closer to the reality of night and day, the sun, the earth and the year.

Time has its own dimensions, and neither the sun nor the clock can encompass them all. All we can do with the astronomical absolutes of time is note them, divide them as we please, and live by them in our daily routines. Beyond that, our own emotions, our hopes and fears, our worry and our relief, shape not only our days but our hours with only casual regard for absolute or arbitrary time. The busy day can be brief, the suspenseful hour endless. Who can prove, by any clock ever devised, that time on occasion does not stand still? The interval between heartbeats can be a terrifying eternity, and the pause between two spoken words can shape the dimensions of all our tomorrows.

Time is all around us, the time of the hills, the time of the tides, the lifetime of a man or a tree or an insect. We participate in time, try to shape it to our own necessities; but when we change the clocks we aren't changing time at all. We are playing with figures on a dial that denotes but cannot alter the flow of forever.

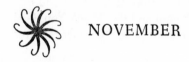 NOVEMBER

November   *November 1*

November is the aging year, a woman whose Springtime children
have grown and gone their way but whose hair is often spangled,
whose gray eyes are often alight, and whose dress of grays and
browns is neither dour nor dowdy. November is berry-bright and
firelight-gay, a glittering night, a crisp blue day, a whispering
wind and a handful of determined fence row asters.

November is the lithe hemlock in a green lace party dress, and
a clean-limbed gray birch laughing in the wind. November is
apple cider with champagne beads of authority; it is a gray squirrel in the limber top of the hickory tree, graceful as the wind; it
is a doe and her fawn munching winesap windfalls in the moonlit
orchard. It is a handful of snowflakes flung over a Berkshire hilltop, and a woodchuck sniffing the wind and retreating to his den
to sleep till April.

November is a rabbit hound baying the hillside; a farm boy
in a canvas coat and a red cap, the 16-gauge in the crook of his
arm, on the hills of the upper pasture; a grouse bursting from underfoot with a roar of wings and rocketing into the thicket. It is
hog butchering and cracklings and sage and pepper and fresh
sausage. It is a fox barking in the starlight and an owl in the old

dead popple asking midnight questions. It is high-heaped fire-wood and leaf-banked walls and buckwheat cakes for breakfast.

And November is the memory of the years. It is turkey in the oven, and plum pudding and mince pie and pumpkin and creamed onions and mashed yellow turnip. It is a feast and cele-bration; but it is also the remembering and the Thank You, God, and the understanding. That's the heart of it: November's matur-ing and understanding.

The Hurrying Wind   *November 2*

Wind and weather move more swiftly now. Dakota's storms come whirling east with little pause along the way, and the Mid-west's frost-edged winds sweep up and over the Alleghenies. Summer's mildness and leisure are things of the past, memories of July and clover and bee hum. November is the fallen leaf, the bare branch, the early setting sun. And the hurrying wind.

You can hear the wind, in the sighing pines, the whistling maples. You both hear and see it at the roadside, the rustling skitter of the crisp leaves, the swirling leaves in the gust, still restless, not yet settled into their Winter bed. In the weeks to come you can hear and see it in the swish of snow, the restless, shifting curtain of snow hung against the Winter sky. You can see it, when Winter takes command, frozen into the swirled drift, the crystal curve of the fluid wind shaping the earth to new dimensions.

Even the days move more swiftly now, with late dawn and early dusk and the sun marking a smaller arc off there to the south. The days march toward the solstice like a Winter farm-hand with the wind at his back. And the long nights are the sleep of the earth itself, the rest, the waiting. The fox barks on the hillside in the starlight, the deer shelters in the hemlock thicket, the woodchuck sleeps. But the hurrying wind whistles up the hounds of Winter in the distance, the impatient wind of November.

Autumn's Clutter

The Autumn countryside has a ragged, unkempt look. Nature isn't neat in these matters. Rural roadsides swirl and rustle with fallen leaves. Dried goldenrod stems strew seeds at random. Gaping milkweed pods spill fluff in all directions. Wild grapevines and woodbine dangle in random loops from trees and bushes. Withered grass obviously needs combing and brushing. The little backwater bog is a jumble of disordered reeds and fraying cattail heads.

On the floor of the woodland is a litter of dead twigs and branches pruned and left to lie by wind and rain. The pines have shed their extra needles, which scatter like wasted straw. Ferns lie withered and crumbling where their fronds waved gay and green two months ago. The oaks are dressed in brown tatters and the box elders emphasize their nakedness with loose tufts of ripe seed keys. Jack-in-the-pulpit is reduced to a papery curl and a tight bunch of red berries. The abandoned oriole's nest begins to fray at the limber tip of the elm's topmost branch.

Man feels the need to rake leaves, clean up the Summer's remnants, proclaim his tenancy by making things neat and tidy. Nature doesn't bother. The tree thrives on its own trash and the seed sprouts in the parent plant's midden heap. Each new season grows from the leftovers from the past. That is the essence of change, and change is the basic law. Nature hasn't time to be neat and tidy.

Plenty, and to Spare

Mingled with the leaf litter beneath the maples is a generous sprinkling of maple keys, nature's original helicopters. Ripe and loosened like the leaves, they came spiraling down, each key's own broad vane like a wing that flips and sails it away from the parent trunk. At the base of that broad vane is a fat kernel, the seed itself, from which, if all conditions are favorable, a seedling will sprout next Spring. Every maple in the woodland has matured enough seeds to plant a small forest. But only a few of them will survive the hunger that prowls the woods and searches the litter.

Those maple keys are typical of nature's generosity, which man sometimes has difficulty understanding. It is so uneconomical! Virtually every plant that produces seed produces a hundredfold as much as will grow or can grow in the soil available to it. Nature has no truck with the theory of an economy of scarcity. Nature produces to the utmost of her capacity, whether it is wild berries, cattail fluff, maple seed or domesticated wheat. Man is the only living thing that ever says, "Too much!" Man with his self-made complexities, his own systems of economy.

Periodically man apologizes for his own plenty, or he tries to limit production, trapped in his own devices. And year after year, as certain as Autumn comes, nature goes her own way, oblivious. The whole natural system is based on abundance, plenty, more than enough. And the paradox becomes evident on every hillside to anyone who will look. There it is now, even on suburban streets where the maples cast their Summer shade. The winged seeds come spiraling down, writing, "Plenty, plenty," on the Autumn air.

Why? *November 5*

These are fireside evenings, a good time to ponder, though not too deeply, some of the questions characteristic of mid-Autumn in any year. Why, for instance, are andirons sometimes called dogs? And, in that connection, why don't more fire tenders know that a hearth fire burns better and holds fire longer with a good bed of ashes around the andirons? The hearth broom should be used to sweep ashes into, not out of, the fireplace.

Why do barking foxes sound as though they had advanced cases of laryngitis? A human being with such a rasping voice would be packed off to bed and the doctor would be summoned. Why are there only a few partridgeberries this year? Is it because of the drought? The drought reduced the crop of many wild berries, but it didn't seem to hurt the apple crop. Even in old, abandoned orchards back in the hills the windfall apples are plentiful, to the benefit of deer, opossums, grouse and other wild folk.

Why do willows, particularly weeping willows, hold their leaves so much longer than, say, the maples? In favored spots the weepers are foundations of gold even now, and the maples are stark limbs against the November sky. Those who study and tabulate such matters say that chickadees' normal diet consists of 68 per cent insects and 32 per cent seed and other vegetable matter. How can they maintain a normal diet in the Winter when they spend all day and every day cracking and gulping sunflower seeds at the window feeder? Doesn't the gravity-defying nuthatch ever fall on his upturned nose? Apparently not, but why?

Star Nights   *November 6*

November nights are star nights. The leaves have thinned away so that lifted eyes can see a whole sky, and that sky now begins to show the Winter gleam and the Winter constellations.

The Dipper hangs low and Cassiopeia, the Queen, reclines in her chair far overhead. Orion, the Hunter, is there above the eastern horizon, with Rigel, its chief star, bright enough to catch any eye turned in that direction. And above Orion is Taurus, the Bull, with Aldebaran its particular bright star. Still higher, and in the same quarter, are the Pleiades, that dim cluster which none the less catches the eye whenever it looks to the east.

In the west Aquila, the Eagle, flies low, skimming the horizon, a constellation that has caught the eye of westward travelers since this land was new, caught and beckoned. Overhead, to the south, is Pegasus, the Winged Horse, which is the Great Square, though it is an irregular square. And all across the sky sweeps the Milky Way, growing milkier night by night, intensifying with the chill until, on frosty nights to come, it will fairly dance and glitter with its own brightness.

Spring nights are balmy and Summer nights can be and often are breathless, but the stars seem then to have retreated into some distant depth of the sky. By November the remoteness is gone. Stars sit on the next hilltop, and constellations array themselves in the high, bare branches of the big elm just down the road. If one were to go to the far ridge and reach, full arm, one might almost grasp a handful of stars, the lesser ones, of course. But that's in November, when there is no wind save the whisper in the crisp oaks down the valley.

The Owls of Autumn   *November 7*

The owls are calling, these early November evenings, perhaps no more insistently than they did last Spring but more noticeably now because they have the nights to themselves. Sometimes it is the call of the little screech owl, sometimes the deep, gruff hoot of the great horned owl, sometimes the varied calls of the barred owl. All of them seem to have a chilly note, a frosty edge of Winter.

The screech owl's call is neither a screech nor a hoot, actually. It is a quavery, lonesome wail that starts high and slurs down and off. It can be surprisingly loud for the size of the bird, which is no larger than a robin. The barred owl and the great horned owl are the big ones, though neither is much larger than a crow. They look bigger because they are so fluffy feathered. And their voices are big; they hoot, and no mistake about it. The barred owls hoot in varying pitches, sometimes making a chorus of their calls, and it takes little imagination to hear them saying, "Who cooks for you? Who cooks for you all?"

Why do owls hoot? For the same reason, basically, that crows caw. Sometimes they are talking to each other, sometimes they are proclaiming ownership of a territory, and sometimes they simply like the sound of their own voices. Happily, they aren't as insistent as crows, or as repetitious as whippoorwills. But they can and often do make a frosty night seem 10 degrees colder, especially in the outer reaches of the city or in the suburbs. In the country they are just a part of the Autumn.

❦ If these comparisons of size seem surprising, look in any good bird guide and see for yourself how big the owls really are, and how big are crows and robins. The owls do have longer wings, though.

Brown November   *November 8*

Those who speak of gray November must be describing their own mood, not the landscape; for this is the season of browns, not grays, the warmest, richest browns of the whole year. The vivid colors of October are past, but they are succeeded by colors that range from the rich golden tan of the sere milkweed leaf to the earth brown of the oak tree's trunk, from the blond ripeness of the corn husk to the lively russet of the apple twig.

Behold the sleek, polished mahogany acorns in their tam-o'-shantered caps of rough country tweed. See the creamed-coffee shells of the hickory nuts. Hold the brown ripeness of a white pine's cone in your hand, and know the bronze spruce needles in the woodland duff. See the key tassels on the box elder, a livelier shade than that deceptive maple's leaves ever achieved. Admire the polished, leathery, maroon-brown pods of the honey locust.

Goldenrod is a brown tangle of stems and tawny plumes at the roadside. Queen Anne's lace has become an intricate ball of weathered copper filigree. Fern fronds are tangles of cinnamon-colored curls, and spore heads of the ostrich fern might have been carved from polished walnut wood. The meadow margin and the fence row are dappled with rust and terra cotta, ginger and snuff, in outworn leaf and crisp stem and ripened seed.

The spectacle of gold and crimson falls and fades, but it leaves no monotone, no colorless gray world. This is brown November, a chromatic triumph as spectacular in its own way as was green April.

"Birds" *November 9*

Back in the hills they are seldom called grouse or partridges. They are simply "birds," and that distinction is a kind of index to the status of *Bonasa umbellus,* as the ornithologists list the name of the ruffed grouse. For this is not only one of our most valued game birds; it is a kind of embodied spirit of the open woodlands, admired and respected by everyone, and not only for the flavor of its flesh.

Grouse once were called "fool hens" because they were so tame and seemed so stupid. But they learned, as they were hunted. Few birds today are more canny or more wary. Some hunters insist that all the stupid ones were killed off, a few wise ones survived, and today's birds are the descendants of those wise ones. True or not, that's a proper tribute, well deserved.

One doesn't have to be a hunter to know the grouse. Those who know back-country woodlands and explore abandoned farms grown up to brush often see them at this time of year; hear them first, in that startling roar and rush of wings as they take off, then see them for an instant, a blur of wings beyond the nearest trees. Fortunate ones sometimes hear a cock partridge drumming in the Autumn woods. When snow comes, one may see them in old orchards or stands of birch, eating the dormant buds which are an important item on their Winter menu. Next Summer a hen partridge and her flock of chicks may be seen occasionally on the brushy margin of a country road.

But they aren't really grouse or partridges to those who know them best. They are "birds," the sole proprietors of that name.

Evening of the Year

Our Northern land begins to tuck itself in for the Winter. Frost, wind and rain bring down the leaves and the season's coverlet starts to take shape in the woodlands. It is still restless, the gusting wind rustling and shifting the leaves even in the hillside thickets, strewing them over the meadows, heaping them in the fence corners. Sometimes it seems that the leaves themselves are restless, reluctant to be earth-bound. After all, they are winged and they had an airy lifetime, and now they are free to ride each passing breeze. But the restlessness will pass. In a few more weeks they will have settled down to blanket the earth, to dull the fang of frost for the wild seed and root and bulb.

Just now it doesn't look like a blanket at all. It is, rather, a colorful patchwork quilt, rich with reds and tans and yellows. But sun and weather will leach away those strong colors and by the time the wind is freighted with snow instead of leaves there will be a faded blanket in the woods, a washed-out old outdoor blanket already showing the signs of wear. Then Winter will spread a brand new cover, a gleaming puff of white, the snow.

November is the evening of the year, the bedtime of the green and flowering world. Now comes the time for rest, for sleep. So the coverlet is spread, the tucking in begun. Next should come the lullaby, but the lullaby singers have all gone south. The pines and the hemlocks will whisper good night instead.

Mr. Loudmouth

The crows may not be much louder now than they were all Summer, but they certainly give that impression. Raucous braggarts that they are, they seem to be saying that with the migrant songbirds gone or going the world now belongs to the crow tribe. They even call conventions to proclaim this from the leafless treetops, and a convention of crows is one of the noisiest bird assemblies in the world. Actually, three crows are enough for a quorum.

The crow's devilish cleverness has made him practically a folk character. His very name has become a part of the common language. If we would go anywhere directly, we go "as the crow flies." If we have an argument, we "pick a crow" with someone. When we have to make abject apology, we "eat crow." If we have a worthless horse, he is "crow bait." And one of the blackest colors is "crow black."

In many ways the crow's reputation is as black as his feathers. He is a bully and a thief. He robs bird nests, kills young chickens, eats sprouting corn. He also eats many beetles, grasshoppers and caterpillars, but he makes his virtues a secret and parades his vices. He seems to enjoy a bad reputation. And he hasn't even the saving grace of song.

But when the leaves fall, the flowers wither and the real songsters depart, even Mr. Loudmouth is welcome in many places. The world would be a lonely place without him. Maybe that's why he stays around all Winter. Anyone as clever as a crow could figure that out in five minutes. He knows what he's doing, and enjoys it.

The Long Sleep   *November 12*

The long sleep has begun. The trees stand stripped for Winter, next Spring's buds, germinal leaf and blossom, there on the twig but dormant as the monarch butterfly's eggs on the milkweed stem; jack-in-the-pulpit berries are a cluster of rubies among the crisp maple leaves, but life has retreated into the acrid root from which, in the way of such life, it will offer its green response to another April. The roadside aster's blossom has gone to seed, but it, too, sleeps at the root, where life's energy is conserved for another year.

The woolly bear caterpillar has found a nook and curled itself into a furry, sleeping ball. Come Spring and it will rouse, feast on a plantain leaf and build a cocoon from which it will emerge in pink-and-yellow glory as a Summer butterfly. The young queen bumblebee, fertile with a new generation, sleeps in a deserted mouse nest in the meadow, ready to waken and hatch a new colony when Winter is over and gone.

On the hillside, in a den among the rocks, the woodchuck sleeps, and near by in a lesser burrow the chipmunk goes to bed. Their sleep is nearer to nonhibernating man's understanding, but still a mystery. Somehow they quiet their nerves, ease their vigilance, slow their heartbeat and their breathing, and let Winter spread a comforting blanket. Theirs is the long, deep sleep that outlasts the deep cold and the bitter wind. For them, too, the long day of Summer is ended, the long night of Winter is at hand, and the sigh of November is the year's lullaby.

Bold Simplicities   *November 13*

November nights are long and chill and full of stars and the crisp whisper of fallen leaves skittering in the wind. November nights are good for walking down a country road, when the world comes close about you, a world drawn in bold charcoal strokes against the sky.

Perhaps it is that night and darkness simplify that world to a point of understanding. The far hill is any hill, with substance but no detail. The valley has depth without contours. The shrunken pond is a little patch of sky with a handful of stars wavering in the rippled footsteps of the wind. The clump of cedars at the far edge of the meadow is thick, restless shadow leaping, like a black hound, at the horizon. And the houses down the road are blinking yellow eyes, windows with no walls around them.

This is no complex world. It is a world of simple things, now brought to rest. Who can make complexity of wood smoke, so sharp in the night air, from a fireplace chimney? Or from the barking of a dog announcing footsteps and leaf rustle on the road beneath the hill? And what is so simple as an elm, its leaves all shed, silhouetted against the skyline?

To walk in such a night is to know that the only mysteries are the great mysteries of all time—the stars, the heavens, the restless wind tides, the spinning earth, and man himself. Daylight and sun time are the time to explore these things; nighttime and darkness are the time to accept them and build dreams and poems upon them. Night, when the cool of the year has come, is the time to walk with them and know intimately the bold simplicities.

Jaybird   *November 14*

If the blue jay were one of those migrants who stop in for only a few days each season, he probably would be known as an exotic bird of unusual beauty. Some jays do migrate a little way, but few places in their range are ever without them. The jays and the crows keep the Winter landscape alive and lively.

Watch a blue jay on a frosty morning and you can see a caricature of the pompous alderman of the old school. His feathers fluffed against the chill, he sits and scowls. His vest is snug across an ample chest. He even seems to have a series of chins, and his crest is a kind of avian topper which gives him dignity. Until he opens his big mouth. Then he rasps, always indignantly. The climate, the landscape, the meals or the company always seems to be subject to criticism. Jays flock together and seem to quarrel incessantly.

But there is this to be said for the jay: He has an immaculate air. The white cravat at his throat, the white bars on his wings and edging on his tail are crisply white. The blue of his wings is a clean, rich blue, particularly against a gray Winter sky. He has an air, definite and definable. He can sit stock still and strut. Yet, for all his pomposity, he has frivolous moments. On a lively morning two jays will sometimes play tag in the tangled branches of an old apple tree. And when nobody is in sight, a jay will occasionally whisper a sweet little song, soft and melodious and almost sentimental. At such times one thinks of him as a character actor always cast as a colorful old villain, but who has a secret yearning to play the romantic young hero who gets the ingenue.

Rise early, on a crisp November morning, and look out at the frosty world before the sun has climbed more than a couple of rungs on its tall, blue ladder. The grass is crisp and glisteny, brown goldenrod stems are beaded with crystal, and the last few deep crimson leaves of the huckleberry have a fringe of frost. For a few moments there is the illusion of a first light snow, filmy as sugar dust, spread over the nearby world.

Then the sun climbs another rung, tops the trees and touches the slope beyond your own; and in a matter of minutes the gleam is gone from the sunlit grass. The frost-white meadow turns brown, as it was at last sunset. And with the lifting of the sun the brown line creeps eastward, frost vanishing under the warm sunlight touch.

But it is no ruler line, nor yet a hilltop line, that creeps across the meadow. It is a sawtooth line, the silhouette of the leafless trees laid flat across the grass. And as you watch, you see the shadow of each tree, white shadows etched across the brown, the November sere. It is a strange reversal, white shadows overlaid on a darker world. It is, if you will, the shadow of white days to come, when every tree will be outlined in the clinging snow; when not even sunrise and the warmth of day can leach away the frost.

And so you watch, and the sun is higher still. The white shadows shrink away, and it is a November morning, brown with Autumn, the frost gone as your white breath went in the sunlight.

The Winter Light   *November 16*

No matter whether the temperature is unseasonably high or low, the season's change is here when dawn and dusk are times of slanting Winter light, when the sunrise and sunset are far off to the south and the midday sun sweeps into the south windows.

And if the sky at dusk is rimmed with faint greenish light, you can be glad for a full oil tank, a heaped coal bin or an ample supply of firewood. Winter is there in sight, in that icy band of sky; very likely it will be nipping at nose and fingers by morning after such a dusk.

Each season has its own light, its own sunrise and sunset. Spring is a lightening of the sky, a new clarity of the blue, an absence of that feathery snow threat that is so typical of March. Spring is an equinox and sunrise square with the compass. Summer is a dazzle, though often gauzed with heat haze of high-flown dust. And the northing sun marks the Summer, early sunrise, late sunset and a lingering dusk. Autumn is a time of crispness, even in the air, and the light is like a burnish for the changing leaves. Autumn sunrise often seems to reflect the flaming maple and the golden birch; and Autumn is another equinox, sunrise and sunset once more square with the directions.

Then comes the southward shift toward Winter, the sky clarifies itself with frost, and the light begins to shimmer. Late dawn with a long, slanting light that touches the leafless hillsides with a brief, rosy glow. Then comes the cold, and the icy green at sunset; and after that comes the snow, and the Winter light on the snowy land is full of blue and purple which lie like lakes among the drifts. Then the solstice, Winter at its depth, and deep, long starlight. We can see it coming now, the slanting Winter light, the icy green at evening, the short days, Winter itself.

The Nest   *November 17*

Last Summer's oriole nest hangs high in the elm, in plain sight now that the leaves are gone. The orioles too are gone, and after a frosty night the nest sways in the morning sun like a gray purse spangled with brilliants. Snow will come, in due time, and fill the woven pouch where eggs were hovered and hatched. Winter gales will whip at it, and still the nest will remain, anchored to the slender twigs, a fragment of Summer gone and a reminder of Spring to come. A reminder of orioles, and bright plumage, and rippling bird song.

Meanwhile, the blue jays seek out the apple trees, peck at the frosted fruit still hanging there, and proclaim themselves possessors of the November world. Feathers puffed against the chill, the jays have a pompous insolence; and when they fly past the elm with the pendant oriole nest they seem to jeer. A jay builds no such nest, and a jay does not migrate to escape the cold. And it is useless to speculate on why the jay lacks the weaver's skill, or why he lacks the migrant's instinct. Enough that he also lacks the song of the oriole.

There is the temptation, on a sharp morning, to draw broad conclusions about art and industry and song and cynicism and the bullies of this world. But it leads nowhere. An oriole is its own excuse for being, on a warm June day. It is one of the bright and happy phenomena of this world. And if it follows the sun southward, it also follows the sun when the season brings it north again. The jay remains, to scoff perhaps; but there, too, is that nest swaying from the high elm tips, frost spangled in the thin November sunlight.

Twilight   *November 18*

Twilight comes early, now, with the sun taking the short-cut arc across the sky from southeast to southwest, a late rising and an early set. Twilight comes by five o'clock, with a blue light that fades on the hills and deepens in the valleys and shimmers only on the cold ponds that lie in the hollows of the land. And all across the western sky are the merging bands of dusk purple and dusk blue and cold-evening green, shades so fugitive and so blended that they darken and are gone even as you watch, and you wonder if they were there at all.

You watch from the hilltop, and the dusk begins to hide the valley, all but the pond that still holds that strange evening light. Then you go down into the valley, and somehow the twilight has lessened; it is one of those strange illusions of a November evening. The rounded hills with their leafless trees are like boys with crew haircuts, and beyond them the sky is luminous with the cold blue-green light again, the light that hints of stars and growing moonlight.

The moon is there, almost overhead, almost half full, and it begins to glow. The green fades in the west. It is a blue sky, now, the blue of full dusk but still so luminous that only the brightest of the evening stars can be seen. The faint outlines of the Big Dipper are there in the north, down close to the horizon, where the dusk seems deepest. And in the east are the still fainter outlines of Orion, the Hunter.

Then the west, too, is dark. Blue evening cups the world, blue and the shine of the growing moon overhead. But in the hollows of the land the ponds still hold the twilight glow, the quiet ponds that wait for another, shorter day of sunlight tomorrow.

The Hearth   *November 19*

There is this about a chill November: It makes one appreciate a fireside. And there is this about a hearth: It calls for small company, for companionship.

A hearth fire is a wasteful thing, in terms of economics. But so is much of the talk that generates beside an open fire, for it seldom settles big problems and it never pays the taxes. Much of it, like the heat from the logs on the andirons, goes up the chimney. But when you have said that, you have pretty well exhausted the case against the simmering log and the slow talk and the leisurely evening. And there still remains the reflected glow, which is its own excuse and needs no defense.

There are times and occasions when quick heat and sharp words are among the world's largest inefficiencies. Some things, and friendship and understanding are high among them, mature best by emberlight and in a small company. It is doubtful that mob rule was ever inspired by the slow gleam of a fireplace. The tinder of violence and fanaticism requires a bigger fire and larger arena. Philosophy and faith are companions on the hearth, and ever have been.

There are better ways to heat a house, true; but neither love nor friendship is concerned too much with economics. Man built a home around his fire, and there the family grew. To his fireside he brought his friends, and friendship grew, and understanding. So hearth became home, and home became heart, and it has little changed over the centuries. What greater friendship than understanding? What deeper understanding is there than which stands, back to hearth, and faces outer cold and darkness?

Chickweed   *November 20*

The goldenrod is through, most of the wild asters have been frosted into submission, and even bouncing Bet can muster only an occasional stunted blossom. But chickweed persists, green as June and with a few flowers, on any sunny morning. Chickweed never gives up. It doesn't exactly thrive on the icy blast of Winter, but unless it is buried under a foot of snow, it will be in blossom at Christmas and it will be in bloom again, practically vernal in vigor, during the January thaw.

As a plant, chickweed doesn't amount to much, and as a flower it is even less important. One of the least of the pink family, it seldom grows more than three or four inches high, and its thin-petaled white blossoms are little more than an eighth of an inch across. But it grows in the garden, on the lawn, in the path, at the roadside, on the ash heap, anywhere there is root room. And even in this latitude it can often be found in bloom every month in the year.

Like the gnat, chickweed proves the staying power of the inconspicuous weakling. One plant doesn't seem worth weeding out. Leave it undisturbed and tomorrow there will be a dozen plants, next week a hundred. It's as ubiquitous as grass and twice as stubborn. Equipped with neither thorn nor noxious juice, it can outstay the bramble and the poisonous ivy or the nettle. It seems to have little purpose beyond adding a little to the earth's natural humus, though some birds eat it sparingly. But it does prove that even Winter, even ice and snow and steely frost, have only limited triumph.

The Enduring Voices   *November 21*

Now that Autumn's silence is upon the land, one can hear the big, enduring voices which seldom shout the things they have to say. One can hear the earth declare that ice, the counterpart of fire, must be reckoned with. One can hear the hills assert their stony structure which forever underlies the soothing green of leaf and shade. One can hear the wind and water discussing polar regions and the fundamental wedge of frost that can level mountains. Listen closely, and one can hear the patient throb of almost suspended life in the root, the bulb, the seed, the egg, waiting for another Spring.

It is pleasant to walk with May and hear the song of mating birds and see the glint of fresh violets in the new grass. It is satisfying to sit in Summer's shade and know the fragrance of roses and the hum of bees through the long afternoon. It is exhilarating to watch the color come to the woodlands and feel the lure of wanderlust in blue sky and opening horizon. But when the blossom has become the seed, when daylight has been abbreviated by the southward swing of the sun, when the trees stand naked in the frosty woodland, such transient pleasures give way to the big assurances.

Now we approach the nadir of the year, the neap tide of daylight. But the earth still turns, the stars are still there, the seas maintain their vast expanse and the hills still stand. Another Spring is already patterned, as inevitable as sunrise. Time flows, and with it life and change. That is what the enduring voices are saying, if we only listen.

The Paper Makers   *November 22*

In this age of the printed word we tend to think that man invented paper. That isn't so. The hornets did, and a walk in the leafless woods will prove it. Somewhere along the way one probably will find a gray paper ball at least a foot in diameter hanging from a low limb. It will be a hornet's nest, to be avoided all Summer but now deserted and safe to examine, since all the hornets except the queen are dead and the queen is hibernating elsewhere.

Ever since there were hornets and trees, hornets have been making wood pulp, softening it with their own saliva, and building such nests of it. The nest usually has double walls for insulation—another hornet invention—and inside is a complex of cells, hundreds of them, the original of the apartment house. And every square inch of material in that nest is paper, hornet paper, the first paper ever invented.

The nests are never used more than one season. Next Spring the queen will come out of hibernation, build a small new nest, lay eggs and hatch a brood of workers. They will gather wood pulp and enlarge the nest, which by mid-Summer will be a fearsome hive of hornets. It may even be a colorful hive, since hornets keep up to date—now they use painted wood, sometimes, to make their paper, and even chew up bits of the discarded paper and cardboard which litter the roadside. But it will be paper, the primitive kind of paper hornets were making long before man tamed fire, let alone learned to write or print or bind a book.

The Simplicities   *November 23*

One thing about late Autumn, it displays the stubborn simplicities of the earth. Man may contrive himself into all kinds of human complications, but this earth which bore him and will be his home until the end of his days seems to settle back periodically into quiet contemplation. There stand the hills, rugged as time, and there lie the valleys at rest. The sun cuts its small arc in the southern sky and the long night is the counterpart of June's long day. The tree stands stark, life at rest in the root, and the meadow is sere with frost. The goldenrod is a dead stem and a waiting seed, restless in the wind.

The simplicities are everywhere. The cicada and the katydid have retreated to the silence of the egg. The partridge feeds on the bud and the berry, no longer urgent with nesting. The frog has buried himself in the mud and the woodchuck sleeps only a few degrees this side of death. The owl hoots in the cold moonlight, and the fox prowls and barks his ownership of the night. The brook hurries noisily toward the river, and the river carries Autumn's remnants toward the sea. Leaves begin to molder in the simple economy of nature, last Summer's shade leaching back into the soil.

The urgencies are eased for another season. Only the wind hurries now. Soon even the rain will flake down, wafted crystal drifting on the brittle air. Ice, the most stubborn of all simplicities, will pry at the fundamental rocks. And out there in the depth of the night the whole universe will still be in eternal order.

Beaver Moon   *November 24*

In the days of woodsmen and Indians, when there was a harvest moon and a hunter's moon in September and October, November brought the beaver moon. One reason was that by November the beaver pelts were prime. Another was that by November's time of full moon the beavers, wise in the way of the seasons, were ready for Winter. Their dams were sound, their ponds were full, their houses snug and well supplied with food; and any countryman with half the sense of a beaver had his own establishment similarly prepared. November, in those days of early Winters and long ones, was the last chance a man had to get ready for what

December and January, and often February as well, would bring in the way of snow and cold. The farmer who hadn't worked like a beaver was in for some unhappy times.

Weather has changed somewhat, and conditions otherwise have changed even more, but by the time Thanksgiving is past the provident countryman still is ready for what may come. That's why you see the leaves snugged around the foundations of old country houses by now. That's why the pump house, with its electric motor and throbbing pump, is banked and insulated. That's why the silo is full, and the mow, and the granary. That's why the freezer lid will barely close on its store of garden harvest and butchering product. That's why the blade is all ready to attach to the tractor, to keep the lane and the barnyard clear when the snow piles deep.

It's still the beaver moon, that full moon which comes tonight, though it is seldom so called. It means snugness for the Winter, and it means that November has been a beaver-busy time for the family which still lives within whispering distance of the weather.

The Turkey   *November 25*

That big, colorful, meaty bird which makes the table festive for America's traditional Thanksgiving is surrounded by strange and contradictory legends. It is an American native, unknown elsewhere until the sixteenth century. It is generally believed that the name "turkey" came from the early discoverers' belief that the America they found was Asia; but logically, even under that misapprehension, the bird should have been called a Cathay hen. Confusion persisted when it received its scientific name, Meleagris. Meleagris literally means "guinea hen," a bird with no relation to the turkey.

The natives of Mexico and the Southwest had domesticated the turkey long before the Spaniards came, but in the Southwest it was grown for its feathers, not its flesh. The Spaniards took turkeys back to Spain, and thence they were distributed throughout Europe. Early English settlers brought turkeys to New England, only to find the woods full of wild turkeys. Later, when a national bird was being chosen, Ben Franklin and others urged the turkey for that honor. They lost the fight to the bald eagle.

The wild turkey, the deer and the buffalo sustained most of the pioneers as the frontier moved west. And the turkey, deprived of formal honors, eventually ran away with the November holiday.

Even there it comes to an ironic fate, colorful with cranberries, savory with sage, tasty with stuffing and gravy and mashed potatoes and, if you will, onions and turnips, mincemeat and pumpkin. The turkey, the all-American bird, provider of feathers and feasts, misnamed and imported to the land of its origins, symbol now of Thanksgiving. Long may the turkey gobble!

The Beginning   *November 26*

And when they had given thanks for life, for loved ones, for the purpose that had brought them here, they went about their tasks. And the dusk of Winter evening came early upon them, for Autumn was at its end and long nights were closing in.

Summer had not been easy, for it was a time of labor; but they had given thanks for that, too, for the chance to labor for themselves. And Autumn had not been easy, for it was a time of garnering, of gathering the small harvest from the woods and fields; but they had been thankful for the harvest, the chance to lay up the substance that must sustain them till another Spring. And now Winter was at hand.

They went about their tasks, cutting wood and snugging houses and caring for the beasts. The simple work, the drudging work, of living. And night closed in, the long night when ice would fringe the river and the trees in the forest would sigh in the toothed wind. The women spun, and the children combed the wool, awkwardly but persistently, and the men carved patiently at new porringers and wiping rods for their muskets and yokes for the oxen. The hearth fire eased the darkness and drove back the cold a little.

And one man looked up from his wood shaping and said, "We have made a clearing in the wilderness, and another year will see a larger clearing. A better garnering. We have made a beginning in a hostile world." And all who listened knew that it was so. Beginnings are the most difficult, next only to the dream itself, which is the great beginning of all enduring things. They had the dream, and now they knew that it would endure the Winter and live on and on.

Season in the Sun   *November 27*

The leaves lie deep in the woodland and the slanting sun lights the floor of the deepest thickets, and the rest that is Winter seems to have come over the land. But go there now and you may see the humbler greenery of this world, the venerable ancestors of those big-boled oaks and broad-topped elms and white-barked limber birches. Now the mosses and the creeping pine and cedar and the hardy ferns have the sunlight to themselves.

In green Summer they are lost to the eye. You feel the deep mats of tree moss underfoot in the shade where the meadow meets the woods, but you see the grass. The teeming colonies of hair moss and broom moss are there at the gnarly butts of the swamp maples, but the violets catch the eye, and the buttercups and the wild geraniums. And the ground cedar is lost in the green shadows of the underbrush.

Now you see them, unexpected green gleaming through the rifted leaves. The persistent fronds of the Christmas fern spread their grace against the gray stones of the old wall. The grape fern, beginning to turn purplish bronze, thrusts up through the dead grass. And the tangles where shadows once lay so deep are now alive with the green runners and spreading heads of creeping pine and all the other Winter greens that are known as club mosses.

They are old and humble and patient dwellers of this earth. Their kind are found in fossil beds, so like those we have today that there is no mistaking them. They were here long before the oaks and the maples, yes, and the violets and buttercups. It is good, and it is healthily humbling, to see them now, when the long, cold days stretch ahead. All things come, in due course, to their season in the sun, and this is theirs, literally as well as figuratively.

The Quiet Time   *November 28*

Quiet has come to the country, the Winter quiet that waits on no arbitrary season of calendar or solstice. It is not only an aural quiet, but a visual one, something seen and felt as well as heard. The insects that buzzed and hummed and scratched are silenced now, save for an occasional fireside cricket. And the songbirds have gone south with the sun, leaving the countryside to the crows, the jays and the lesser birds that may gossip among themselves but do little town crying and engage in no concerts. It is a quiet in which one will be able to hear snowflakes nudging each other as they fall.

The visual quiet is almost as complete, for now we have a world of muted colors. Maples stand in gray and brown nakedness, even the drifts of their leaves dulled by early leaching of rain and frost. Oaks, their trunks black with the damp of morning mist, wear the tatters of old, worn buckskin in their clinging leaves. Beeches stand stiff and silvery, stripped to the restless wind. And the sumac is a lifting of gnarled, frost-blackened fingers toward the distant sun.

The pines stand green, and the hemlocks, looking greener than they did in September but still subdued. The quiet of their green needs a backdrop of snow to call the eye to attention. The cedars dull into the background, the anonymous cedars.

Here and there one sees the blush of wild rose haws or the warmth of orange fruit on the bittersweet; and back in the woods is the occasional twinkle of partridgeberries. But they are the gem stones, the rare decorations, which make the grays, the browns and the greens seem even more quiet, more completely at rest.

Hoarfrost

This is the season when hoarfrost comes in the night to make magic of the commonplace. Walk abroad before the sun has risen more than a hand's breadth, and if the night has been seasonal, there is a crisp white filigree on grass blade, weed stem and withered leaf, a tracery of crystal that came in the damp, cold darkness and will vanish in the first warm breath of daylight. Walk across a lawn and the grass is brittle as spun glass. Scuffle a drift of leaves and you are shattering delicate crystal. Look at the newly risen sun through frosted branches and your eye is dazzled by the glint of ten million prisms.

Hoarfrost is ice crystal and almost as fragile as a snowflake. It fringes everything it touches. It makes a dead goldenrod stem a thing of grace and glitter. It transforms the withered flower head of Queen Anne's lace into an elaborately curved and carved chalice. The hoarfrosted milkweed pod is such a shell as no sea ever cast up, diamonded and decked with gleam. The blackberry bramble is no longer thorned, but fruited now with glistening frost berries. The reddened strawberry leaf has become all ruby and diamond.

Hoarfrost comes from the mysterious insistence of cold water to become a solid. It does this with magnificence and generosity, transforming everything it touches. It makes December blossom, for a few hours. It recasts a world that put away its finery a few weeks ago, gives it transient beauty again. Hoarfrost is the elaboration, the wonder and mysterious crystalline order, of a starry night brought down to earth.

The Certainties

The wind sweeps out of the west with the faint breath of blizzard far away; but the skies are clear, without even the shredded, high-flying clouds of storm. And so November leans toward December, and late Autumn creeps past, silent as the stars. The hush of Winter approaches, and short days lie upon the land.

Now is the time when the countryman has the country to himself. The visitors are gone, vacations over. Even the migrant birds are gone. The squirrels go quietly about their business. And a man has time to survey his world and understand his own place in it, if he is ever to understand.

Now it becomes clear that it isn't the little pleasures of the country that make life worth living there. It is rather the big assurances. The little pleasures are for the casual visitor; but one must live with the wind and the weather and know the land and the seasons to find the certainties. The flash of a goldfinch or the song of an oriole can delight the senses; but the knowledge that no matter how sharp or long the Winter they will be back again for another Spring provides an inner surety. To see a hillside white with dogwood bloom is to know a particular ecstasy of beauty; but to walk the gray Winter woods and find the buds which will resurrect that beauty in another May is to partake of continuity. To feel the frost underfoot and know that there is both fire and ice in the earth, even as in the patterned stars overhead, is to sense the big assurances.

Man needs to know these things, and they are best learned when the silence lies upon the land. No one can shout them. They need to be whispered, that they may reach the questing soul.

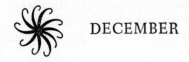

DECEMBER

December

December is the year in age and wisdom, a woman with starlight in her frosted hair and a snowflake on her cheek and a sprig of holly on her coat. The light in her blue eyes is young as this morning and old as time. She has known youth and love and age and heartbreak, and she still can smile, knowing that life is not all of either. She is December, which is a kind of summation not only of one year but of all years' ending.

For December is bare trees and the evergreens, it is rustling weed stem in the ruthless wind and a partridgeberry on the hillside. It is ground pine, older than the hills where it grows, and it is a seedling maple from two years ago clinging to one last scarlet leaf. It is a stiff-tailed young squirrel scrambling up an oak tree, and it is a mask-faced coon in the moonlit cornfield, listening for the hounds. It is ice on the pond and lichen on the rock and a flock of chickadees in the pine thicket.

December is a blizzard in Wyoming and a gale on the Lakes and the Berkshires frosted like a plate of cupcakes. It's fir trees going to the cities by the truckload, and red ribbon by the mile and tinsel everywhere. It's so many days till You-Know-When. It's the Winter solstice and the shortest day, and it's a snow shovel and galoshes and a muffler round the neck. It's 30 below in Medicine Hat.

December is the hungry owl and the fugitive rabbit, the woodchuck abed and the crow all alone in the pasture. It's soup in the kettle and a log in the fireplace and long wool socks. It's a wind at the door and a whisper in the air and a hush on the evening when the carols are sung. It's the wonder and the glory, and the Nativity.

Winter Color   *December 2*

The color, we say, is gone, remembering vivid October and verdant May. What we really mean is that the spectacular color has passed and we now have the quiet tones of Winter around us, the browns, the tans, a narrower range of greens, with only an occasional accent in the lingering Winter berries. But the color isn't really gone.

The meadow is sere tan, but that is a tan of a dozen different shades from gold to russet. The fallen leaves have been leached of their reds and yellows, but theirs is no monotone by any means. The bronze curve of the goldenrod stem emphasizes the ruddy exclamation point of the cattail. The rough brown bark of the oak makes the trunk of the sugar maple appear armored in rusty iron. The thorny stalk of the thistle stands beside the cinnamon seed head of the pungent bee balm. Dark eyes stare from the white parentheses of the stark birches, bronze tufts of one-winged seeds tassel the box elder, miniature "cones" adorn the black-brown alders at the swamp's edge.

In the woods, the insistent green of Christmas fern and partridgeberry leaf compete with the creeping ancients, ground cedar and running pine. Hemlock, spruce and pine trees cling to their own shades of green, individual as the trees themselves. And on their trunks are paint patches of the ancient lichen, tan and red and blue and green, like faint reflections of vanished floral color.

The color is still there, though its spectrum has somewhat narrowed. Perhaps it takes a Winter eye to see it, an eye that can forget October and not yearn for May too soon.

Snow

One of the penalties of modern life is the loss of appreciation of snow. The countryman realizes that snow nourishes and protects his fields and pastures and even helps to seal and insulate his house and barns against the cruelest bite of Winter. The youngster with a sled and the grownup with a pair of skis know the satisfaction of a snow-clad slope. But in city and suburb, snow has become a cold and slushy nuisance when it isn't a costly problem. To travelers everywhere snow is a blinding, slippery hazard to foot and wheel and wing.

Yet the snowflake, of itself, is a thing of fragile, evanescent beauty. It is a delicate water crystal, one of the most transient of all natural forms, a wisp of mist that has briefly acquired tangible shape. A snowfall can transform a woodland into a place of magic, a meadow into a shimmering wonderland. A snowdrift is the frozen grace of the wind, perfection of line and curve and form. Snow can temporarily restore the lost innocence to a scarred and naughty world of disillusionment and folly.

We know these things. We can believe in them for a little while at the beginning of any Winter. Then our comfort and our convenience are threatened, and we forget. We, and the snow itself, become victim of our own way of life. Snow becomes a problem, another phase of nature that man must be at war with to maintain his own elaborate complexities of living.

Shortest Month   *December 4*

December is the shortest month of the year. No argument will be accepted, if it is to the contrary; and those who point to February are merely making gestures. True, December does have thirty-one days, such as they are. But can you really call days those hurried little spans that come zipping past, once Thanksgiving is behind and Christmas lies just ahead? Certainly not. Why, if you even pause to check them off on the calendar, you have no time for anything else! The Thanksgiving turkey vanishes, and you turn around, and there is the Christmas tree waiting to be decorated. New Year's Day is here, and January. December is gone again.

There is no illusion about it, except for those who are innate sticklers. In round figures, December has only 288 hours of daylight; and that counts in even those dreary times when the sun sulks behind a mass of clouds all day. Even March, of evil reputation, can muster that many hours of daylight in twenty-four days. And June, magnificent June, does as well by us in only nineteen days.

What is a December day, anyway? Nine hours of daylight, with a few minutes left over at each end to turn the lights on and off. And fifteen hours of darkness. With a moon, to be sure, and a great many stars. But darkness, just the same. You eat breakfast by lamplight, hurry to work in half-light, and get home in darkness. You have four weekends in which to watch the sun scurry across the southern quadrant of the sky.

December? By sundown tonight we will have had just a little over thirty-seven hours of December daylight. Enough said?

The Lantern   *December 5*

This used to be the season when the farmer did his chores by lantern light, morning and evening. Nowadays electricity lights the barn and the barnyard in all but the most remote rural areas,

but almost any farmer with gray in his hair can recall the days of the kerosene lantern. And so can his wife.

The lantern smelled of kerosene, it gave only a feeble light by modern standards, and it was a constant fire hazard among the livestock. But it was as much of a necessity on the farm as the milk pail or the farmer's Winter boots. It was a portable lamp, a fuel can with a wick and a glass globe to enclose the flame, and a bail to carry it by. Farm work couldn't be done without it.

The farm wife knew it well. She saw that its tank was kept filled with kerosene, that the wick was trimmed or renewed, that its globe was clean. She hated it, but respected it, because it smelled of kerosene and sometimes leaked; and kerosene was not only a fire hazard, it polluted every scrap of food it reached. But it had to be kept in working order. Without the lantern, farm work couldn't be done.

The lantern lighted the way to the barn, the corn crib, the hen house, the woodshed. It hung on its peg in the barn while the milking was done. When a trip had to be made after dark, the lantern sometimes hung from the end of the wagon tongue to light the way feebly. More often it sat at the driver's feet, under the robe, to fend off chilblains. It was better than an open torch or a candle. But nobody regretted its passing. And nobody who ever did the chores by lantern light has forgotten.

❧ Kerosene? In the days I am here remembering, it wasn't called kerosene by those who worked by lantern light. It was coal oil, a plain, forthright term of Anglo-Saxon origins. Coal oil sold for about ten cents a gallon. If you asked for kerosene, the storekeeper gave you a quick look and a faint smile, filled your can from the coal-oil barrel and charged you twice as much.

The Night   *December 6*

No night, not even the Winter night, is quite as dark and silent as it seems. Go out and accept the night on its own terms, even now, and it takes on new or long-forgotten meaning. Walk a country road and you can see as well as feel the Winter night, light and alive in its own proportions.

Starlight is strangely brilliant, once you accept it. The whole sky has its own glow, which silhouettes the trees and the hills. It comes to life on a slope of frost-bronzed grass. It is reflected from the frosty trunks of the birches. It is magnified in the roadside pond, ice-silvered to mirror sheen. It almost gleams from a rooftop, and it is reflected from a darkened window. It is a cold, distant light, yet it is light that marks a path through the woods and gives shape and form to the roadside walls and rocky banks.

And though the insects are gone, the night is not silent. No fox may bark, no owl hoot, and yet the night is alive with sound and movement. The subtle movement and the infinitely varied voices of the wind. A leaf scuffs along the road. An oak tree, not yet completely naked, rustles crisply. The grasses sigh. There is the soft, intermittent whisper in the high tops of the elms. And the towering hemlocks murmur among themselves with a voice quite different from that of whispering pines.

You walk, and you see and you hear, and it is ancient knowledge re-remembered. No night is quite so dark as it seems, once you explore it; no night is without its familiar voices, once you are prepared to listen.

Chickadee Weather   *December 7*

Cold nights, chilly days, frost on the grass, perhaps snow in the air—such is chickadee weather. Now the little black-capped birds come down from the woodland to the dooryard, jaunty little beggars who can make out very well on their own but who amply pay for handouts with minor but gay song and friendly entertainment.

As birds, the chickadees are quite remarkable. A full-grown chick seldom weighs more than half an ounce, about the weight of the average letter we get in the mail. Inside that tiny body is a heart that beats close to 700 times a minute, so fast that in a stethoscope its sound is practically a buzz. Its body temperature ranges around 105 degrees, which in part accounts for that high-tension activity. On a cold day it needs its own weight in food to keep the inner fires burning. Its small fraction of an ounce of feathers, which can fluff it to the size of a sparrow, helps hold this inner warmth, and the dark color of its back and head gathers additional heat from the Winter sun.

But these are details and this bird is more than the sum of its anatomical parts. It is a lively spark of personality. It can be a ham actor, a bully, a wheedler, an acrobat, an unpredictable little gamin. It loves a human audience and comes to the dooryard feeder as much for companionship as for a snack. As an entertainer, it is all pro, the feathered song-and-dance performer who gets, and deserves, top billing on the Winter circuit of the dooryard feeders.

The Pause   *December 8*

Now the year begins to sum up in its own inconclusive way. In our own area, Winter is with us, whether the calendar admits it or not, the year's fourth season, rounding out a cycle. And, in the continuity of time, Winter overlaps the years and makes any summary incomplete. There have been sprouting and leafing, there have been flowering and maturity, there have been harvest and the falling leaf. Now there is rest, quiet, a time of forces consolidated, which is as near to a summing as any year affords.

Life is not all of a piece, and never was. Life is change, as we can see in any round of the seasons. Life is cause, and life is effect, and there is no escape from that. Those who would put a price on things can say that December is the price we pay for June. Others may say that June and December are opposite sides of the coin, that December's long nights are the dark equal of June's long days. But even that distorts the impersonal cycle of nature.

The hills now are enfolded in the sleep of the year's night, the time of rest. The busyness of sap and leaf has ebbed. The insect hum and scurry lie dormant in the hidden egg and pupa. The frog and the salamander hibernate in the mud and the woodchuck sleeps. The songbird's nest is abandoned. Life awaits the turning of the earth for a new burgeoning. And so there is a kind of summarizing in the pause, the hoarding of strength, with a quiet knowledge of a June to come, another Summer. For now it is the year's Winter, which is no more than a recurrent pause in the long span of life and time.

The Snowbirds   *December 9*

Of all our Winter birds, only two are known as snowbirds, and both are as true to the weather as the barometer. Just now our only snowbird is the junco, the genial slate-gray dooryard bird that comes south ahead of the snow. But when Winter really arrives, with a biting wind and swirling snow, our mid-Winter snowbirds, the snow buntings, will seem to come on the very wings of the storm.

Small wonder these little buntings are sometimes called snow larks or snowflakes, for they are the whitest of our land birds. Like the snow-clad weed patches they haunt, they are marked sparingly with black and brown above. On a blustery day they ride the wind like real snowflakes, and a flock rising from the ground seems to roll right over itself, like drifting snow. Find a wind-blown, Winter-bound weed patch, especially of ragweed or pigweed, and you almost certainly will find a flock of snow buntings making a meal. Listen between gusts and you will hear them, twittering as though they actually revel in rough weather.

It is still junco weather, and nobody is begging for a change. The juncos are pleasant company in any dooryard. But snow-bunting weather is sure to come eventually, and when it does it almost certainly will bring the mid-Winter snowbirds. They won't improve the weather one whit, but they will make it official, in a way, and they will add a cheery note even to a stormy day. Meanwhile, the juncos are quite satisfactory snowbirds to have around.

Fence Posts *December 10*

The sound of the ax in the back-country woodland these days doesn't necessarily mean that somebody is cutting firewood. Now is the time when the farmer "gets out" his fence posts. He is harvesting his pasture cedars, those slim, straight, blue-green trees that fill the open spaces and creep out onto the grassland. For the brush land just below the rocky ledges is not wasteland; it grows a crop that every farmer needs, fence posts.

They are red cedars, those trees, technically junipers, and their wood rots slowly. They have small blue berries, dark blue with a whitish bloom, and birds eat the berries and plant new cedars with their droppings. So now, when the farmer cuts his cedar posts, he thinks well of the birds which relieve him of one job of planting.

There he is on the ridge, cutting cedars, and the bite of his ax is good to feel. The echo is loud and lingering in the crisp air, and after a while the jays come to see what is going on and the chickadees come closer. A man cutting posts can create a good deal of excitement in the woods, and yet he is somehow at home there, and the birds know it. He's a little like a tree himself, rooted in the soil and living with the seasons, shaped by the weather and patient with the years.

So he cuts his posts, and he thinks that maybe no man should quarrel too much with the world around him. Good things grow in odd places, and what's poor land for one crop is good land for another. It depends on what a man wants and what he needs. Crop land needs fences, and fences need posts, and posts grow where crops for market won't grow. Maybe it all evens out. It seems to, in a minor way, when a man is up there on a December day getting out his posts.

A Song for Supper   *December 11*

Among the daily customers at the Winter bird feeder, the tree
sparrows are almost as common as the chickadees, and usually as
welcome. One reason is that the tree sparrow, that fellow with a
single dark button on his light gray vest, will volunteer a song for
his supper even in the midst of a snowstorm. He doesn't go into
ecstasies over the weather in December, perhaps, but he is more
than a mere twitterer even now. By January he will be as much of
a songster as a chickadee, and by February he will sing about
Spring, regardless of the weather.

The name is deceptive, for this fellow is essentially a bird of
the bushes and the underbrush. Even at nesting time—and the
tree sparrow nests up around Hudson Bay—these sparrows stay
close to the ground. And the Summer habits are carried south in
the Winter. For the tree sparrow is a migrant, sometimes going as
far south as the Carolinas. Those that Winter here will be on
their way back north no later than April.

Every farmer and every gardener who knows his birds wel-
comes the tree sparrow, who probably consumes as many weed
seeds, ounce for ounce, as any bird alive. In a state the size of
Connecticut the tree sparrows alone will eat as much as eleven
tons of weed seed in a single season. What they eat at the feeding
station is small pay for such a service. And even the handouts are
paid for in song as well as service. Who could ask more than that?

Wind and Weather   *December 12*

When storm sweeps across the land or when sudden cold grips
with icy fingers, there is the temptation to say that nature is giving
man a hard time of it. But the fact is that nature is neither
vindictive nor benevolent. Man merely finds conditions to his
liking or his distaste. The wind and the weather are as unware of
man as they are of the hibernating woodchuck or the migrating

bluebird. The only emotion involved is man's emotion. The big primal forces, of which wind and weather are prime examples, were doing pretty much these same things before man appeared; and if man should vanish as a species, they would go right on doing those things.

Humility is not one of mankind's outstanding attributes. It seems to be instinctive for man to look upon the world as something made especially for him and to regard natural hazards as an affront to his status. Actually, every accomplishment of any consequence, from the taming of fire to the development of an atomic power plant, has been a kind of adaptation by man to his environment, not the other way around. And so is the fact that man still wears a raincoat when it rains and mittens when a cold wind blows.

In a cosmic sense, this must have its amusing aspects. Man, the master of his environment, facing a snowstorm and an icy wind in an overcoat and mittens! Strange armor indeed to wear when facing a vigorous opponent. But the fact is that man, so armored, has survived some pretty rigorous battles. It could be that man needs his strangely oblique arrogance. Maybe that is one of his major weapons in this endless battle with such impersonal forces. And that, too, might call for an appreciative cosmic smile.

That Thermometer   *December 13*

What is there about a thermometer that rouses the competitive instinct in a man? Particularly in the Winter. Once the first breath of chill December has been felt, man—particularly rural or suburban man—gets out his warm coat, his muffler, his gloves, his galoshes, and makes sure the outdoor thermometer is where he can see it the moment he gets up in the morning. Then he begins competing—with the weather man, with his neighbors, with his office mates, with everyone in sight.

Does the weather report say it was down to 25 this morning? Ha! Now at *my* house it was down to 22! Or 21, or maybe even to

20. And the man with a thermometer looks around for a challenge. If someone else can match his temperature, that's verification. If someone can better it—and "better" in this instance means lower, not higher—there is reason for chagrin. That evening he must move the thermometer away from the warm house, preferably into the path of the raw night wind.

And so it goes, the official temperature skidding slowly toward January's zero, the thermometer man's reports always, if he can manage, at least one degree lower, preferably two or even three. And he can usually manage, since his is a run-of-the-mill thermometer and his front porch or back stoop is not really sheltered. The official temperature becomes par, and the man with the back-porch thermometer breaks par steadily.

And why not? Winter's supposed to be cold, isn't it? If it's cold, we want it to be icy, bone chilling, awesome. What's the use of having a thermometer if it doesn't give a temperature worth talking about?

The Trumpeter   *December 14*

Cygnus, the Swan, is in full flight along the lower reaches of the Milky Way these December evenings. Go out a few hours after sunset and look just a bit north of west, and there not far above the horizon you can find the constellation, which some know as the Northern Cross. Its major stars do, indeed, form a large cross, with Deneb at the top and Albiero at the foot. And not far from Deneb is a dark gap in the Milky Way known to lay observers as the Northern Coalsack. Deneb, according to those who measure such matters, is 10,000 times as bright as the sun and is 650 light-years away from the earth. To the naked eye it is just one of the brighter stars in that area.

The constellation actually looks no more like a swan than it does like a duck or a pigeon or any other bird with outstretched wings. For that matter, it could be the Iceboat, if one so imagined. There is the long keel, there is the cross-member, there are the runners and the mast, all marked out by the stars. But Greek mythology had no iceboats, and it did have swans.

Know it as the Swan, and it flies out of the north, which is altogether proper even here in America. Our native swans nest in the north and migrate south, and seldom are they seen on the Eastern seaboard; you have to look westward to see them even at the height of the migration, which is no longer anything approaching a mass flight. A good many of us will never again see a wild swan on the wing. But there in the northwest, winging through the stardust clouds of the Milky Way, is Cygnus. And if we were of a mind to, we could very well call it the Trumpeter, honoring one of the most magnificent swans that ever bowed a pinion over this earth.

The December Wind   *December 15*

The December wind, like a December day, seems always to be in a hurry. Winter has no time for breezes. Even the weather systems that move across the land travel faster than they did last Summer. And if a cold wind feels stronger than a warm wind did, that is no illusion. Winter's cold air is literally heavier than the warm air of mid-Summer and exerts more pressure, even at the same velocity. Its force, as well as its chill, is concentrated.

The December wind hurries over the hilltops and down the valleys, and the leafless trees offer little restraint. Their bare branches shiver and rattle and the wind rushes on, swishing and whistling. Even if it is a wind freighted with cold rain, there is no heartening promise in it. There is, instead, the threat of sleet or snow, for the winds that sweep down out of Medicine Hat and Bismarck have teeth, however hidden, that were whetted on sterner fare than the milk of moderation.

And in the quick December dusk the wind has the voice of the running wolf and the hungry owl. It snarls, it keens, it howls, even among the pines. It hurries toward the night, when it can be as cold as the Winter moon, as impersonal as the stars. Small wonder the woodchuck hibernates from it, the bear retires to its den, and the deer huddle in the hemlock thickets. Even the hills seem to hunch their shoulders and brace themselves against the hurrying Winter wind.

Balancing the Year   *December 16*

The short days are upon us. It will be another week before the Winter solstice, but the day's change now is slight. Daylight, sunrise to sunset, will shorten only another two minutes or so before it begins to lengthen. The evening change, in fact, has already begun; the year's earliest sunset past; but sunrise will continue to lag on through the year's end.

Thus the year balances its accounts. In our latitude we know that each year brings the time when not only the candle but the hearth fire must burn at both ends of the day, symbol not of waste but of warmth and comfort. The sun cuts a small arc far off to the south and shadows and cold lie deep. It is for this time that we, if we live close to the land, lay up the firewood and the fodder. Now we pay for the long days of Summer, pay in the simple currency of daylight. Hour for hour, the accounts are balanced.

And yet, the short days provide their own bonus. The snows come, and dusk and dawn are like no other time of the year. We come to a long Winter night when the moon rides full over a white world and the darkness thins away. For the full-moon night is as long as the longest day of Summer, and the snowy world gleams and glows with an incandescent shimmer.

Year to year, we remember the short days but we tend to forget the long nights when the moon rides high over a cold and brittle-white world. Not only the moon nights, but the star nights, when it seems one can stand on a hilltop and touch the Dipper. Who would not cut wood and burn a candle for a few such nights a year?

Winter has its purposes, no doubt of that. If there weren't such a season, someone would have to invent it. Or decree it; though no season ever was or will be amenable to decrees. We need Winter's whimsicalities and extremes, and even its simplicities.

When except in Winter can one watch the sun rise at a decent hour? Seeing the sun rise may not seem to be a basic necessity, but everyone should have the experience a few times. And when, except in Winter, can one learn about ice? Ice is comforting in a glass, but man should know more about ice than can be learned from an ice cube. Ice is a primal element. Or snow. Some of a snowflake's beauty can be transmitted in a photograph, but until one has seen a snowflake in the air, felt it crowding down one's neck or faced it atop a four-foot drift, what does one know about snow? Very little.

Take less evanescent matters, such as soup. Nobody can really appreciate soup until it becomes more than a minor item on a long menu. Soup comes into its own only as a body-and-soul-satisfying meal. In Winter. Or a hearth fire, which is a cheery companion on a Fall evening but becomes a deep and abiding comfort when Winter's icy knuckles are at the door. Or a house, which never reveals its true character until you've spent a Winter in it.

But the enduring factor, the really indispensable one, is simplicity. Of all seasons, Winter is the only simple one. And man, who can ensnarl himself unbelievably in problems of his own making, for once in the year faces two simple problems, warmth and food. Winter gets down to essentials, and it does its best to get man there, too. We all struggle against it, but for a few months we get a glimpse of stark and even painful simplicity.

White Birch

Of all the leafless trees in the Winter landscape, the most eye-catching and spectacular is the white birch, particularly when seen against the grays and browns of a snowless hillside. It has a grace of line, a slimness of bole, a clean, sleek look that is sheer beauty.

From the earliest days the white birch has been storehouse and source of elemental materials for both the settler and the woodland wanderer. Its bark provides a usable paper, tinder for fires in the wet woods, enough nourishment to save man or beast from starvation; and from it came the canoe, shaped and sheathed by the tough, enduring bark itself before man adapted cedar and canvas and, eventually, aluminum, to the same purpose. Wigwams were roofed with that bark, and buckets and boxes were made from it. And in the Springtime the rising sap of the white birch was boiled down, like maple sap, for a syrup and a sugar that sweetened the woodsman's diet and disposition. The white inner wood, easily worked, provided an infinite variety of woodenware for the pioneer cabin and still provides everything from spools to bowls for the contemporary household.

One can scarcely imagine our Northeastern hills without the white grace of the birch against the gaunt Winter hillsides of naked oak and maple or the deep greens of pine and hemlock. Other birches have their own qualities and virtues, but the white birch is the noblest of them all, beautiful to look upon and full of simple utility. In Spring it rouges the gray hillside with its buds. In Summer it is a whispering canopy of shade. But in Winter it is simply beautiful, white beauty in a drab gray world.

A Man Must Go and See

A man can go out now and sense the dimensions of his world. If he's a countryman he may take his shotgun or his ax, and he probably will whistle his dog along; but gun or ax is an excuse, not a reason. The reason is that a man needs to go up onto the ridge or down across the pasture and along the fence row, just to look and feel and know.

It's an open world, now, where a man can see. He can see out of his own valley and beyond his own hills, and even in the woods there are vistas, distances. All Summer long the countryman's world was bounded by fences and stone walls that marked his fields. They were reminders that life has boundaries and that a man who would reap must first sow and then tend his crops. Then came Fall and the final harvest. The barns had to be filled, the cribs loaded with corn, the cold pantry and the root cellar amply stocked. The place had to be snugged for Winter. Life still had its boundaries of duty, and man couldn't deny it.

But now the snugging is finished. There are still chores to be done, morning and evening, and one of these days there will be snow to be cleared in the barnyard, paths to be shoveled, roads to be opened. Winter will set in. But for a little while, just now, there are hours in the day when a man can say, "I think I'll go look at the cedars, see how many posts I can cut when I get to it." Or at the pines, which can provide a few sawlogs. Or see how the fences are. And he can shoulder his ax or his gun and go. And maybe look at the cedars, or the pines, or the fences, but mostly just look, just look and feel and know the dimensions of the world.

The Abandoned Farm   *December 20*

Leave the main highways, take the back roads, then get out and walk. Up the hillsides you may find the old farms, long since overgrown, cellar holes caved in, barns now a rubble, dooryards occasionally marked by a gnarled old lilac bush. The hayfields and upland pastures are thick with oak and ash and maple, the farm roads are mere traces, gullied and overgrown. Those who lived there worked the land out, grew old, and passed away.

Often there is the persistent remnant of an orchard, a few old apple trees with frosted little apples like colorful balls on grotesque gray Christmas trees. Ground cedar often grows there, adding green festoons, and pine and cedar form a backdrop. Deer come there for the frosted apples, and foxes for rabbits. Grouse roar in sudden flight at human approach. Jays jeer and chickadees call from the pines. It is a strangely busy and even festive place, deserted though it is.

Practical people wonder why those forgotten hillside farmers left the valleys. The valley land has deeper soil, better shelter, more water, is easier of access. But when one stands on such a hillside and looks out across the valleys, one comes to at least a glimmer of understanding. There always have been among us those whose eyes need distance and whose minds refuse to see the hills as barriers or the valleys as refuges. Always there have been those who found satisfactions in living a little apart, and for them the easy way never is the happy one. Those farmers are gone, but their human strain lives on, leavening the race, knowing that ease and efficiency are not enough.

The Clown   *December 21*

Of all the Winter birds, the clown of the lot is the nuthatch. Not that he shows any sign of conscious clowning; far from it! The nuthatch is as serious a bird as you will meet at any feeding station. That is a part of his absurdity. He is short and fat. His bill is ridiculously long, and slightly tiptilted. His tail is too short. So is his neck. And his beady black eyes are set so close together he looks either cross-eyed or ridiculously near-sighted. And, to cap it all, he doesn't know that a bird can't go down a tree trunk headfirst. Not knowing it, he turns his stubby tail to the sky and blithely walks down, headfirst, searching the bark for bugs as he goes. Maybe other birds can't do it, but the nuthatch can.

And his voice! Technically, and by ornithological definition, the nuthatch is a songbird. He has vocal organs. And how does he use them? To utter a nasal *yark, yark, yark,* a little petulant, a little questioning. No variation. Nothing approaching a melody. Just *yark, yark, yark,* always in the same key, always the same note, whether he is gloating over a fresh piece of suet or warning a chickadee to stand off. In the Spring the nuthatch has what passes for a song, a mating song. It is something like *too-too-too,* as tuneless as the *yark* call, but in a different key.

None of this is to belittle or berate the nuthatch, an exemplary bird if there ever was one. He is not quarrelsome, or noisy, or pilfering. He is a good neighbor, and a welcome Winter guest, and he eats his full share of noxious bugs the year around. But he is a funny bird, for all that. He would look right at home with a slapstick tucked under one wing and a jester's cap with bells on his head.

WINTER

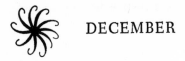 DECEMBER

The Rhythm   *December 22*

So we come to another solstice when, by the calendar, Winter begins in our northern hemisphere. We know the precise day and hour and minute when it will happen. We no longer do as the ancients did, pleading with a sun god for mercy, performing elaborate rites to persuade the sun to return from its six months' southing. We know, rite or no rite, that the sun will climb the sky again, as we say, and dark nights shorten and daylight lengthen into eventual Spring and Summer again.

And yet even this knowledge cannot take away vast and basic wonder. For the Winter solstice, immutable and predictable as it is, is but another phase of the rhythm that beats through the least of the atoms, through the throbbing of the human heart, and through the seasons and the years themselves. There it is, in our very breath, our words, our songs, our birthing and loving and growing old.

The solstice is no more, and unmistakably no less, than another beat in the pulse of time. All life partakes of that pulse, and even the ancients who performed the rites knew and revered the rhythms. There was an almost sacred order to the seasons, an order still unchanged and unchanging. Man lived by the rhythms, and he knew it. And no matter in what language we disguise them, man still lives by the rhythms.

A solstice, and another Winter. Change within the eternal constant. And there lies the great assurance for man, whose pulse, whose breath, whose very life is of a rhythm beyond his understanding.

The Greens   *December 23*

And now we gather the greens, the festive greens. Townsmen, villagers, and countrymen, going to the florist, the corner store, the upland woodlot, returning with the pine and spruce and hemlock, the mistletoe and holly, for wreaths and sprays and the tree itself. The greens, the needled and bright-berried symbols of life and hope and belief which we gather as the Winter solstice nears. Not for the solstice, knowingly, but for the festival of faith which comes so soon after. For Christmas.

They are old, the greens we gather, old in geologic time and old in man's veneration. Since man has known Winter, they have stood in the cold and the snow and the darkness as reminders that all Winters have their end and that life endures. Long ago the ancients brought the green boughs into their firelit halls at the time of the solstice, when night lay long and cold and deep over the land, as reminder that life and leaf would, without fail, return and endure. And when the new faith, born with the Child in Bethlehem, came to those lands it gave new and deeper meaning to old customs and beliefs. The wreath and the tree of evergreen took on a symbolism that reached beyond the solstice to the soul itself.

Thus the beginnings of a solemn festival of peace and hope and understanding in which nations the world over join this week. A festival of life newborn when the year is at its nadir, of faith and hope in the midst of Winter dark. A festival of lights and greens and gifts and prayers, for its symbols and its ceremonies are many and diverse among the nations. But everywhere a festival of peace and goodwill, vigorous and verdant as the greens we gather now.

Holy Days   *December 24*

We call them the holidays, too seldom remembering that they are holy days, days of reverence for life and the spiritual meanings implicit in it. Root meanings that go back to pagan times relate the word "holy" to "whole" and even to "healthy," in the sense of completeness. Even in the early days of the Christian era, holiness and a degree of reverence extended to a host of everyday things and natural phenomena that we now have made commonplace, to our loss.

There were holy plants, among them the holy mallow. We still know it, still grow it in our country dooryards, but today we call it the hollyhock and forget its earlier significance. There were holy trees, each for a particular reason, among them one with thorny green leaves and bright red berries. We grant it holiday status today, but in the way we spell and pronounce its name, holly, we ignore the meaning it once had. There were even holy fish, among them the *holi butte,* in Middle English terms. It was a holy flounder, but we now call it the halibut and only the philologist recognizes the original meaning in the name.

There was mystery and there was reverence for the whole of life, healthy mystery and holy reverence, before man began saying he knew all the answers. The basic mystery prevails, and on occasion man can even admit that he neither made the earth nor set the stars in their courses. The holidays we now celebrate are such an occasion, holy days for reverence and humility.

The Wonder December 25

Not the least of the wonders we commemorate this week was the simplicity surrounding the Birth itself. A carpenter named Joseph went with his young wife up from Nazareth to Bethlehem, the town of his fathers, to enroll for taxation as the governing Romans had ordered. Bethlehem was a simple hill town of no particular consequence at the time. Joseph and Mary arrived late and weary, to find that the inn was crowded; so they took shelter in the stable with other latecomers. Second best, but humble travelers could not choose. And there, in the stable, the Child was born.

Thus the simple beginnings. Add the shepherds on the night hills, the appearance of the angel, their journey to the stable, and it still remains one of the least adorned of all the great stories we cherish. It is as simple as was the Man himself and His teaching. As simple as the Sermon on the Mount, which still remains as the ultimate basis of Christian belief and, in its essence, of the belief of free men of goodwill everywhere.

There were the night hills, with the little town among them. And in a stable there was born One who came to speak to multitudes about freedom and justice and fundamental right. One who spoke in a simple tongue, in terms of the beasts of the land and the birds of the air and the lilies of the fields, and of man's responsibility to man. The Kings and captains were marching up and down the land, in full panoply, even as He was being born, and in the end they seemed to silence him. But it is His simple words that still live, not theirs; and it is the Birth in the stable that we solemnly commemorate now, not the gathering at the crowded inn.

The Next Day December 26

In the dawn of the next day the shepherds returned to their flocks out among the hills. The stars were gone with the night. Looking back at the little town there on the ridge, they could see the inn, but not the stable; and in the first, long-shadowed sunlight they could see a few early-risen travelers in the courtyard preparing to resume their journey, unware.

The shepherds hurried on. Their flocks would be leaving their bedground to graze on the dew-wet grass from which they got most of their water in this sparsely watered land, and the boy helpers left behind would have trouble holding the various flocks apart.

But even as they hurried, one and another of them looked at each other. Outwardly it was like any other day they had ever known. Yet they had seen a wonder, felt a remarkable thing, and they looked at each other to see if all had seen and felt these things. They had. The wonder shone upon their faces.

Then one among them paused to tie a loose sandal thong, and when he stood up he looked back whence they had come. One thing he must know. He looked back at the humble village of Bethlehem-Judah. Then he looked beyond, over the hills to the north, where lay Jerusalem, busy metropolis and center of the priesthood. And he said to himself: "It was for simple men like me. So it would happen in Bethlehem-Judah, not Jerusalem. Even in a stable."

And he was content. He hurried on to join the others. It was a simple wonder, revealed to simple men. It was for all men, not merely for the lawgivers and the ritemakers in the temples. And so, with the wonder of Bethlehem upon them, the shepherds returned to their flocks in the bright light of the morning.

Questioner   *December 27*

The owl, that bird of onomatopoetic name, is a repetitious question wrapped in feathery insulation especially for Winter delivery. He is the Winter's equivalent of the Summer's whippoorwill, the persistent night crier, especially the bird often called the hoot owl. Strictly speaking, there's no such thing as a hoot owl. The bird so referred to usually is a barred owl, occasionally a great horned owl. Both of them hoot, though in different keys and with different emphases. But many owls are popularly misnamed. The small screech owl, for instance, whimpers and whines and whistles but doesn't really screech. And only an occasional barn owl lives in a barn.

The barred owl, the most common of the hooters, is a big bird, somewhat larger than a crow. He has a claw for a beak, he seems to wear spectacles over his big eyes, and he has no feather tufts that look like ears. The great horned owl is still bigger, often with a wingspread of five feet, and he does have the ear tufts which excuse the name. Both are night hunters of renown, but while the barred owl seldom tackles anything bigger than a rabbit, the great horned owl can kill a woodchuck.

We know them by their voices, primarily. The barred owl's call consists of six or seven repeated notes, usually with a rising, questioning intonation at the end. Two barred owls hooting at each other on a Winter's night can sound like a whole flock. The great horned owl has a deeper voice and more of a challenge. He can make the darkness tense and quivering. And either of them can make a December night seem full of omens. Who else can ask so demanding a question on a brittle, star-bright night?

The Winter Stars   *December 28*

The Great Bear is now down on the horizon at evening, come down, the legends say, to wash his paws in the deep December lakes before they are all iced in. And the Little Bear hangs by his tail from the North Star. Cassiopeia, the Queen, sits high in the sky, and off toward the west Cygnus, the Swan, is in flight toward another hemisphere, the eternal migrant. The Big Dog and the Little Dog, off to the east, watch Orion, the Hunter, as he faces Taurus and the zenith. Almost overhead are the Pleiades, those seven shy sisters who are best seen from the corner of the eye.

These are star nights, with the moon late rising, in its last quarter today, and with Winter-brilliant skies. Walk the countryside these evenings and the whole universe accompanies you, for the earth is all open now to the starlight, leaf fall complete. The stars lean so close that if one stood tiptoe on the highest hill he might grasp at least one star in his tingling fingers.

It is illusion, of course, but the December stars seem twice as brilliant as those of June, for the sky is doubly clear, the mist chilled out of it and the dust of Summer settled at last. An illusion, but a pleasant one on a brittle night; the sun seems so far away that the stars should come closer. We should be able to glimpse eternity through those spark holes in the blanket of the long night. And perhaps we do. Where else is such order, such an eternal pattern, as in those stars that light the Winter sky?

Ice   *December 29*

Perhaps it is because ice is so common that it seems so simple. After all, ice is only frozen water, and we live with it every Winter. In one form or another, we plow it, shovel it, ski on it, skate on it, skid on it, bless it and curse it. Ice is frost and sleet and snow. It is the glacier, the hard surface of a Winter pond, the icicle on the eave, the treacherous glare on the highway. It is marvelously varied and infinitely complex.

As frost, it heaves and aerates the farmer's soil. It turns your breath into a shimmering cloud on a brittle-cold day. It creates patterns of fantastic beauty on a window pane, creates halos around the sun and the moon; it jewels weed stems and bushes. It also bursts water pipes, heaves foundations, splits rocks, alters the shapes of mountains. Evanescent as mist, frost is also one of the most powerful levers there is, an elemental force.

As snow, ice becomes one of the most fragile and beautiful crystals we ever see, incredibly various in detail, awesomely persistent in its sixfold pattern. Drive those flakes with a gale and chill that wind with zero temperatures and ice becomes a blizzard that can paralyze a countryside and cripple a city. Compact those fragile flakes and they create a glacier and carve valleys.

Ice can dam a great river. It can maim a whole woodland. It can choke a port, even change a climate. Ice is never simple, never trivial. It is one of the earth's very fundamentals.

The Tomorrows   *December 30*

The old year dies and we face the new year as though it were an entity, new as a newborn babe. A new calendar with twelve leaves, one for each month. Something in us, some need for the specific, the orderly, the mathematical exactitude, calls for such a demarcation. Yet any year, regardless of arbitrary time, is like a circle; you can start at any point upon it and, following the circle, you come back to that point. Our year, our circle, happens to be a cycle of the seasons, planting, growing, reaping, resting; and thus it is a part of the earth, the soil and the flowing waters as well as of the stars by which it is gauged.

No year stands by itself, any more than any day stands alone. There is the continuity of all the years in the trees, the grass, even in the stones on the hilltops. Even in man. For time flows like water, eroding and building, shaping and ever flowing; and time is a part of us, not only our years, as we speak of them, but our lives, our thoughts. All our yesterdays are summarized in our now, and all the tomorrows are ours to shape.

No year is complete. Even the seasons into which we divide the years overlap the arbitrary markers. Winter ends one year and begins the next, and the growth of each Spring is from the root and seed of the past. It is the continuity that matters, the inevitability of tomorrow, which gives meaning to the numbers themselves. Ten or a hundred has no meaning without the continuity of numbers behind it, other numbers beyond. Tomorrow implies a now and a yesterday. And year's end is neither an end nor a beginning but a going on, with all the wisdom that experience can instill in us.

Year's end comes on the wings of a chattering jay and a cawing crow, and a wind that rustles the sere oak leaves in the star-glimmered night. The jay chatters of short Winter days, and the crow caws of the long Winter nights. And the wind's song is the song of time, of the years, the endless round of the years.

No year is complete in itself. There is the overlap, the continuity, the seasons in order and in unaltered and unalterable sequence. Even Winter belongs to no one year, complete. It closes one year, by the calendar, and opens the next, the new. Snows heap the meadows and ice stills the brook, and the wind of one year passes over; and the snow still whitens the hilltops, the ice still seals the flowing waters as another year wheels into line.

There is no end and no beginning save as one life ends or another begins. And the lives themselves flow one into another, the wisdom, the understanding, the hopes and dreams and aspirations. It is on the dreams of yesterday that tomorrow's reality takes root. The generations rise one upon another. But they rise, and the dreams become reality.

Time, the years, the seasons, the dreaming and the hopes which throb with life even under the ice and snow. There is an order to all things, a pressure of progression, and the winds themselves will die into nothingness and the tides wither away before the hopes shall have ended, the aspirations frozen forever. Year builds upon year, even as the seasons follow. And year's end is no end at all, but only a pause, a time for the deep breath that marks the next step forward. There is no halt, no turning back. Tomorrow rises in the east, and all the tomorrows.

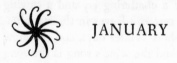 JANUARY

Another Year   *January 1*

The old year is gone, the new year begun, and those of us who
set store by the calendar draw a line to sum up a total, since it is
man's habit to count the minutes and the days and try to map
time. Nature, of course, has her own map of time, and although
man's calculations may approximate it, they miss the mark re-
peatedly. If we insist on starting the year in mid-Winter, the
solstice would be the logical moment, and the solstice occurred
nine days ago. The ancients, being practical people, started their
year with the vernal equinox, the beginning of Spring.

But, being insistently illogical, we follow long habit and in-
grained tradition and give this day unwonted significance. We
draw a mythical total line, hoping somehow to stop time long
enough to sum up. But even before we have totted the first
column, time has gone beyond us. Time doesn't wait for totals.
Only the tax collector can command time, and even he can't
check the sun in its course. The sun already leans toward Spring
and another Summer.

A new year begins, as we say. And the latent bud on the branch
doesn't stir one whit, the blossom in the bulb sleeps undisturbed
in the frozen ground. The woodchuck's hibernating pulse doesn't
quicken one beat, and the deer in the thicket is just as hungry as

he was yesterday. Man is the only animal to whom this new year is important. All the others live by the day and the season.

The old year passes. We draw up the totals, and the stars wheel and the sun slowly widens its arc, creating their own years. Spring is already on the way, the Spring that knows no calendar.

The Cold Slope   *January* 2

Now comes the long, slow haul up the cold slope toward Spring and April. The cold days and the long nights are ours, the best and the worst of Winter. Long nights and early evenings, fireplace evenings for long thoughts and simple comforts. Star nights, when the old patterns in the sky gleam with a promise of the nearest certainty, the most enduring continuity, that is visible from any Winter window or any snowy road. Late dawns, when the gray world comes alive after darkness and chill that seemed so deep they might last forever. High noons, with a sun so far off to the south that only the faith of generations can believe that it will be overhead again, come June. Winter, which drives man in upon himself and tests his mettle and his understanding.

January and February are the darkest months, and the coldest, and the snowiest. In our part of the world this is the time when the rocks lose the last of their Autumn heat and the earth itself heaves with frost. Now the seep among the stones turns to ice and levers the stones apart. The ice shoulders the river valleys and splits the cliffs and loosens the soil in the meadows. This is the time of cold, inexorable force working silently all around us.

But the ice will pass, with the passing of the long nights. Streams will flow free again, and the rocks will lie warm in the sun, and birds will sing and trees bud and leaf. Spring will come. Already the days lengthen. The sun is already in the sky almost four minutes longer than it was a week ago. By January's end the daylight will be almost three-quarters of an hour longer than it was at the beginning. The slope lessens as we climb from Winter's nadir. That we know, for it has always been so.

The Killer Wind

Cold can maim, but the wind is the killer. Those who live with blizzards every Winter know this and have a deep respect for the wind. Still cold, even well below zero, is tolerable because it saps the warmth of life slowly and can be endured with ordinary precautions. But when wind is added to such cold, the inner fires of life are endangered because the wind sucks away the vital warmth faster than it can be renewed. From time to time, we in the Northeast have to learn again to respect the Winter wind and fear its consequences. We have to recognize it for the elemental force it is.

To a considerable degree we have tempered the direct effects of Winter weather by our modern way of life in the city, the suburbs, even in the country. But the barriers we have built, dependent as they are on power and transportation, are themselves vulnerable. Combine wind and cold, add snow, and the whole intricate web begins to give way. Highways are blocked, power lines crippled, communities isolated. Then we are doubly at the mercy of the weather because we have delegated not only our comfort but our safety to the machines and those who can keep them running.

We have never really mastered the Winter wind. At best, we now can hide from it a little while and hoard our inner fires. But our safety eventually lies in the weather itself, in the relaxation of the storm. Those who repair the vulnerable web ease the danger, but until the killer wind has died we live beleaguered.

Days Lengthen

January 4

The change is slight, but the span of daylight now lengthens toward March and the vernal equinox. That is one thing you must say for any January: Its daylight hours increase rather than diminish. Cold may strengthen, as the old saying goes, and snow may deepen and ice may thicken on pond and river, but sunset comes later, day by day. The long, cold nights are being nibbled away.

Sunrise still lags, and it will continue to lag for another week. But sunset has already begun to change. At the season's earliest, sunset occurred at 4:12, and now it is delayed until 4:25, a clear gain of thirteen minutes of daylight. A week from today sunset will come at 4:31, another minute of gain each day. By the end of the month sunset will be still another half-hour later, and by then the sunrise will be enough earlier to make a total gain of almost three-quarters of an hour of daylight.

Thus do Winter's days change, even as molasses-slow January flows past. And by February, no matter what the weather, Spring will be within hailing distance. You can see it, even through a haze of frost crystals, in the earlier dawn. You can see it, even behind a bank of snow clouds, at dusk. Spring will be there, waiting out the lengthening days; and you will know that the day and the night partake of change, even as the wind, even as the temperature. You know, by then, that Winter has an ending.

You know it now if you watch the sunset closely. That ice-green band of light may mark the horizon, and that knifing wind may rattle the door, but they come later than they did a week ago. That's the promise. That's the proof.

Winter Dividends   *January 5*

Now is the time when the countryman gets his dividends on last summer's work. It's all a part of the old, old pattern, but on a short Winter day one is forced to review it and even to admire the venerable truth in which it is grounded. A man does his best by the land, gives it his sweat and his muscle ache, and it yields its corn and oats and hay. Being a reasonably provident person, a man stows away the yield of the annual season of growth. Now he feeds that harvest to his cattle, Winter-bound in the barn, and they convert it into milk. So, through these cold months, last

Summer's sun and rain and lush green growth go off to market in the milk tanker. And the countryman's daily schedule slacks off a bit, with time to catch his breath. Last Summer's overtime is evened off.

Somewhat the same thing happens in the country kitchen. Last Summer's garden is there in the pantry and the cold cellar and the freezer. The war with the weeds and the insect pests is all over with and the aching back can now relax. Potatoes are in the bin, beets and carrots are in the sand box, tomatoes are in the jars. And the jams, the jellies, the relishes, the pickles and all the other items of the garner, the sum of seed and tending, wind and weather, plucking, picking and preserving. Summer is there, ready for the countryman's Winter fare.

None of it comes free. It was all bought and paid for with sweat-stained, weary hours and days and weeks. And that's the basic truth that one remembers. You work for what you get. But it is comforting to sit back and enjoy it now.

Dogwood   *January 6*

Next Spring should be a magnificent season for flowering dogwood. The leafless trees now are heavily laden with flower buds, which will brave out the Winter and burst into white loveliness next May. If all goes well, they should be a dazzle in the woodlands, for the buds are both big and plentiful; every twig seems to be nobbed with at least one bud.

Look closely at these buds and you get a false sense of Spring just around the corner. Their stems are a faint lavender-green, a lively color. And the base of the bud itself is that soft, new green of a garden pea fresh from its pod. On top, the buds are an inconspicuous reddish-brown, but if you crouch beneath a tree and look up you see the green undersides like a dappling of young leaflets in April.

The buds even now are as much as three-eighths of an inch across and seem to be almost bursting their skins. Roughly four sided, they show a clear seam across the middle, where they will eventually open. Peel the scales away at the seam. Two of them will come off, each like a cupped hand, and the other two scales will be seen clasping the central cluster of green pinheads which are the true dogwood flowers—or will be, come Spring. The white "petals" of the dogwood bloom are more leaf than petal; they are, in fact, those four bud scales, grown big and white. And the flowers, which form the red berries harvested last Fall by the birds and squirrels, are the little cluster in the center. Each cluster may contain as many as twenty-four florets.

Dogwoods tend to have alternate years of scant and abundant flowering. This year should be one of superabundance.

Snowbird   *January 7*

Just why the snowbird should be called a junco nobody seems to know; but Junco is the scientific name and is more and more used as the common name. Even the ornithologists hesitate before they say that the Latin word for seed is *juncus;* the snowbird eats quantities of weed seed, therefore junco may be a logical name.

Anyway, there is the snowbird, or junco, in dark gray full dress and white bosom, his tails neatly piped in white. He is beautiful against a snowy background, and while one hesitates to suggest that his esthetic sense dominates his habits, he certainly thrives in snow country. Sometimes it seems that it takes a snowstorm to bring the snowbirds, for they come wheeling in flocks as a storm approaches. Give them any encouragement in the form of grain or crumbs, and they will remain, almost as tame as the chickadees.

Technically, they are of the same family as the sparrows. This is easy to believe when one sees and recognizes the young snowbirds, for they are dressed in juvenile plumage that looks, at a glance, like that of the adult song sparrow, streaked and speckled. And the adults have a little song that reminds one of the more melodious of the sparrows, the trill a good deal like that of the chipping sparrow. Never is it a loud song, but sometimes it is elaborated into a soft warble that has echoes of the song sparrow's best melody.

It would be all very well to call the snowbird a junco in Summer. But in Winter the name has no color at all, no matter what its derivation. In Winter it is a snowbird, and that's all there is to it.

Moonlight on the Ice   *January 8*

There's deep ice on the pond, a nip in the air, and a moon practically at the full. It's a night for skating, pond skating, with a bonfire on the bank and stout clothes to fend off the January wind, and older folk as well as youngsters on the ice.

There is routine, but little ritual, about moonlight skating. The walk to the pond, which gets the circulation going and warns the lungs of frost in the air. The lighting of a fire designed for light as well as heat. The deceptively easy change from shoes to skates —the change back will be quite a different matter, confounded by chilled fingers and tangled laces. And there's the talk, the discussion of ice and weather, the local chaff, the Winter news and gossip.

Then the skating itself, the bite of sharp blades on smooth ice, the sense of speed and freedom. And the ice rhythms that never vanish, once acquired, and never date. They are best, of course, with a skating partner, on a moonlit night, one who knows those rhythms and who has the instinctive grace of a dancer. Blades flash in the moonlight, and the ice sings, and there is music in the heart.

The evening deepens, the hush is borne in upon even the younger skaters, and the night and the moonlight and the ice become all of a piece, beauty that touches the quick of understanding. You have come for the night as well as the skating, and now you know it; for here is the night around you. And when at last your stiff fingers have untangled the laces and you are on your way home again, arm in arm, the magic is still there. It's more than a country pond; it's ice, and moonlight, and an old, old song.

Change   *January 9*

Now is the time when the mountains wear away and the rocky knobs that core the hills are wedged apart and broken. Ice is at work. The slow seep and the midday melt are creeping into the rocks, and the midnight frost is prying open spaces where roots will find their way, come Spring.

Heat and convulsion lifted the mountains, and cold and slow time are eternally struggling to level them once again. Cold, and a water crystal, loosen them up. Time and growth and the breath of wind and the flow of rain move mountaintops into the valleys and round the jagged hills into rolling uplands.

A water crystal and a creeping root are the two great levers of nature. Man does the job with clanking drill and booming blast, but nature does it silently, save when a riven rock loses balance in a Spring thaw and nudges a whole hillside into motion. Thus does granite become gravel and gravel become sand. Thus are the ledges worn away.

Pile and compress the ice into a glacier, and nature has a plow that can rip away whole mountainsides, level a range of hills in one slow stroke. Combine glaciers into an ice sheet and the character of half a continent can be altered, as was the northern half of the United States a relatively few thousand years ago.

But it takes neither glaciers nor ice sheets to do the job, in time. Winter frost does it, eventually. For change is eternal, and no mountain, no hill, no stone, will last forever.

Indians called it the wolf moon, knowing well the time when fangs were eager and hunger drove the pack. Most of the wolves are gone, but the fangs remain, fangs of ice and cold, the great primal forces of winter's depth. The wind courses the valleys and harries the hills, and the long nights sharpen its fang. The ice lies deep.

In some lands there are mountain barriers to the winter wind; but our geography has no such design. Our mountain chains, for the most part, lie with the wind which moves down from the north. The great valleys merely funnel the gales so that they howl unfettered and roar out across the flatlands until they have worn themselves out. Our winter winds have few barriers. Even the trees stand naked, to sigh and moan as the wind whips through them, freighted with snow or ice or merely with cold. And the hills lie open to the elements.

Ice sheathes the ponds and clogs the streams. It thrusts at the banks with its own fangs. But more than that, ice gnaws at the hills. It thrusts a hidden fang into the granite of the hilltop and rips the rocks apart. Ledges that can defy all other elements crumble away beneath the ice, which can come from as impalpable a thing as a wisp of mist or as fragile a thing as a snowflake. Ice, the sharpest fang of all, and the most persistent.

The wolf moon, they called it, listening to the howl of the pack in the Winter valleys. And the howl we hear tonight will be the wolf howl of the wind in those same valleys, the voice of primal forces at work in the Winter world.

Mr. Downy *January 11*

Downy woodpecker is his accepted name, though here and there he is called Tommy woodpecker, black and white driller, little guinea woodpecker, even little sapsucker. This last name is in error, for the downy is not a sapsucker, but all the others are quite in order, even that of little guinea, for the downy's black and white feather pattern has some resemblance to the coloring of a domestic guinea fowl such as used to be common on many farms.

By any name the downy is a shy but friendly bird common to most wooded areas and often seen at or near the bird feeder at the window sill or in the back yard. When he comes to the feeder, however, it is for suet rather than for seeds. Three out of every four mouthfuls of the downy's food consists of insects, worms, larva or, if he can find it, suet.

The downy is a small bird, just a bit larger than most warblers, just a bit smaller than a bluebird. In Winter he usually looks even larger because he fluffs his feathers to keep warm. But if he looks as big as a bluejay, he isn't a downy. He's a hairy wood-pecker. The hairy and the downy are full cousins, marked exactly the same, even to the scarlet skullcap the male wears. They even have the same cheery, chirpy voice, though the big hairy is more of a baritone.

Mr. Downy has about him something of the cheerful air of the chickadee, though with a diffidence quite alien to Mr. Chick. He is more self-sufficient, perhaps, and a little less truculent. He is just about the perfect Winter guest, one whose swooping flight is a melody of motion and whose tapping on a dead limb is very close to song.

Ben's Stove   *January 12*

It must have been about this time of year that Benjamin Franklin first had his idea for a stove. He was about to begin his thirty-eighth year, an age when a man would have had enough of chill and scorch from a fireplace. Ingenious as he was, he knew that a fire in an iron box open to the room on all sides would radiate much more heat than a fire in a wall. He may even have known that such fireboxes, or stoves, were used in Alsace back in the fifteenth century, then forgotten. At any rate, in the year 1744 Ben Franklin had an iron founder cast the plates for a stove of his own design. Thus was the Franklin stove born.

It wasn't elaborate. It was essentially a free-standing fireplace, a cast-iron, open-front box in which wood was burned. The fire heated the iron box and the iron box heated the room, its smoke drawn off by a pipe or flue. It still had the cheer of an open fire. But in it was the germ idea for all the stoves and most of the furnaces that have followed it.

Unlike so many early inventions, the Franklin stove persists even today. It is an antique and in many places a rarity, but not many of those fortunate few who have one would willingly be rid of it. Anachronism that it is—and somehow it seems even more out of date than a fireplace—it has an honored place in many a New England country living room. Men love it, particularly in January. Dogs bask in its gentle glow. And wherever you find one, there is the spirit of Old Ben, his back to its open glow, beaming, satisfied, content that his firebox was as important, in its way, as his kite.

❧ Franklin stoves are still being made. L. L. Bean, in Freeport, Maine, sells a model, fresh from the foundry, almost exactly like some of the antiques I have seen. Most of the Bean stoves go into Summer cottages and hunting and fishing cabins, but not long ago I saw one in a contemporary, flat-roofed house and it looked right at home. Very cozy on a Winter night, too, with all those glass walls around.

Winter Wind   *January 13*

The Winter wind is like a cold surf beating through the bare tree-tops and sweeping through the valleys. It roars in the night, an elemental voice; it whistles at the house corner and it rattles the shutter and the pane. Listen to it, and you are hearing the mighty currents of the air rushing down the latitudes of the earth, currents from the Mackenzie and the Athabasca and the Saskatchewan, and from the prairies and the white tundra.

It is a homeless wind, forever on the move. It cannot pause on any hilltop, and if it seems to relax in some deep valley, it is only gathering strength. It bows the oaks and goes on and on. It brings a freight of snow and swirls it over the land, and it thickens the ice on the lakes; but the wind itself is forever on its way, driven by the weight of its own motion, drawn by the vacuum of a risen wind in some far place.

It is restless as the human mind, strong as the drive of passion. It matches strength with strength, tests the fiber and tries the earth-bedded root. The rocks shoulder it aside, but the sand rolls with the wind, and the hills and dunes take on new shapes. The weak gives way and the uncertain alters its course as the wind dictates.

We sit before our fires, themselves wind-blown by the chimney gusts, and cherish our warmth, our snug security. And we know that the rush of wind just beyond our stout walls is the rush of Winter passing. It is the fierce breath of change itself. The earth turns and the winds eddy and swirl; and one fine night there will be a whisper of Spring in the wind, and another Winter will have blown itself away.

Ice Flowers   *January 14*

They bloom in a crisp, cold night when the air is still and the stars lean close, and they are called ice flowers or frost flowers. You see them on the new black ice of a river or pond, and they are pure crystal, dazzlingly white and amazingly beautiful. Sometimes they look like small tufts of the finest miniature ferns, sometimes like the softest of feathers. There may be only a few fronds in a clump, or there may be a tussock several inches across and two or three inches high. Sometimes they dot the ice in all directions. If all conditions have favored, the ice around them may be strewn with feathery frost patterns such as form on Winter windows, as though some exotic Winter bird had shed its plumage in the night.

These ice flowers are a form of frost, another example of the incredible loveliness with which ice crystals can arrange themselves. They are related to the snowflake, to window frost patterns and to the intricate forms of hoarfrost. Their masses of infinitely delicate crystals are built from the vapor that has drifted across the ice from some patch of open water, and unless deep cold persists they are almost as ephemeral as mist. A gusty wind will shatter them, and a few degrees of warmth that even the far-off Winter sun generates can soon destroy them.

Winter is full of its own wonders, and the most spectacular of them are elemental—the wind, the snowstorm, the snowdrift, the ice sheet, the glacier. But Winter is also the spectacle of the ice crystal in its infinite variations; and he who has seen the ice flowers has seen a masterpiece of such crystalline perfection.

Snow Night   *January 15*

Even under an overcast sky, a snow-covered night is not a night of darkness. It is a night of black and white and gray, all faintly aglow; and once the human eye has accustomed itself to it, there is much to be seen and even more to be sensed. But it is seen and sensed in different terms than by daylight.

First, it is a world totally lacking in shadows, for what light there is comes from the snow-covered earth rather than from the sky. Trees are stark outlines, bushes are vague heaps of darkness, and snowdrifts vanish into a common blur that has no small contours.

When one has accepted this shadowless world on its own terms, the next thing that strikes the consciousness is the absence of color. True, there is little color to the human eye in any night, but in this world of strong contrasts one is more aware of this than on a Summer night under a full moon. What we see in this darkness is seen with other vision than we use in daylight; the daytime part of our eyes blanks out, and night vision takes its place. Our night vision is simplified, color sensitivity sacrificed so that we may gather every bit of the thinner light now available. Our night eyes gather contrasts so that we may identify shapes, whereas our daylight eyes bring us color and detail.

So we walk abroad, on a snowy night, into a world whose magic is created of light and darkness, its subtlety all in grays. We walk in another world, use new senses, find new values in the darkness that is the night of Winter.

Why?   *January 16*

These are fine evenings to sit by the fire and listen to the wind and think leisurely thoughts about the winter's questions. Why did Canada's climate have to move in on us this year, for example? What unplotted force drove those bitter winds our way so early, and so persistently, and why? Where now are those who not so long ago were saying with such assurance that our Winters were getting warmer? Why don't we hear from them now?

How do you suppose those robins who chose to winter over in the North are taking it? Are they huddling in the hemlock thicket and hatching rebellion against the persuasive young leader who said, last October, "Why, there's nothing to it! Stick around, boys, and have the place to yourselves." And is the jeering of the jays inspired by those hapless robins?

Why did the opossums ever come north? True, they have fur coats; but they made out very nicely down below that line drawn by Charles Mason and Jeremiah Dixon until twenty-five or thirty years ago. Now they are up here, and well north of here, all year round, and a possum in a snowbank on a zero day is a thoroughly pathetic sight, with watery eyes, a red nose and a frost-bitten tail. And not enough sense to go indoors. Why didn't possums stay where they were well off?

Why hasn't any poet celebrated winter in a big way since Whittier wrote "Snowbound" in 1866? Have all our poets become softies? Or isn't winter as romantic as it used to be, now that all the sleighs and sleigh bells are in antique markets? For that matter, why are the oldsters huddled by the fire right now? Why aren't they out enjoying one of those Winters they used to brag about?

Winter strips the trees to their essentials. They stand now in bare bones, except the pines and spruces, and you can see what stands behind their graceful Summer shapes.

That elm against the sky, which in mid-Summer is a great green featherduster—see how its sturdy trunk divides some distance from the ground, and divides again and yet again. It reaches upward, widening like an inverted cone, and all its branches point toward the sky.

Across the way is a scarlet oak. It has a trunk three feet through, and your eye can follow that trunk to the very tip of the tree. But its branches start not ten feet from the ground, and they reach toward the horizon. Here's a tree as broad as it is tall, and rounded, even in leafless winter, like a great dome.

The ash, whether white or black or red, is essentially a tapering trunk with whorls of lesser limbs—a pole with slender branches now; a svelte and graceful tree in full leaf.

Maples tend to branch like oaks, but with less spread and more lift. The sycamore, which shines as though perpetually frost-coated, divides like the elm and branches out in all directions. The tupelo, or sour gum, is a central stem with a hopeless tangle of branches crisscrossed on each other, a veritable confusion of a tree without its leaves.

But of all, perhaps the most beautiful against the winter sky is the little flowering dogwood, with its horizontal limbs that reach skyward at the tips and form a fine lace pattern. The dogwood is a picture tree, Summer or Winter.

Sun Dogs   *January 18*

The snowflake and the ice crystal have their own symmetrical beauty, colorless as water; but a cloud of minute ice crystals flung across the eastern sky at sunrise on a frosty morning can produce sun dogs which are as colorful as rainbows and are sometimes mistaken for rainbow fragments in the wrong part of the sky. Sun dogs are vivid spots or short columns of color, red usually predominating, which appear in the eastern sky just above the horizon on each side of the sun. Country folk, who know them well, know them as warnings of an approaching storm.

Sun dogs and rainbows are related, since both are caused by sunlight's being reflected and refracted from moisture in the air. The rainbow is sunlight broken down into the spectrum by the curved surfaces of raindrops; the bow is all the way across the sky from the sun. Sun dogs are sunlight broken into the spectrum by the prism surfaces of ice crystals, and sun dogs are seen in the same area of the sky with the sun. The ice crystals are very small. They make up those cirro-stratus clouds which ride high in the sky far ahead of a Winter storm center.

There are also moon dogs, which appear in the Winter sky on each side of a newly risen moon near the full. They are essentially the same as sun dogs except that the light which creates them comes from the moon, and they can be eerily beautiful on the horizon of a snowy Winter world. But they, too, tell of an approaching storm. Just why they are called "dogs" nobody seems to know, but the term is venerable. And sun dogs and moon dogs are as beautiful accents to a Winter day or night as the rainbow is to a showery Summer day.

Firelight   *January 19*

Say what you will about January—which hasn't a mere two faces, like its mythological namesake, but a full thirty-one—it makes a man happy to be the owner of a roof and a fire. And to have someone to share them. January is for companionship. January justifies that overworked word "cozy," which itself comes from the cold Norse countries where *kose sig* meant to make one's self comfortable.

Mid-January seems to have been put in the year to provide fireside evenings, leisurely reading, quiet, friendly talk. The simpler inner resources, so easily glossed over when the world is full of golden sunlight, green shade and soft Summer starlight, now come into their own. One feels no urgency to be gregarious or full of busy, bright, warm-weather chatter. One needs only to toss a log on the fire, find an easy chair, and let the heart do its own talking, in its own time.

It's a strange paradox that the warmth of friendship so often runs an inverse ratio to the height of the mercury in the thermometer. Cold nights call for close friends, and the number is important primarily as a limitation. No lawn party groups now, no houseful, but rather the intimate few. And the talk now has range and depth rather than deftness and volume. Thoughts seem to prosper in a warm room with a cold wind at the door.

Snow and ice clarify the mind as well as the air, and firelight better illuminates the reason than moonlight. Maybe that's one reason for living in a latitude where Winter has a degree of authority; it gives a man time to explore his thoughts, to look at his own heart and to approach understanding.

Sawlogs   *January 20*

The upcountry farmer getting sawlogs out of his wood lot this week is timing it just about right. It's mid-January and the moon is in the last quarter. Those logs will be seasoned to make good lumber, straight planks and flat boards.

In the old days, when most farmers cut their own sawlogs, you didn't mean that lumber had dried out when you said it was seasoned; you meant that it had been cut in the right season. And the season was governed by the moon as well as the month. Timbers cut during "the old moon of January"—sometimes they said February—would always stand straight and true. But if you cut your logs "when the moon is new to full, timber fibers warp and pull."

Such sayings were typical of a time when a countryman

equipped with only an ax, an auger and a knife could build, furnish and equip a house from the trees in his own clearing. Wood was his most versatile material, and what he didn't know or learn about it wasn't worth knowing. When he began to build with sawed lumber, he carried this knowledge right into the sawmill and back, with the boards, to the building site.

The old houses and the old barns prove that the men who chose the lumber knew what they were doing. It's still good lumber, true and straight, after all these years. How much the moon's phases had to do with it can only be guessed, but there's no denying that the wood was seasoned to perfection in almost every case.

Farmers are essentially practical people and no more super-stitious than city folk. But if a man wanted to get out a few sawlogs for his own use, he certainly couldn't be blamed for look-ing at the calendar first. A calendar with the moon's phases clearly marked.

Winter Music   *January 21*

Is there a colder sound than the whine of snow underfoot on a night when the temperature is flirting with zero? Possibly the popping of trees in the deep woods on a bitter night, or the boom of ice on a deep-frozen lake. But the creak of snow under a boot also has something of ruddy cheer in it, perhaps by contrast. It goes with a hearth fire and sudden laughter in a warm room, and glowing cheeks and frosty windows full of light.

In the days not too long ago the music on such a night came from sleigh and cutter and pung. The whine of their runners on the icy snow could be heard fully half a mile away, and it was unlike any other sound in the world. Even if the horses wore no bells, there was a song in that sound, a song that leaped to the low stars and seemed to echo from all the hilltops.

On such a night nowadays we hear, instead, the metallic chain clink on the highways, punctuated by the staccato bang of broken chain on echoing fender. The music that remains comes from our own footsteps. And it is cold music, make no mistake about that. The temperature has to be well down toward zero before the snow begins to sing. But when it does sing underfoot, the stars dance and the owl hoots from the dark hemlocks across the valley and our breath is a gleaming crystal cloud in the moonlight.

We walk abroad on such a night, to hear the snow sing underfoot; and we come back tingling in every nerve, back to the leaping fire. For that, too, is a part of any night when Winter whistles through its cold white teeth and the snow is full of crystal music.

Those Winter Robins   *January 22*

The ways of birds persist in baffling mere human beings. This year, for instance, there seem to be more robins than usual braving out the winter here in the Northeast. Sizable flocks have been seen as far north as the Berkshires. Why they have stayed, nobody really knows; and why they chose this, of all recent Winters, is beyond understanding. But here they are, in considerably greater numbers than usual.

The evening grosbeaks, those Winter-colorful finches from the Midwest and the Northwest, are somewhat more numerous too, for equally obscure reasons. The grosbeaks move from west to east in Winter, at least those we see, and presumably they come east in search of food. When did they start this migration? It is rather common belief that they are newcomers here, unknown until twenty or twenty-five years ago. Yet they were recorded in New York City in 1911, and in 1916 a large flock was seen in Portland, Maine.

Perhaps these new range patterns are not as "new" as we sometimes think. Qualified observers were nowhere as numerous even fifty years ago as they are today. The professional ornithologists knew their subject, but they hadn't the help of today's tens of thousands of volunteer bird watchers. It may be that their knowledge of migration was more limited than we yet realize. Even today we must admit that there are persistent puzzles in the subject.

And among those puzzles are the flocks of this Winter's robins. They know why they are here, and they undoubtedly have their sound reasons for staying. Mere man can only guess and wish that the birds spoke a language more easily understood.

Winter's Spangles   *January 23*

Walk the country roads and ridge paths now and you will be discovering little mirror ponds at almost every turn, winter ice pockets that will either be dried away or hidden completely once the first green of Spring has touched the woods. They are the cold-weather seep and the snow's melt, caught in the hollows and frozen there through the cold weeks.

Catch them on a bright day and they have the shimmery blue of the Winter sky. Come upon them when the sky is Winter gray and they are steely in their cold reflection. They reflect the sky's mood and the mood of the weather even more clearly than does a Summer pond. A drifting of snow hides them completely, of course, even the thinnest of snowfalls. But when the woods are gray in snowless nakedness, they are like jewels on the landscape.

Another two months and they will be merely muck land, where the skunk cabbage lifts its purple hoods and the purple violets are preparing to bloom and the trout lilies are hurrying to blossom before the shade has closed in upon them. They may even become the swampy source of loud frog calls when Spring evenings are warming the hilltops. Marsh marigolds will bloom there, if all goes well, and giant Solomon's seal will spread its generous leaves over their tufted dampness.

But now they are ice gems set in a dull landscape, eye-catching spangles which wink with starlight and shine with moonbeams in the brittle night. They are scraps of tinsel left in all the little hollows by a frosty gentleman who walks the woods with icicles in his hands and an overflowing pack of glitter with which to frost the landscape.

January Thaw   *January 24*

If the January thaw could be predicted like an eclipse or an equinox, it would be just another annual incident. But the prophet who forecasts one takes his reputation in his hands, and usually at a time when his fingers are stiff with cold and uncertain in their grasp. It is even precarious to predict that there will be a January thaw, let alone when it will come. But if there is a thaw in January, it usually comes about now. If it lags into February, it is just another warm spell and has no significance.

The January thaw is special because it opens Winter's door a crack just when it seems that the ice has locked it tight. Through that crack one can see the certainty of March and April somewhere up ahead. And on a warm and melting January day even the hours of daylight seem hopefully longer. Actually, the sun now is in the sky less than forty minutes longer than it was in the depth of December, but because most of the gain is in the evening it seems greater.

The worst one can say about any January thaw is that it never lasts. It lifts the heart, then drops it with a cold thud when the warm spell passes and the chill congeals the earth again. It raises hopes that, in the nature of things, cannot be realized. Not yet. February still lies ahead, notorious for its snow despite the groundhog legend. And after February comes March, windy, unpredictable March. And finally April.

But when January does relent, even for a day or two, we can celebrate, cautiously. No fanfare. No dancing in the streets. Just a quiet thank you for that glimpse of Spring in the distance.

The Diversions

There are two seasonal diversions that can ease the bite of any winter. One is the January thaw. The other is the seed catalogues.

The January thaw—it comes about four years out of every five —usually arrives on the heels of a blustery snow or sleet storm. It arrives as a high-flying southerly wind, a warm front crowding a retreating cold front. As the cold front retreats, the warm front settles down, usually full of fog, always full of melting ice and snow, slush and mud. It may last only a day or two. It can persist for a week, raising hopes of early Spring and the imminent arrival of migrant robins and bluebirds. Then a new cold front comes whipping in, and that's the end of the thaw. We are back in the midst of Winter.

The seed catalogues also come quietly, through the mail. They have colorful covers, full of tantalizing flowers. They have color plates inside, full of luscious tomatoes, toothsome sweet corn, ruddy beets, crisp carrots, snap beans, squash, pumpkins, peppers. And petunias, asters, pinks, zinnias, daisies, dahlias. Within half an hour they have the living room overflowing with blossom and the kitchen overwhelmed with garden produce. They are wonderful. At the back of the catalogues, illustrated in black and white, if at all, are also insecticides, spades, forks, hoes, rakes, even wheelbarrows and sprayers. But not one liniment for sore muscles is listed; say that for them.

January wouldn't really be January without them, both the thaw and the catalogues. But even with them it is still Winter, though April is a week nearer than it was a week ago.

Snowdrifts

A snowdrift is a beautiful thing—if it doesn't lie across the path you have to shovel or block the road that leads to your destination. In the open a snowdrift is the sculptured figure of the wind done in crystal. In the woodland it is the path of the wind pirouetting around the trees and curling over stumps and stones. If there were such a thing as frozen motion, surely it would be a snowdrift, new and gleaming and softly curved.

Big drifts are magnificent. They show how the wind can walk with giant strides across the land. But there is a simpler beauty in the little drifts, the feathery drifts that trail away from the weed stems in an open meadow. They are the filigree of the wind, the fine detail of the snowstorm, and one must look close to see them unless the long light of morning or late afternoon has drawn its blue shadows across the snow. Then they stand out in all their fine-detailed beauty.

That, of course, is the best time to see the clean sculpturing of any drift, when the long light touches the crests and the shadows lie like pools in every hollow. Then you can follow the wind along the hilltop and down the valley and see the full pattern of its path. Nowhere else is the record so clear. Sand dunes show it, but not with the fine detail of a new-fallen snow.

A snow, of course, that you don't have to shovel or struggle through with a smooth-tired car. In those circumstances a snow-drift is just so much snow, sleek and wet and very much a nuisance. It is, in fact, too much snow to be beautiful at all.

Almost Half Over   *January 27*

There is an old rural saying, here in the Northeast, that a farmer can last out the Winter if he still has half his wood and half his hay when February arrives. The Winter was supposed to be half over by the end of January, and while a man couldn't exactly relax, he could at least begin to think about April, up there ahead. By the last week in January he began saying to himself, and to his neighbors, that every day the sun shone was another day nearer Spring. The dark days, the days when the wind howled and the snow fell, didn't seem to count either way; they were days to be endured.

So here we are within a week of February, and by the old criteria Winter is half over. We don't hear anybody complaining that it went too fast. By tradition, January is supposed to be cold, and it has been. By the same tradition, February is supposed to be snowy, and it may be. But every day now certainly is another day nearer Spring, whether the sun shines or not. Ice lies deep on lake and pond and river, and has for weeks, and frost has bitten deep into the earth. But we all admit now that they will relax, in due time. March will come, and April, and even May. So will new leaves and Spring flowers and migrant birds.

Maybe the old traditions were a little lax, but the hill farmers were not inclined to excessive optimism. They knew Winter rather intimately. They didn't hibernate, as the woodchuck. They lived with the weather, the year around. Not many of us have hay or woodpiles to measure this week, but we can begin to think about April for a change. Why, April is only a little over nine weeks ahead!

Winter's Moon   *January 28*

Mid-Summer's moon is the serenader's moon, sentimental as the rhymes that go with it. Autumn's moon is the golden harvest moon, big as all outdoors. But Winter's moon is queen of the sky. It hurries the sun to bed, banishes all but the brightest stars, and blazons the frosty night a full fourteen hours in remote and solitary grandeur.

The January moon is no moon to dream on or bask under. It is a distant and icy moon that glitters the hills and glints the frozen valleys. It may dance a stately pavane on the frost-flowered surface of a silent lake. It may dazzle the crystalled air over a frost-defying brook. It may etch whimsical hieroglyphics on the snow beneath the naked trees, but it is brittle as spun glass, sharp as the talon of a hungering owl.

The Winter's moon makes magic of the night, but it is a sharp and frosty witchcraft. The fox knows it, and so does the hurrying hare darting from shadow to shadow. The night walker sees it in his own spangled breath, senses it in his whistling footsteps. The late homecomer sees it in the shimmer of his own rooftop, smells it in the slow curl of smoke from his own chimney. Even the night wind knows it.

Mid-Winter moonlight is no hearth glow reflected in the sky. It is the cold beauty of a whole Winter wrapped and rimed into one long January night.

The Creeper   *January 29*

Every Winter the casual bird watchers have kind words for the chickadees, the nuthatches, the titmice and the kinglets that visit their feeding stations. Now and then someone says, "There was a brown creeper on the apple tree, too, but it wouldn't come near the feeder." And that dismisses the creeper.

The brown creeper is easily dismissed. It lacks the color of the titmouse and the kinglet, the pertness of the chickadee and the absurdity of the nuthatch. But in its own way the creeper is the busiest bird of all, and far more independent than most. If it comes to the feeder, it's only for a quick nip of suet; then it's off again, back to the tree trunks, for it is one of the most thorough insect gatherers of all the Winter visitors. It gets little attention because it is shy, busy, and needs no companionship.

The creeper is about the size of a chickadee, but it looks smaller. On a tree trunk it is sure-footed as a fly though, unlike the nuthatch, it can't walk downward. It starts at the base and swarms up, not missing a crack or crevice that might hide a sleeping insect or dormant egg. It feeds on the run. In an hour it can cover a dozen trees, top to bottom.

Its family life is equally unobtrusive. It wedges its nest behind a loose slab of bark on a fir tree, lays six or seven white eggs dusted with brown, and tends to its own affairs. It has only a minor song. It never raids garden or orchard. Each Winter it comes south and lives on the fare the nuthatches and woodpeckers miss. If it were the color of a goldfinch, it would be celebrated and cherished. Instead, it is often mistaken for a field mouse.

Snowstorms and Blizzards   *January 30*

The argument about whether it was or wasn't a blizzard that hit us a few days ago can go on for years. The late Dr. Charles F. Brooks, noted Harvard meteorologist, once said, "The true blizzard is almost unknown in the East. Its native heath is the Great Plains." He defined a blizzard as a snow-driving northerly gale of zero cold. Dr. Brooks may have been biased in this matter. Most Westerners are, and he was a native of Minnesota.

Anyway, it was snow aplenty, with vicious wind and cold that flirted with zero. And, we are reminded, the blizzard of '88 was a real blizzard. It can happen here.

As for snow, the Northeast is getting a full budget this year. New York's annual average, according to the records, is only 30.1 inches. The same records show that Denver and Duluth average 56 inches. But for real snowfall one must go to Silver Lake, Colorado, or to Paradise Ranger Station in Rainier Park, Washington. Silver Lake once got 76 inches in 24 hours, 95 inches in 48 hours. And Paradise Station averages 576 inches a year, was buried under 1,000 inches the Winter of 1955–56. And they call it Paradise!

Whatever it was that the Northeast got last week, it wasn't really needed. It wasn't even needed out in the country where snow is less of a nuisance and life is somewhat less at the mercy of the weather than in the city. In fact, the keepers of the traditions out there are still snowed in. There hasn't been a peep out of them about those old-fashioned Winters they are so fond of recalling. They are too busy shoveling out.

The wide blue sky of Winter, when nature is less visibly busy, invites mental excursions. It is a very different sky from that of, say, July or August, when every tree is in full leaf and every ridge is fringed with trees. Boundaries are everywhere then; in Winter the boundaries are all here on the ground and the sky itself is boundless.

There is a fiction that living with the land somehow fixes one, mentally and emotionally, in a conservative orbit. The fact is that knowing both the Summer and the Winter sky, and the Summer and the Winter earth, gears one to change. How can one ignore change, or deny its inevitability, when faced with change day by day and season by season? No two days are the same, when you face them whole; and, facing them, you must somehow yourself change. Trees grow. Valleys deepen. And there is the horizon, the wide, blue sky that has no boundaries.

There have always been two major problems, man and man, and man and earth, his environment. Neither stands alone, and the false solutions always turn out to be the ones that ignore that eternal kinship. So, too, with the false philosophies. But for those who would understand, there are the times of clarity and simplicity when the Winter hills are naked and the Winter sky is wide, inviting exploration. The time when boundaries we set up for ourselves are less constricting. Man and man, and man and earth, stand forth more clearly.

There is clarity in the Winter sky that holds its own challenge. It promises change, and it invites the mind to match that change.

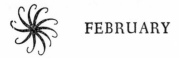 FEBRUARY

February   *February 1*

Here comes February, a little girl with her first valentine, a red
bow in her wind-blown hair, a kiss waiting on her lips, a tantrum
just back of her laughter. She is young as a kitten, changeable as
the wind, and into everything. She can sulk, she can beam, she
changes from one minute to the next. February is a phase, a short
phase at that, and she has to be lived with.

February can't be taken seriously too long at a time. It starts
with Groundhog Day, which is neither omen nor portent, but
only superstition, and it ends, often as not, in a flurry of snow.
It is sleet and snow and ice and cold, and now and then it is
waxing sunshine and tantalizing thaw and promise. February is
soup and mittens, and it is a shirt-sleeve day that demands an
overcoat before sundown. It is forsythia buds opening in the
house and skid chains clanking on the highway. February is
sunrise at 6:30 for the first time since November.

February is a gardener pruning his grape vines today and
shoveling a two-foot drift off the front walk tomorrow morning. It
is a farmer wondering this week if his hay will last the Winter,
and next week wondering if he should start plowing. It is tiny,
tight catkins on the alder in the swamp and skunk cabbage

February / 303

thrusting a green sheath up through the ice. February is the tag end of Winter—we hope. But in our hearts we know it isn't Spring, not by several weeks and at least a dozen degrees.

There's no evidence to support it in the dictionaries, but some say that February's name comes from an ancient and forgotten word meaning "a time that tries the patience."

Contrast   *February 2*

Against a gray Autumn hillside a crow is just a crow; but put a group of crows against a white Winter landscape and they become spectacular. More spectacular than the blue jays, even, for the crow is so black and the contrast is so sharp. Two or three glistening crows strutting across a snowy field will make even a farmer look twice and secretly admit that, under some circumstances, a crow can be pretty.

The white backdrop does it. It makes the black twice as black. It makes an old apple tree a thing of grace and beauty. It makes a rusty pasture cedar green and rather wonderful. It makes a stone wall a thing of startling color, with all the grays and greens of moss and lichen on the stones. It turns the swift water of the brook almost crow black, with white ice on the banks and gray alder stems and willows forming a graceful tangle, all curves, against the white fields beyond.

The color is there, but it takes the snow to bring it out, the stark and dazzling white. It won't be very long till other color will begin to show, particularly along the stream banks where willow brush and osier stems will show their reds and ambers. But that will be a different color, and there will be a different kind of light in which to see it. And when that time comes the crows will be only crows again, strutting the muddy fields and not being spectacular at all. Waiting for someone to plant corn. And the spectacular birds will be the first robins, the first bluebirds, the early goldfinches. But now, against the snow, the crows are something to see. And don't they know it!

Purification

If February turns out to be capricious, as it usually does, there is some excuse. It is the last full month of Winter, by the almanac at least, traditionally full of snow and always a time of warring weather systems. It begins with the absurdity of Groundhog Day, celebrates romance in midmonth, and includes an extra day every four years. In a sense, February is a throwback to ancient times, for it is the only month we have that still approximates the lunar month, one of man's earliest units of time. Yet on occasion February can pass without a full moon.

According to the old chronicles, February was first inserted in the calendar by Numa Pompilius, legendary second king of Rome. It was named for Februarius, the feast of purification, and on the old calendars it was the year's final month. It ended with the feast of Terminalia, a kind of New Year's Eve celebration that lasted several days. Then came March, the vernal equinox, Spring and the new year.

So we inherited February, a whimsical month that can smother us in snow or set the sap to flowing, immobilize us with sleet or brim all the brooks. Its daylight is as long as that of October, but its nights can be colder than December's. Februarius and Terminalia have vanished from the calendar; but February still purifies us, in a rugged way, and when it goes we bid it a glad good-bye. February may not be exactly a mad month, but it can be decidedly eccentric.

A Short, Lively Life

Man, who beats back the cold with fire and shelters himself from the icy wind with walls, sometimes wonders how less provident creatures survive when Winter days pile one upon another. The junco, the chickadee, the small woodpeckers, all those lively feathered ones who are so active through the Winter days—how do they make out?

A bird's life is finely balanced simply because birds are warm-blooded and because birds spend so much energy, so much vital force, in the fundamental process of living. Few other warm-blooded ones burn their food as quickly as the birds or run the engines of their vitality at such speed. Winter is difficult, but in any normal weather the cold probably takes no greater toll of birds than do their natural enemies awing and afoot. An ice storm may decimate a flock by locking away their essential food, and a bitter gale may take a serious toll. But only such extremes cut greatly into their numbers.

The average life of small birds is seldom as much as ten years. Most songbirds apparently live only about five years, eight years at most. Owls, on the other hand, sometimes live for fifty years. Pelicans also achieve the half-century mark; but pelicans live in a milder climate. Canada geese often live twenty-five years or more; but the geese, too, go south for the Winter, escape its rigors.

To a degree, man makes his own climate, at least indoors. The Winter birds live with the weather, whatever it is. The marvel is that they live as long as they do, with the hazards so high. But for five years, perhaps as much as eight, they survive and make Winter lively and somehow brighter for sheltered man.

The Interim   *February 5*

No matter what happens now, the year has committed itself, January is past, this is February, and up there ahead lie March and April. And May. But since man is man, not woodchuck, he has to live with the interim, not sleep it out and emerge into a green and vernal world. Incidentally, there weren't any woodchucks out in this neck of the woods on Groundhog Day. If the alarm clock went off, they let it ring, as they usually do.

This is probably as good a time as any to remember that it is only 85 days until May Day, when violets will be in bloom and the lawn will need mowing again. And it is only 149 days till the Fourth of July, when the beaches will be jammed and sunburn will be as universal as sniffles are now.

And it is only 208 days till Sept. 1st. That won't be the end of Summer by the almanac, but to all practical purposes Autumn starts with Labor Day. Back to the desk, back to work, back to school. And the next thing we know, it will be October and first frost and Columbus Day and the height of the color in the trees in New England. And before you can catch your breath it will be Thanksgiving. How time flies! If you really must know, it is only 323 days till Christmas. And then it will start snowing again.

Maybe we shouldn't have brought the matter up to begin with. But it is February, after all, only 85 days till May Day.

Skunk Cabbage   *February 6*

Look closely in the iced-over boglands and you can find, even now while the frost strikes deep, the stubborn greenish heads of *Symplocarpus foetidus,* the skunk cabbage, jutting toward the sun. Earliest of all Spring flowers, it sometimes thrusts through the frozen muck as early as December, and often it comes to light in January.

What can be seen now is merely the tip of that strange hood which shields the primitive flower stalk. And the hood will not open until there is considerably more show of warmth, probably not until well into March. Then, however, it will lift its head, almost overnight, and show characteristic streaks and blotches of red and purple and yellow-green, as exotic as the strange flower knob that will be revealed inside.

As the hood opens, the characteristic fetid odor of the plant will creep through the bogland. It is the "perfume" of the flowers, and it attracts early insects, which are often trapped inside the hood. To some observers it is the odor of decaying flesh; to others it is more like the odor of a mustard plaster seasoned with onions or garlic. The onion odor is typical of the full-grown plant; when you cut or break one of the broad leaves in mid-Summer that odor is strong and persistent.

Yet the skunk cabbage is cousin of jack-in-the-pulpit and the pretty little swamp flower called water arum. They are arums, all of them, perennials with a peppery juice in their stems and a love for damp footing. Other members of the family, however, have more respect for the season. Skunk cabbage is a rank individualist.

Patience   *February 7*

February rain isn't any wetter than that of March, and February snow isn't any colder or slushier than the snows of January. Nor is the sun actually Summer-hot on an occasional mild and balmy February day. They just seem that way because, at this time of year, our weather nerves are right up on the surface. The bad seems worse and the good seems better than reality. We would give anything for a fine Spring-fever week and a little sunburn. And down in our hearts we know we aren't going to get it—yet.

It sometimes seems that our forefathers, who lived closer to the soil and the seasons, were a little more patient. In public print they wrote of February: "Now comes the deepest snow; now we receive the remainderment of Winter." But look at their private letters and you see another picture of them: "February is a miserable time. I would gladly pass it by . . . I yearn for March, inclement as it often is." And in their journals you will find laconic weather records that make chilly reading indeed, cold and wet and disappointing.

They, too, got Winter-weary. They had their troubles, and they were impatient about them, down in their hearts. But, partly because they lived close to the land and understood the leisure of the changing seasons, they put up with them and saw them through. Spring was not only relief from Winter; it was work, hard work and long hours, planting for the Summer's growth. No year, no season, was without its pains and worries. But there was comfort in the knowledge of change, and even security. No troubles lasted forever, nor did any weather, good or bad. Winter ended, eventually, and Spring came. And thus it is and always will be. In that knowledge they lived out their Winter-weariness, even as we shall live out ours.

It Won't Be Long   *February 8*

A thaw in February has a different feel from that of the January thaw. The bite of February cold and the drift of February snow are not so different, but a few warm February days—and it's a rare February without them—persuade one that April and May as well as March lie just ahead.

Ponds are still iced. Ice still lies on rivers and chokes the brooks. It may go out and come back again. There's still skiing for those who look for it. A few days ago there was snow back in the hills, and even a warm spell will not melt it from all the hemlock groves. But on warm afternoons the trickle of flowing water, which was all but silenced from end to end of January, can be heard. Hill-country farmers still getting out saw logs know that they haven't much more time. Maple-syrup makers take a look at their pails and pans and spouts, thinking that it won't be very long now.

Each day is another day toward Spring. We still have weeks of impatient disappointment, for we always want April before March has arrived. But even that yearning has its reassurance. We know that Spring will come, and we want it next week, or week after, at the latest.

The important thing, as we creep toward mid-February, is that now the time is measured in longer days and shorter nights. Now the sun is noticeably swinging north. Now sunrise comes earlier and sunset later. Now we can count the time ahead in weeks, not months. It's less than six weeks till the vernal equinox.

The Deliberate Migrants   *February 9*

A few unseasonably warm days make us look and listen for robins and redwing blackbirds. It is that time of year when we hope for the impossible, even though we know that the first migrants can't properly be expected much before the vernal equinox, and that is almost six weeks away.

But the season is already on the march, down toward the Gulf and the Caribbean. With almost ten and a half hours of daylight here now, the frost line has already begun to move north. The early birds follow close behind the 35-degree isotherm. That line retreats from time to time, but Spring is gathering momentum and the surge is steadily northward.

Instinct probably dictates migration, but the actual timing seems to depend on food supply. Apparently vitamin D is a critical element, and since insects are specially rich in that vitamin the early migrants seldom travel ahead of the emerging insects. They, too, have their logistical problems. Even the seedeaters of the finch tribe that Winter over in the North wait for the insect harvest before they nest so they can stuff their young with vitamin-rich worms and bugs.

Some of the restless travelers are already in the lower Carolinas. Each warm day they are moving a little farther north. By the end of the month they will be in Virginia. But until mid-March we probably won't see a migrant robin or a redwing with sunburn on his shoulders.

Those Snowy Owls   *February 10*

Snowy owls have been coming south this Winter, but not because we have had more snow and deeper cold than usual. The big white owls get down this way every four or five years, and now it is known that their coming coincides with the fluctuations of the lemming population up north. Lemmings furnish a major part of the snowy owl's diet, and when they are scarce the owls move south to feed on other fare.

Why the lemming population fluctuates as it does is something of a mystery, but those little northland rodents periodically over-populate their area, then die off of crowding and disease. The cycle runs about four years. Northern hares and foxes show the same population cycles and there are even such cycles in the salmon catch. Studies have been made of this phenomenon, which some think may be related to sunspot cycles. Anyway, the lemmings come and go, and when they go, the big white owls come south.

The snowy owl is a spectacular bird, big as the great horned owl but white flecked with a darker scalelike pattern. This one is a vigorous hunter and a daytime bird, as a good many truculent crows find out too late. But the white owl, when it comes down here, lives mainly on mice and rabbits. On occasion it goes as far south as Virginia. But its presence doesn't always coincide with a severe Winter. It simply gets starved out up North when the lemmings are at the bottom of the periodic population cycle.

❧ Unhappily, many of these owls never return to Canada. They are killed by stupid hunters who either shoot at anything in sight or think all owls are predators who rob them of rabbits and game birds. True, if the snowy owls hid in the evergreens during the daylight hours, as our native owls do, they wouldn't be such inviting targets; but that isn't the way their lives are patterned.

The Price of Spring   *February 11*

There used to be a country saying that you have to earn Spring, you have to work your way through January and February for it. By mid-March, or whenever Spring really arrived, you presumably had done enough Winter penance and shoveled enough snow and toted enough wood to entitle you to it.

By mid-February many of us are inclined to agree. The bright sheen of Winter has worn off. Whether there has been much snow or little, there has been cold enough for anyone in any Winter. Maybe the sled generation will bemoan the date, and maybe those who got new skates for Christmas are more interested in ice than in valentines. But Papa will be very glad indeed to see the first dandelion and the last fuel bill. Papa has earned Spring and it can't come too soon.

There are, as always about now, signs to be seen. Someone reports a flock of robins. Not a mere one or two, but a whole flock. They may, of course, have come north a little while ago in desperation, when Florida and its environs were knocking the icicles off the eaves. But robins have come north in February before this. On south-sloping hillsides where the snow in the hills has thinned away the giant mulleins show signs of life. Before long someone will be finding coltsfoot in bloom and then hepatica.

But the unfailing sign comes every evening, at sunset. The sun sinks now, officially, forty minutes later than it did a month ago. And it rises almost half an hour earlier in the morning. The daylight has lengthened an hour and a quarter. There is the infallible sign. We haven't yet paid all it costs for Spring, but the installments are getting smaller. One of these days we'll have a receipt, paid in full. And Spring will be here.

Hunger Moon   *February 12*

To see the full moon as it rose in the brittle eastern sky last evening was to know both awe and shivering wonder. It was round as a medallion, bright as burnished brass, but its light had no more warmth than the frost cloud of a man's breath. It was a false and lifeless sun that made false daylight of the night. It killed the lesser stars and reduced the constellations to fundamentals. It burned the darkness with neither heat nor smoke, strewing the snow with charred skeletons of the naked trees. No wonder the Indians knew the February full moon as the hunger moon.

Yet, as it mounted the icy sky, the moon set stark patterns of beauty. Footsteps in the snow became laced traceries of purple shadow. Roads became black velvet ribbons with winking frost sequins. Starless ponds of night sky lay in the meadow's hollows. Pines became whispering flocks of huge, dark birds on the hilltops and pasture cedars were black candle flames. Warm-windowed houses and frost-roofed barns were all twins, each with its cold counterpart beside it on the snow. And no man walked alone as he hurried toward warmth and shelter.

Last night it was the perfect Winter moon. Tonight its edges will be frost bitten and it will rise an hour later. Tomorrow night it will be still another hour laggard and its rim will begin to crumble. And night by night more stars will creep back to claim the darkness, and day by day the true sun will move a fraction of a degree toward March and the equinox. The hunger moon has passed its prime.

Why? *February 13*

While the frost is still on the ground, before it's time to think about gardening or fishing or plowing the lower forty to put in corn, is a good time to ponder some of the lesser questions. Sit and watch the birds at the feeding station, maybe, and wonder why anyone ever thought of bird life as peaceful existence. Why do they squabble the way they do, when there is enough for all? More than any two tree sparrows can eat, anyway, or even a couple of blue jays. And why are the jays so skittish at the station? Guilty consciences, maybe?

What does a chickadee do when he isn't feeding? That takes up most of his time, of course, burning up energy the way he does. But there must be a few minutes of daylight when he is at leisure, so to say. What is there in a chickadee call on a bright, sunny afternoon, even now, that speaks of Spring? The notes are no different, but the whole intonation is new. Do the birds know when the sap is about to rise in the maples? Can they hear the preparations, there in the roots, and the slow opening of the pores in the tree's cambium layer?

What are the jays talking about now, and the crows? They are loud and persistent, and it isn't all complaint or boasting. The jays, in fact, are twittering rather sweet calls, bell-like in tone. Are they practicing for later, for the mating season? Are these trial phrases for serenades? And is anybody listening?

When will the whitethroats be singing again? And the song sparrows? How have the robins who didn't migrate been making out? When, by the way, will that first flock of migrant robins arrive?

Nonhibernating Man   *February 14*

There are days, particularly at this time of year, when one wonders why man's primitive ancestors gave up the habit of hibernation, why they turned warm-blooded and began to roam the earth in all kinds of weather. It is doubtful that the climate, in those remote days of change, was uniformly hospitable the year around. Yet here came man's progenitors to face all kinds of weather, awake and vulnerable.

Man still faces it, while the cold-blooded ones, and even a few of the warm-blooded creatures such as woodchucks, go to sleep and wait for better days. Man wallows in snow and slush and risks his cranium and coccyx in sleet. He shovels coal and he tinkers with his oil burner. He muffles himself against winds from the pole, and still his marrow congeals. He puts up with it, because he can no longer hibernate.

Then February flips on its unpredictable axis. The sun shines and the temperature rises. Ice begins to melt. Sleet and snow creep away in trickling rivulets that sing like penitent birds. A tempered wind comes up from the south. February puts on its best face and life is worth living again.

Even wise men cannot say when this will happen. It isn't even as predictable as the January thaw. But when it comes it warms the heart of technically warm-blooded man. It lifts his soul. It isn't really compensation for storm and flood and sleet and snow, but it is the best that February can do. It is worth being awake to know, and for a little while one knows why man does not crawl into a hole and stay there for weeks on end. It could happen tomorrow, but don't count on it.

The Heavy Wind   *February 15*

February winds have a bite, and no doubt about it. And that bite is more than a matter of temperature, though the temperature does give it authority. The winds of Winter not only blow stronger; they have more weight, literally, than those of any other season. The reason is that Winter's cold air is more dense, there is more of it to the square foot. Those who measure such matters say that a January or February wind may have 25 per cent more force than a July wind of the same velocity. That is one reason the past week's wind could force its way through an overcoat or the walls of a normally weathertight house.

Perhaps because of the cold air's weight, Winter storms move more swiftly across the land than the storms of Summer. The cold air of Winter in the North is much heavier than the cold air of Winter in the South, so the differences in atmospheric pressure are greater. The "highs" are higher and the "lows" are lower, and the air moving from a high-pressure area into a low-pressure area goes racing along. Summer storms normally move across the country at about twenty miles an hour. Winter storms whip across at thirty miles an hour. This makes swift and sometimes sharp weather changes at any given point.

That is a part of the price we pay for living in a land of four seasons. Our Summers are marked by heat, rain and thunderstorms, and our Winters bring snow, sleet, blizzard and sometimes bitter cold. This Winter has brought all of them. But with February more than half over, Spring isn't too far ahead. And Spring is really quite wonderful. Remember?

When the Sap Flows *February 16*

It won't be long now before the sap begins to rise in the sugar maples, and—regardless of anyone's opinion about where the best sugar originates—the first sap flow is as happy an event as February ever offers. It means that March is coming, and the equinox, and the buds and the leaves and Spring itself. It means that Winter has an ending. And all the ice on the river, all the cold in the thermometer, can't check it when the time comes.

We see the sun rising a bit earlier, setting each day a little later, and we know that the old earth is turning as usual, on its axis and in its orbit. We see the moon following its phases. We see the pines and the hemlocks on the rocky hillsides, shrugging off the snow and sheltering grouse and chickadee. Things are in order, and we know it. But it isn't until the sap begins to rise that we really feel it. There is the substance of knowledge, but there is the essence of belief which must rise from inside; it, too, has its season.

You have to be sick to know you will recover. You have to be cold to appreciate warmth. Maybe you can best believe in the change that is Spring when you are most in need of it. Certainly there are few enough signs of Spring when the sap begins to move. But something happens down at the roots and there is the response. Snow and ice and sleet and biting cold, and in their midst comes a warm day and there is the sap. And you know that Winter's days are numbered. It's as simple as that. You know. And from there on you look ahead, confident. Sap rises and hope becomes certainty.

❦ Anyone who could predict, even within a week, when maple sap will begin to run could make a modest fortune. In this book, as in the maple woods themselves, the sap flows several times and on various dates. It all depends on the weather. I will say that the flow begins sometime between February 15 and the latter part of March—usually.

Leaf and Bud *February 17*

The beech trees still cling to their brown papery leaves, or at least a share of them, with March less than two weeks away. So do some of the white oaks, making russet splotches in the woods. But look closely at the beeches and you will see lance-tip buds half an inch long, and there are bud clusters at the tips of the oak twigs, more reluctant in their growth.

There is a theory that the clinging leaves shelter the new buds from the rigors of Winter. And, indeed, the oak leaves do cup the buds with their stem bases; but there is little shelter in the slim clasp of a beech leaf. Yet it is the beech which swells its buds earlier, so the theory sags under the weight of what anyone can see with his own eyes.

The beech buds invite inspection. Peel one and you are stripping back layer after layer of soft brown tissue; at heart you will find a feathery tuft—a twin tuft, in fact—of white, silky catkin-to-be. This will become the staminate flower of the beech, which will appear in May along with the leaves. The pistillate flowers will open at that time too, but they will be very small and inconspicuous; their time of display comes in the Fall when they have fattened into soft-prickled burs enclosing the sweet-flavored beechnuts.

The reluctant oaks are more chary with their secrets. The buds are both small and tightly closed, and even if you can pry into the green mystery there you will need a strong glass to identify the nucleus of leaf or flower. They bide their time. But meanwhile both oak and beech cling to last year's leaves, rattling in late Winter's wind and keeping their own conservative counsel.

Twilight *February 18*

We call it twilight, and we cherish it now especially because it helps the days in their slow reach toward Spring. It shortens the nights, which are so reluctant to relax their cold grip. It makes the sunset seem later than it is and somewhat eases the dimensions of our late Winter lives.

We cherish twilight, too, because it not only has the glow of departing day but a special beauty of its own. It is neither sunlight nor starshine and moonlight, though it borrows somewhat from all of them. It can be hauntingly memorable over a snow-covered meadow or in the leafless woodland. Its shadows are soft-edged, velvety. It spreads blue-black pools in all the hollows. It touches the horizon line of the sky with the green of lake ice freshly cut. The air of twilight may be brittle, but the light itself has the soft, elusive texture of mist.

Even the sounds of late Winter dusk have that special quality of twilight. The jays and crows are silent, their day ended, but the great horned owl's mournful wailing from the dark pine is less ominous than it will be at midnight. The voice of the red fox challenging the farm dog hasn't quite the sharp, staccato note of darkness in it. The countryman's footsteps on his way to the woodshed make Winter music in the crisp snow, but it is a whistle, not a frigid whine. February twilight is glow without glitter, a song that is never shrill.

The Twelfth Sign   *February 19*

The celestial signs change now, as the ancients said, studying their zodiac. They change from Aquarius, the water bearer, to Pisces, the fishes, from the symbol of moisture itself to that of the water dwellers. And ahead stands the equinox, the astronomical turn from Winter to Spring, when the round of the zodiacal signs starts anew. To the ancients, this was a wet time, floods and mud and dripping skies.

To us, in this time and latitude, it is a time of noticeably lengthened days. Some years it brings the season's heaviest fall of snow, but only often enough to keep us aware of tradition's fallibility and to add another figure to the records. In almost any year it is a wet time indeed. And continued wet it usually is, with brooks running nearer bankfull than they have run all Winter, with mud in the meadows, with frost beginning to ease out of the open ground. The fishes of our land, as well as the fishes of the zodiac, now have enough water, and to spare. For a little while there is even water left over for people.

And in any year the longer days mean that Winter, no matter how it may try, cannot linger too long. Winter thrives on the short day and the deep cold of the long night. It weakens, even as the root strengthens, under the sun climbing toward the meridian again. Sun warmth and water nourishment encourage the roots now, whether it is water from melting snow or from slow rain that has not yet felt the warmth of season's change. And overhead the sun moves steadily through the venerable sign toward the vernal equinox, which means that April is just over the brown hills that wait for Spring.

Songs of Promise   *February 20*

We now begin to hear the still, small voices of change, particularly in the sound of running water, since this is the season of increasingly warm days and still cold nights. The brook that will be silent in August now rushes and gurgles at midday, and the ice on the hilltop begins to ooze away in little runnels down the slope.

It is the ancient process, this inevitable shift and change of the elements that comes in any land of changing seasons. Basically, it is an inanimate process, yet out of it comes new life rousing from a time of dormancy, and we think of it in animate terms. The first robins to come back make their own small songs, and we think of trickling waters as making equal songs and for the same reason.

Winter has been a time of essential silence, with the wind and the ice the loudest of the silence breakers. But as the time of new life stirring approaches, we think of that time in terms of our own living and endow it with voice. Waiting for the new bird song and the cry of the Spring peepers, we hear voices in all the small events of the season. We give voice to the wind and we give voice to flowing water because we would hear voices and listen to music.

Mankind is a talkative race and we somehow evolved song out of our emotional heartbeat. Spring is a time of singing, and if growing leaves and opening buds made even the least of audible sounds we would hear words and music in them. Meanwhile, we hear songs of promise in trickling water.

Big Thaw   *February 21*

A big thaw, whether it marks the end of Winter or only a break, has the drama of eons in it. One day the land lies white and silent under ice and snow; then a warm wind comes. Temperatures climb. The ice grip relaxes. Water, the concerted melt of all the hillsides, begins to flow. You hear it. You see it in a mist over the thinning snow. You feel it soggy underfoot. And you know you are witnessing, on a minor scale, what happened when the glaciers began to melt back. One Winter's ice age is beginning to go.

A day passes, and a night, and great bare patches show in the pasture. The rocks on the hillside are in sight, black and wet, centers of warmth. Fence posts stand in deepening hollows in the snow. Beneath the ice in the gully you can hear the brook begin to talk; and if you follow the brook you will see it open to the sky in a few places, where it has eaten away the ice. Rivulets from the whole hillside have concentrated to clear the brook's channel. They talk in many voices.

Another night of warmth and the hollows have become ponds. The brook leaps, now, its channel clear, and the big river comes to life. The ice in it begins to move, to break into floes and shards. Thus rivers came to life when the great ice sheets began to recede. The pasture shows faint green at the grass roots along the brook. The hillsides, by afternoon, are bare of snow.

You watch the river and listen to the brook and feel the softness of the sodden earth with its icy solidity untouched a few inches down. But you forget the deeper ice and look at the trees, expecting to find fat buds. Expecting to see flocks of Spring birds, You look for fresh miracles, as if the big melt itself were not miracle enough.

Trickling Waters   *February 22*

Man is not an aquatic animal, but from the time we stand in youthful wonder beside a Spring brook till we sit in old age and watch the endless roll of the sea, we feel a strong kinship with the waters of this world. We marvel at the magnificence of a snowflake, a water crystal. We sleep content with the drone of rain on the roof. We slake our thirst with the cool waters of the earth. And we go forth at this time of year to see and hear the little streams trickling down all the hills of Spring.

It was such little streams, grown big with melting snow, that carved our valleys. The silt they carried from the hilltops enriched the meadows and built the delta lands. Grass followed in their wake, and trees. And when men first traveled they followed such streams, first along their banks and then upon their swirling current. They followed flowing waters to the oceans and in due time put forth upon the ocean itself. Their towns were river towns, and their first cities faced the sea.

The trickling waters are awake now and creeping through the grass roots, down the wakening hillsides. The swamps ooze with their slow drainage and ponds brim over at the edge. Streams test their banks. Floods are in the making. The very earth seems sodden underfoot. And if we reach back far enough in the racial memory, we must know that we are seeing the ooze and flow not of one Spring alone but of the very Springtime of the earth, when the land and life itself rose out of the waters of long ago.

The predawn quacking now heard along the rivers back in the hills is as typical of the season as the fluttery call of robins in an upland meadow. From mid-February on, the black ducks are back and feeding in the swollen streams, looking for nesting sites, and discussing whatever ducks discuss. Most of them haven't been far away, though they did move to open water when December and January iced the streams and ponds.

The black duck is also called the red-legged duck, the dusky duck, the dusky mallard and the black mallard. The mallard term is natural, for except in color they are much like the mallard ducks of the West, in size, shape and habits, though they are much more shy. Also like the mallards, the females among the blacks do the quacking. The drakes have only a low, trilling note. And, again like the mallards, they are notably good parents, nesting early in April, hatching a clutch of eight to a dozen eggs, hiding the ducklings in the brush and reeds till they can fly, in August.

The black duck is the common wild duck of the Northeast and is New England's own duck. It isn't really black; it is a brown so dusky it looks black at a little distance, but there are paler streaks, plainly brown, on the head and neck. Its legs and feet are bright orange-red, the reason for one of its common names. How they keep those feet from freezing, only ducks know.

The black duck is not actually a nocturnal bird. It merely seems so because it likes to feed at dawn and dusk, and it likes company, garrulous company, at mealtime. That's why the black ducks are heard now when sensible ducks should be sound asleep.

❧ For the past three years one black duck on the river close by my house has been rousing at 3:30 A.M. and insisting that everyone else wake up, too. All her sisters and female cousins soon are awake and apparently telling her to shut up and go back to sleep. It takes quite a while to quack her down, and by then it is almost dawn. I wish that old duck no particular bad luck, but I do wonder how she escapes the hunters down in Virginia and Carolina every Fall.

The Root of Spring

This is the time when there is a quiet stirring at the root of Spring. It will be some time yet before we see it plainly, but we know it is there; and it is probably more than imagination that there is a quickening in the willows and the osiers that is like a promise on a sunny afternoon. The exact time when this happens cannot be stated, year to year, for it is a matter of sun and temperature as well as of the season, but it comes toward the end of February usually or in early March. It is there, obvious to the eye, by the vernal equinox.

What this means is that sap is beginning to move upward or is about to move. It means that before long there will be small, fuzzy catkins on the willows. But that, too, depends on the day-to-day weather, though willow catkins are early in their habits. What is a more reassuring sign than pussy willows, either big ones at the florist's or the little ones in the bogland?

It means too that before long there will be freshening green along the brooks, especially on sheltered banks where the sun lingers as it never did in January. The grass will brighten there while ice still edges the water. That, too, is for the days ahead. And when that happens, celandine will brighten at the roadside; and after celandine come the dandelions.

It is both easy and tempting thus to project the first stirring all the way into Spring itself. It is the impulsive human thing to do, even now. Or maybe not so impulsive, either. Back in the hills the maple-syrup makers are gauging trees and weather with that speculative eye. They know the time of year.

The Deliberate Buds
February 25

The buds on the lilacs, like those on the dogwoods, always look impatient by late February, no matter what the weather. But they are sealed with caution and are as deliberate as Spring itself.

Unlike forsythia and pussy willow buds, they refuse to be fooled or hastened by being brought into a warm room and cosied in a vase of warm water.

But life is there, and leaf and twig and blossom, in those remarkable buds. And that astonishing little package that is any bud didn't come into being overnight. It began to take shape last Summer, well before the season's leaves fell. The buds on all the trees and bushes were formed then and grew inside the bud scales until hard frost clamped down. Then they hibernated, much as the woodchuck hibernates. They will waken when the sap starts to stir again in response to the vernal sun and warmth.

When the buds do waken, everything in them will grow like magic. The bud scales, no longer needed, will fall in a shower unnoticed but in number even greater than the Autumn's fall of leaves. The new leaves, delicate as a baby's skin, will stretch and expand and be filled with chlorophyll as their "baby color," often pink or lilac, fades. Blossoms will open, often from the same bud. The miracle will happen.

But that is for later. Right now the buds are waiting, a promise of April. The impatience is in us, watching them, hoping, wishing, while the clock they obey continues its slow, deliberate ticking down at the root of things.

February Pattern   *February 26*

Days lengthen, but the nights are still bright with the Winter stars, frosty and sharp in the darkness. The Big Bear, the Dipper, swings to the east in early evening, and the Little Bear walks across the sky, his upright tail tipped with the polestar. The Twins and the Charioteer are almost overhead, and the Pleiades ride high, toward the southwest. The Lion is in the east and the Whale in the west, both within reach of the horizon, reminders of Daniel and Jonah.

February thins away. Before another new moon hangs on the western horizon at dusk, March will be nearing its end and the Big Dipper will be overhead, or at least above the polestar, by midevening. The fang of the night chill will be dulled. Hylas will be shrilling in the lowlands, April at hand.

The seasons turn, as do the stars, and those who live with the wind and the sun understand the inevitability of their changes. The full moon fades the constellations and dims the Milky Way, but it does not halt their progression or change their place in the sky. Come April, and the Dipper stands above the polestar at evening, and buds begin to open. Come October, and the Dipper sweeps the evening horizon, and maple leaves turn to gold and Fall is upon us.

February has its pattern, of stars as well as brown hilltops and leafless trees. But it is a shifting pattern, with movement and change and progression. The sun lingers, the new moon sits on the hills, the early Dipper hangs to the east, and the bud waits on the branch.

The Tides of Spring   *February 27*

February may end in a snowstorm and March may come lioning in and roar for a while, but the season itself won't be bullied for long. The vernal equinox is only three and a half weeks away, and neither a load of snow nor a polar gale has ever yet altered its schedule. One of these days Winter is going to run out of breath.

There are already signs, though most of them are felt rather than seen. Red osier dogwood stems begin to look more lively, red against the snow, than they did a month ago. Willow catkins are still Winter-tight, but the withes have a noticeable tinge of amber. There are a few resident robins and redwings around, but they now seem to be watching for the arrival of their migrant brothers and sisters, who are still down south of the frost line. In sheltered bogs here and there the hoods of time-defying skunk cabbage have melted their way up through the ice. A few warm days would start the sap to flowing in the sugar maples, which set their clocks by the sun, not the calendar.

But it is the sun itself that marks the time unmistakably. It is approaching the rim of the Winter quadrant, rising more nearly due east day by day, and its shadows now point toward Spring. The very sunlight now has a different quality. You can feel it even when the wind forgets what time it is. The trees know and even the buried roots know that the deliberate tides of Spring are already lapping at the latitudes.

The Watery Days   *February 28*

Now come the watery days. The melt sets in, brooks flow, rivers run, even the upland pastures begin to ooze. Not every day or all day even, but with a persistence that only nature and the seasons know. The melt, and then the rain, and the frost deep down begins to leach out, upward by capillary action instead of downward by gravity. And the sap, matching the frost, moves up the trunks and out into the furthest branchlets.

In the big span, life began long ago in the water and the shoreline ooze. And so it is today, and every year. Spring starts in the watery days, in the soggy soil. Water, the life-giver, the prompter of root and bulb and seed and leaf. Water, the solvent which carries nutrients by the ton for the plant life of this earth. A waterless Spring is a dead Spring, as a waterless planet is a dead planet.

Not many centuries ago the year was reckoned from the watery days of March, which is a reasonable plan in any society that lives close to the soil. The last four months of our year still carry names reminding us of that fact; the ninth month of our present year is September, for "seven," and so on to December, for "ten." So we come now to the time of the venerable New Year, when all things green and most things born were at the birth.

We come now to a time of more rain than snow, more melt than new ice. To longer days, which draw the fangs of the cold. To change, slow and creeping change that leaves us impatient with its deliberation. Change that drips from the eaves, and flows singing in the brook, and oozes from the sod, and that, in its own ordered time, will come green across the hilltops.

 MARCH

March   *March 1*

March is a tomboy with tousled hair, a mischievous smile, mud
on her shoes and a laugh in her voice. She knows when the first
shadbush will blow, where the first violet will bloom, and she
isn't afraid of a salamander. She has whims and winning ways.
She's exasperating, lovable, a terror-on-wheels, too young to be
reasoned with, too old to be spanked.

March is rain drenching as June and cold as January. It is mud
and slush and the first green grass down along the brook. March
gave its name, and not without reason, to the mad hare. March is
the vernal equinox when, by the calculations of the stargazers,
Spring arrives. Sometimes the equinox is cold and impersonal as a
mathematical table, and sometimes it is warm and lively and
spangled with crocuses. The equinox is fixed and immutable, but
Spring is a movable feast that is spread only when sun and wind
and all the elements of weather contrive to smile at the same time.

March is pussy willows. March is hepatica in bloom, and often
it is arbutus. Sometimes it is anemones and bloodroot blossoms
and even brave daffodils. March is a sleet storm pelting out of
the north the day after you find the first violet bud. March is
boys playing marbles and girls playing jacks and hopscotch. March

once was sulphur and molasses; it still is dandelion greens and rock cress.

March is the gardener impatient to garden; it is the winter-weary sun seeker impatient for a case of Spring fever. March is February with a smile and April with a sniffle. March is a problem child with a twinkle in its eye.

Partridge in the Apple Tree

March 2

Maybe partridges perch in pear trees at Christmas in some places, as the old song says, but in our part of the world they mark the latter part of Winter by perching in apple trees. When the countryman is startled by the loud whir of wings beating from his dooryard apple tree toward the wood lot, he knows it is early March. The partridges have been down to the house for an apple bud salad.

The ruffed grouse, our common partridge, has an uncanny sense of the season. All winter long it varies its diet of seeds and berries with the tiny dormant buds of birch and poplar back in the woodland. Then the strengthening sun beckons to maple sap and the dooryard apple tree begins to waken. The casual observer can't see much change, but the partridge knows better. It knows, almost to the day, when those buds quicken and start to push against the brown protective scales. Then a new substance and succulence, undoubtedly rich in vitamins, is at work in them. So here come the partridges, to perch in the apple trees and eat as eagerly as the countryman will eat when the first Spring greens appear on his own table.

Some of those eaten buds would make apples, of course. But the countryman seldom begrudges them. Before the buds become blossoms in May, the partridges will be stuffing themselves with bugs and beetles by the thousand. They pay for what they take, in their own coin. And right now, when a man sometimes wonders if the ice will ever break up, a partridge in the dooryard apple tree is worth its weight in hope and reassurance. The bird and the bud both know that Spring is now inevitable.

Spring Tonic   *March 3*

This is about the time of year when Grandmother used to mix sulphur and molasses and prescribe it generously. A Spring tonic was needed, something to lift the spirit and tone up the body. Winter had probably thinned out the blood. Anyway, here came sulphur and molasses, or some other homely elixir.

There was actually a mixture called Elixir, tasting like the essence of gall diluted with tincture of aloes. It was dark brown, in taste and color, and it lifted the spirits in sheer defense; unless the lift was manifest, there was more Elixir.

And, just a bit later, there was rhubarb. It, too, had magic qualities, particularly when it was stewed with a minimum of sugar. If the younger generation raised enough ruckus about it, the powers-that-were sometimes would add raisins and make the rhubarb sauce almost palatable.

Then came the first Spring greens. Dandelions were a favorite, but young shoots of pokeweed also went into the pot. And lamb's-quarters, when it came along. The young and tender shoots of such vegetation weren't bad provender, particularly when seasoned with salt pork; but for a proper Spring tonic the greens must include the older, more authoritative leaves. Then one got all the bitter virtues of a tonic that was aimed at the root of all human ills. The Winter lethargy had to be driven out of the bloodstream. Nothing less than sulphur or Elixir or concentrated rhubarb or dandelion would put that lethargy to flight.

One good effect was that such tonics drove the younger generation out into the Springtime world, merely to escape the bitter brews. There they found the real tonic—the urge and warmth and liveliness of Spring itself.

The Difference

There's one thing about a big snow in March. It hasn't the stay-ing power of a January snow. It can clog and confuse mankind's daily life and make our complex routines both hazardous and difficult for a little while, but snow melts and ice thaws in March as it seldom does in January. March isn't really Spring, in this climate, but it isn't the depth of Winter, either. The sun, as we say, has moved north and those long nights when the snow and cold could sink long fangs that the brief hours of daylight failed to loosen are now past. Midday can now be mild, and the sun's warmth begins to beat back the frigid forces of darkness. The vernal equinox is near.

The implacable strength of seasonal change is visible even against the snowbanks. See a willow tree against the drifted mar-gin of a river. Its long, limber withes have that amber look, the quickening that glows as with promise, as though some kind of golden sap were rising. The buds that hugged the branch so tightly a month ago now begin to stand free, though still furled and waxed. And on the brushy margins of the ponds and brooks the slim stems of red osier dogwood begin to surpass their dull Winter red and catch the eye with livening crimson. Their pulse, too, is rising along with their burgeoning-fever, and the snow-bank makes their flush unmistakable.

The snow comes, and the snow goes. And the sun makes March a time of change. There's the difference, January to March—the sun, the daylight, the urgency of root and bud and sap, the fun-damentals.

Northward Traveler

Discounting local eccentricities of weather, such as March snow-storms, once Spring starts moving north it travels at a fairly regu-lar and predictable pace. The rate is approximately seventeen miles a day. Just for example, if red maples should start opening bud in Washington, D.C., on March 15, which is most unlikely, the same variety of trees could be expected to open bud in Baltimore two days later. And, given normal weather throughout that period, two weeks after they opened in Washington they would open in New York City.

That rate of travel is true, however, only for places of approximately the same altitude above sea level. Another scale of calculation comes into effect when you come to a ridge of hills or mountains. Spring slows up at the foot of a slope, just as most foot travelers do. Instead of traveling seventeen miles a day, as it does on level ground, it climbs only 100 feet of altitude in a day. Spring may creep into a valley with green grass and violets on a Sunday morning and not reach the top of a 200-foot hill bordering that valley until Tuesday noon.

So the dweller on a high hilltop can literally see Spring coming, when the time arrives. He can walk down the hill and meet it and climb back up the hill and wait for it to join him. That's one of the virtues of living on a hill when Spring is about to bow in. And that's one reason the peepers all live in the valleys—they can trill a day earlier than if they lived on a knoll.

The Roots of Spring   *March 6*

The important thing about the first week of March isn't the wind, or the rain, or the temperature, or even the clear blue sky—when the sky is clear and blue. The important event of March is sunlight, lengthened sunlight, almost eleven and a half hours of it now between sunrise and sunset.

All the other things follow, the warmth and the tempered wind and the rain that has the unmistakable touch of Spring. When the sun has climbed out of its deep southern path, so that it comes in the east windows again at breakfast time, then we know that Winter is past and April is not too far away. There it is now, our March sun, coming in the east window. It will be in the west window this afternoon. And it will stay in the sky a proper time for dusk, so that six o'clock comes in early March with a glow instead of lantern darkness. Eleven and a half hours of sunlight, and more each day as the month advances.

There are no violets yet, and there won't be for some weeks to come. But if you know where they bed and if you dig carefully, you can find them budding at the root. And if you dig in the leaf mold on the right south slope, you can even find the pale young rosettes of Dutchman's-breeches waiting under cover for the certainty of Spring. The sun has already warmed them, as it is warming and quickening the buds and roots all through the woods. The sap begins to move. Life slowly stirs.

That is the miracle of the March sun. No matter if the days are chill, or if the rains come, or if the wind blows, the sun is there, stronger each day. And down where Spring waits, where the roots have their being, April begins to stir.

The Winds of March   *March 7*

The winds of March are not only proverbial but, in our latitude, both potent and prodigal and as inevitable as the vernal equinox. Usually, but not always, they are more boisterous and less boreal than the February winds, and in any honest season they take away more snow and ice than they bring. But it is always hazardous to count on that. The one certainty is that March will blow, it will whoop and bluster and buffet and roar, and eventually it will clear away enough of Winter's leftover to make way for April.

Like all other aspects of weather, March winds have their reason. By now the Arctic regions have reached their depth of accumulated cold, and the tropics have begun to simmer under the strengthening sun. As cold air flows down from the north it encounters a stronger flow of warm air from the south. Vast weather systems collide, huge pockets are formed and the outer air rushes in to fill them. When air hurries anywhere the result is wind.

Fundamentally, the March wind is a wind of change. It is the seasons in transition, a part of the eternal rhythm of our spinning planet and the whole solar system. It is a chilly mate of that Autumn commotion we often call the equinoctial storm, but instead of fostering Indian Summer it eventually brings Spring Fever Days. But that's for later, after the March winds have blown themselves out. That's for April and early May, when March winds are only a memory.

Floods, and Their Control   *March 8*

The annual Spring floods have already begun to devastate the inland valleys, with lost life and property and consequent suffering. March will bring more floods, and so will April. It has happened thus ever since man began deforesting the hills and draining the swamps. And soon the perennial demand for better flood control will be heard again.

When we talk of flood control, we usually think of dams and deeper river channels, to impound the waters or hurry their runoff. Yet neither is the ultimate solution, simply because floods are caused by the flow of water downhill. If the hills are wooded, that flow is checked. If there is a swamp at the foot of the hills, the swamp sponges up much of the excess water, restores some of it to the underground water supply and feeds the remainder slowly into the streams. Strip the hills, drain the boglands, and you create flood conditions inevitably. Yet that is what we have been doing for years. And with our increasing urbanization, our "reclamation" of lowlands and our reckless population of the flood plains, we have created at least one new flood factor for every old one we bring under control.

There is no quick solution to the problems of flood. Dams help. Diversion channels help, sometimes; often they merely shift the flood problem to a neighbor downstream. Reforestation of watersheds helps a great deal, but it is a slow process. Conservation of swamplands, however, is relatively easy and is fundamentally essential to any ultimate control. Every swamp that is drained, every bog that is filled, adds to the flood problem. Yet we go on draining and filling—and demanding better flood control. Why?

To appreciate March completely one should go away for a time; to a hospital, say, where neither wind nor weather, sunrise nor moonset, can really penetrate. Then come back to March, and even its temperamental gusts, its snow and sleet and slush and rain are full of wonder. March has a brand new savor. Its gray skies are pussy-willow gray, not leaden; its blue skies are fresh-water blue. Its chickadee song is as gay, if not quite as loud, as that of a May robin. The chuckle of March melt trickling down the hillsides and swelling the brooks is the laughter of Spring just offstage.

To see daffodils thrusting blunt green fingers from the soil is to see March actually growing and greening. Snowdrops always come to blossom about now, but to come back and see them in blossom is to see, suddenly, a lovely facet of the big miracle that stirs the earth and opens petals to the sun. Beside a certain wall hyacinths are coming up, and a few squills are in bloom. No crocuses in sight, but some evening soon the slim sheaths will be seen, and the next day there will be deep chalices of gold and purple. Forsythia buds are fat. Days grow longer, and the tides of sunlight slowly undermine the dam that holds back the floods of Spring.

These things you see and feel. And you feel the indefinable pulse of March, a slowly rising beat that touches the hillside and the woodland and stirs at the root of things. It is like feeling your own pulse again, your own growing strength; and you know that March, no matter what its day-to-day temperament, is a good time to know again, a good time to be alive.

❧ This was written the day after I returned home after five crucial weeks in the hospital. If it seems particularly heartfelt, that is why.

Redwings and Pussy Willows

Robins and crocuses are urban signs of Spring, but country folk look and listen for redwings and pussy willows. The redwing, that blackbird who wears red epaulets, usually arrives ahead of the robins and his loud *o-kal-lee* from the bogside trees and bushes is as clear a summons to the season as anyone could ask. He knows when the swamps begin to melt, and he is usually there to see it happen.

The redwing is a gregarious fellow, but when he starts north he leaves the womenfolk behind. The first redwings to arrive up here are males, and they hold conventions in all the wet places for a week or two before the females get here. Nobody can mistake a male redwing, with his glistening black coat and those scarlet shoulder patches. But the females of the species are easily mistaken, at a glance, for large, dark sparrows; they are speckled and striped with brown and aren't black birds at all, and they are quite lacking in shoulder patches.

Sometimes the redwings arrive in our area toward the end of February. Almost always they are here by early March. Sometimes they get a frosty welcome and sometimes they have to face a snowstorm, but they never seem to complain about the weather. Since they eat weed seed as well as insects—ragweed seed is a staple item in their diet—they seldom go hungry. Occasionally they visit the feeders that people stock with grain, but mostly they stay in the boglands or nearby. When one hears them there, one can begin to look for pussy willows. They both use the same alarm clock.

The Reminders

Snowdrops and crocuses and all the other early Spring bulbs are reassuring things to have around, especially if they are planted in a sheltered spot where they get an inspiring amount of March sunshine. They don't even have to come to blossom to work their early magic. Just the sight of their green shoots lifts the heart and makes one believe that Spring is on its way, reluctant as it can be at times.

The same with robins, and bluebirds. They often winter over, finding warmth, shelter and enough food to keep them going in the thickets of the bogland. But when we see them out and around, in the open, we know that Winter eventually frays out. Maybe they didn't just get off the air stream flowing up from Florida, but they could have. In any case, their cousins soon will be arriving on that air stream. We can believe that in March, even if we are still wearing a Winter muffler around our neck.

And when we hear that maple sap is flowing, back in the hills, and that pussy willows are showing here and there, we can take heart. Sap sometimes flows in February, and sometimes the snow doesn't go off the ground in the sugarbush until well into April. But the very fact that sap is flowing again has its significance. It's good to be reminded of this, to know that sap does flow, and robins do come back, and crocuses do bloom. This also means that apple trees bloom, and lilacs scent the air, and roses unfold their petals. It means that there are such things as Spring fever and Summer sunburn. Not in March, but in June and July. March says, "These things are true. Remember?"

March Visitors   *March 12*

Youngsters may believe it when they are told that pussy willows appear in earliest Spring simply to show off their warm fur coats. But the real reason is that *Salix discolor,* as the botanists call it, is a hardy shrub with early habits. It isn't as forward as the witch hazel, which blooms in the Fall; but it pretty well sets the pace for all the Spring shrubs.

The "pussy," of course, is not the blossom. It is the bud, from which the outer scales have fallen. The true blossoms come a few weeks later, changing the silvery catkin to a more ragged tuft of yellowish miniature flowers. Staminate and pistillate flowers are borne on different trees, as with all the willows. And when the flowers have done their duty, with the help of the early bees, then the leaves will appear.

All willows have catkins, of one form or another, and many of the lesser willow trees, particularly the shrubs that fringe the streams and swamps, can compete in a lesser way with the pussy willows. Even the bearberry willow, which creeps on the windy slopes of the Eastern mountains and seldom lifts its branches more than a foot off the ground, has furry little catkins. So does the even smaller dwarf willow, *Salix herbacea,* which lives on the mountain summits. The really big willows, white, black, crack, and weeping, have catkins that vary from furry little tufts to long, slender plumes. And they all bloom early.

If pussy willows didn't appear until May, they would hardly get a second glance. In March they get praise and a hearty welcome.

The Bluest Blue   *March 13*

There may be others, such as the indigo bunting and the blue grosbeak, who can flash a more brilliant blue than the bluebird, but it seems doubtful in March. A pair of bluebirds comes out of nowhere, and they perch on an apple tree that hasn't even fattened a bud yet, and you catch your breath and tell yourself that nothing, not even the sky after an April shower, was ever this blue. A blue jay flashes past, and you know that he isn't blue at all and never was. Compared to the bluebird, he's gray.

There are robins, too, ranging the open hillsides in pairs and even in small flocks. You think you see them, and then you hear them chattering and you know your eyes didn't deceive you. They take wing and your heart leaps a little, for you know that they'll soon be singing from the high trees at sunrise.

The robins chatter, but the bluebirds come almost silently.

They twitter a little, as though talking to themselves, and on a sunny day they may even sing a simple melody a time or two. But it isn't their song that's important. It's simply their presence. It's their color. They don't have to sing a note. They can simply sit on the apple tree and look at the leafless twigs, and somehow those twigs begin to come to life. Sap flows and buds swell.

Not overnight, of course. But once the bluebirds come, you know that things are going to happen. There'll be apple blossoms again, and lilacs, and shade under the maples. And there'll be other birds, thousands of them. But this is the first pair of bluebirds.

Sugar Time   *March 14*

Sap has begun to rise in the maples back in the hills and sap buckets are out. Sugar making has begun. That doesn't mean that Spring is here. It means that we have had a brief succession of chilly nights and mild days, which can end any time but which also proves that Spring is on its way. The maples are responding to temperature, length of daylight, angle of sun and whatever other mysterious factors prompt the processes which will lead to blossom and leaf in due time.

Sugar of a sort can be made from box elders and birches as well as from maples, but of all tree sugar that of the maples is best, and that from *Acer saccharum,* the sugar maple or rock maple, is best of all. Sugar from the white maples looks just as good and often tastes almost as good, but it contains enough tannic acid to turn tea black. Sugar makers can tell you which variety of maple was tapped after one taste of the syrup, and many countrymen who don't make sugar boast that they can tell.

The sugar maple is a magnificent tree and it grows over a considerably broader range than the rather limited maple-sugar area. It is found and flourishes as far south as Georgia and as far west as Nebraska. But south of Virginia it doesn't produce sugar, probably a result of the climate. Everywhere, though, it produces lumber that makes beautiful furniture, durable floors and tough woodenware. The enduring glory of the tree, however, is in its sap and the syrup and sugar that come from it. And it is always linked with the end of Winter. When the sap flows, the back of Winter is broken. Spring isn't here, but it's coming.

The Voice of Spring   *March 15*

Some years the Spring peepers start calling in mid-March, some years not until April, but whenever it happens the peeper chorus is the voice of eternal Spring. There is nothing else quite like it. Robins sing, crocuses bloom, sap rises, but the peepers in full voice are the ancient and enduring cry of life triumphant and resurgent. The message is as unmistakable as sunrise.

It is one of the pleasant puzzles of nature why this small tree toad, *Hyla crucifer,* this mite of amphibian life which still hibernates as its progenitors did more than 100,000,000 years ago, should so unmistakably personify the surge of Spring. Perhaps it is because Spring itself is ancient beyond reckoning, or perhaps it is because all the life we know had such minute beginnings and because, so far as we know, it too originated in the warm waters of ancient time. But why this voice, this shrill proclamation from such a tiny remnant of the distant past? A dozen peepers make less than a human handful, but their voices can fill a whole evening.

The peeper is prescient of the season, but only a minor weather prophet. Sometimes the peepers emerge, only to be snowed in again. They can be frosted into silence, sleeted back into the mud. But they can't be silenced for long. They are the very epitome of insistent life, making minor compromises with things as they are but never surrendering. When the equinox approaches, you can be sure that the Spring peepers are not far behind. And when the peepers cry, then Winter is on its way out.

The Miracle of Sap *March 16*

Now the red osiers come to life and all the willows quicken.
Those gardeners who have grapes to prune know how early the
sap moves and how full and even profligate is its flow. It is
almost as though the trees and shrubs and vines were ready to
burst with the pressure. One is tempted to say that it is the pressure of the sap which forces the leaves from their buds.

It isn't that, of course; it's much more complex. But the sap is
there, with its own mysterious pressure. The time comes when
days lengthen, frost eases from the ground, and the seep and melt
and rainfall of Spring are everywhere. Then the sap moves. On
a warm day after a chill night it surges upward. Several gallons
will come from a single tap on a maple tree on such a day.
Nightfall and it slackens or stops completely, only to resume on
the next mild day. And not only in the maples. An evergreen
with a fresh gash will ooze for days at this time of year.

Green life is no longer a complete mystery. We know a good
deal about leaves and chlorophyll, and even about the movement
and chemical makeup of sap. But there are some things, even
about such a simple fluid as sap, that still elude us. We know
something about how it travels up and down a tree trunk, and
where, and why and when. We aren't sure just what happens to
it in a leaf, though we now know a good deal about photosynthesis. We aren't quite sure about the upward flow in Spring
and the recession of the sap in the Fall. And we don't know a
great deal about sap pressure. But there it is, the quickening of
the lifeblood of our whole green world. Such a simple thing, and
so mysterious.

First Green *March 17*

It's all a matter of proportion, and of the season. Two months
from now there will be bees and blossoms and balmy air, and so
much green that one new shoot will go unnoticed. But right now

the sight of a crocus poking up and a few courageous daffodil tips showing is reason for exclamation and delight. Spring!

It isn't Spring, of course. Not yet. But those first few tips of green, that venture out of Winter darkness into the light again, mean that things are beginning to happen down at the root. We won't necessarily open all the windows tomorrow, and we certainly won't take down the storm sash or put away the overcoat and the galoshes. Ice isn't yet something that comes only out of the refrigerator, and we still know what a snowflake looks like. But to know again the gold or purple chalice of a crocus and to see the green fingers of a daffodil certainly warms the heart.

Right now, those few shoots of new, fresh green are more important than a whole forest of green will be in May. Those shoots are a promise of May's green forest and the performance of March's seasonal miracle. March, when the hilltops are still as brown as December, when you wonder if you will recognize an oriole's song again, when you think even a dandelion might be beautiful, needs such miracles.

Maybe there aren't many such shoots yet. There shouldn't be, in the order of things. Miracles aren't a dime a dozen, after all, even this kind. But they do catch the hungry human eye and they lift the spirit. We yearn for them, and we cherish them. We haven't yet lost our sense of proportion. We won't, until May.

The Talking Waters   *March 18*

There is much to be said for a house on a hilltop, but the man who lives in a valley beside a brook or a river has the voice of the seasons talking to him the year around. A pond or a lake may be a good neighbor, especially for the fisherman and in the Summer. But still water not only runs deep, as they say; it also freezes deep, and it stays frozen. A brook or a river is flowing water, live water, and it talks of time, particularly in March.

The brooks are talking now. On warm afternoons they are even singing. Brooks are especially responsive to the season, and they are chattering now about snow melting on the hillsides and in the deep woods. They can't talk a bud into leaf, but they do seem to whisper encouragement; and when the song sparrows begin to sing in their marginal alders, the song of the brook partakes somewhat of the vernal celebration. Violets bloom earliest beside brooks, and grass grows greener there. Brooks don't create Spring, but they participate in its coming and they lend their friendly voices.

The rivers are less carefree than the brooks, more sedate. But they, too, have their say. There's something about a river's voice even now that makes one know that redwings will soon be in the big willows and kingfishers will go rattling and diving up the channel. There is even duck talk in the river's voice, and heron talk. There's a hint of April coming, and May.

Live water, flowing water, and an end in sight of Winter's ice. The running waters talk of it, and the man who lives in a valley knows the sound and supplies the words.

Mother Earth   *March 19*

The gardener and the farmer can't keep their hands out of the soil, now that the lasting snows and the deep ice are gone. It isn't so much that they are impatient to plant; they know full well that you plant in season. It's simply that they must touch the good earth, feel its grit and its strength between their fingers, and renew contact with the source of all good and growing things.

Watch a farmer as he walks across his fields on a sunny afternoon. He pauses and scuffs the soil with his heel. He crouches down and picks up a handful. He rubs it, feeling the fine roots lacing through it. He makes a ball of it, a miniature earth. There in his hand he holds the stuff that nourishes wheat and apples and corn and potatoes. Out of such soil sprang the timbers that frame his house, the cotton in the shirt on his back. Out of it grew all the flowers that ever delighted an eye or pleased a scenting nostril.

There is the food of life. It waits only for the warmth of sun, the moisture of rain, the planting of seeds, to produce again the everlasting miracle of green and growing life. There is something eternal about the soil, eternal and somehow eager.

It was no mere chance that inserted into primitive folklore the recurring tale of how the first man was created from the soil of the earth. And ancient people knew the soil intimately, even though they were hunters or herdsmen. From it sprang the very substance of their life. It was Mother Earth. And Mother Earth it remains, no matter how far we travel. It is our yearning and our instinct to touch it now and hold it in our hand. And when the time of planting comes we shall bow down to it as we plant.

The Stuff of Dreams   *March 20*

Whether it's cloudy or sunny as June, whether last night brought rain or a few desperate snowflakes, you can walk into any country or suburban hardware store and think it's mid-May. The snow shovels are out of sight, and the coarse salt and the wild bird seed. In their places are racks of the prettiest spades, rakes, hoes, weeders and trowels ever forged. And bags of patent fertilizers and grass seed and clover. And stands of seed packets, pretty as a flower garden in full bloom. And work gloves.

Go down the street or around the corner to the implement store and it's the same thing on a bigger scale. Tractors, big and little, plows, harrows, seeders, cultivators. And bags of lime and phosphate. And busy men assembling, tuning, repairing such machinery, loading the bags of precious stuff on trucks. Farmers saying, "Tomorrow," or "Next week," or "It's almost dry enough, except in the bottom land."

Then you go home and look at the vegetable garden, and hunt for the spade. And within ten minutes you know it's planting season only in the stores. Maybe you plant a few peas, but that's all. You turn up a few angleworms, cold and reluctant, and you think about the brook and fishing season. You glance at the lawn. And you know it won't be planting time till it's time to fish and mow the lawn and paint and hang the screens and tend the early flowers. And then you wonder again about all those things down at the hardware store. There wasn't any liniment in sight and no mosquito repellent and no sunburn lotion. You know you were tempted by the stuff of dreams, and you go in the house for a warmer jacket and decide to stay there a few more weeks.

Tomorrow's Message   *March 21*

The earth swings slowly but inexorably on its trunnions, and now we in this Northern Hemisphere begin once more to face the sun directly. Sunrise is almost east again, and sunset west; and at midday the sunlight begins to probe the Winter-armored soil instead of glancing off. The vernal equinox approaches.

Man, when he looks to see, finds deliberate and familiar but still astonishing consequences. The willows quicken. Soon, in terms of the year's time, there will be catkins on those ambering stems, those strange, furry catkins we call pussy willows. The streamside brush we know as red osier dogwood seems to pulse once more with its warming crimson color. Life stirs at the root there, too. In sugar-maple country the sap begins to move. And in the boglands those grandfathers of the swamp, the skunk cabbages, unfurl their purplish hoods, green pioneers of Spring.

In the fields, the Winter sparrows reach for song, sometimes achieve it. Crows call in a new register, and jays chatter of new days to come. The chickadees surpass their twittering, and in the nearby woods the woodpeckers drum in a new season. Overhead the squirrels race through the treetops, pausing here and there to taste the coming green in a mouthful of tight-furled buds. On the hillsides the brooks rouse from cold hibernation and begin to chortle. Ice groans in the rivers, nudged by flowing water.

The earth is slowly warmed. Change creeps in. Not overnight, and not in a day or two, but inevitably. March is not May, and snow and ice give way reluctantly. But the pattern is set. The sun is writing tomorrow's message on the earth.

Index of First Publication Dates

NOTE:

Several entries in this list are dated during two periods when *The New York Times* temporarily suspended publication because of strikes. There was no suspension of the outdoor editorials at those times. After the strike in December, 1958, a summary edition of *The Times* was published and in it were included the outdoor pieces written for the Sundays involved. During the three months' strike of 1962-63 the outdoor editorials were read over the air on special *Times* programs each week end, and a number of them were published in the West Coast and Overseas editions of *The Times*.